D1407063

Perfect places for
Afternoon Tea

AA Publishing in association with The Tea Guild
and The United Kingdom Tea Council

© AA Media Limited 2011.

AA Media Limited retains the copyright in the current edition © 2010 and in all subsequent editions, reprints and amendments to editions. The information contained in this directory is sourced entirely from the AA Media Limited's information resources. All rights reserved. No part of this publication may be reproduced, stored in a retrieval system, or transmitted in any form or by any means - electronic, photocopying, recording or otherwise - unless the written permission of the publishers has been obtained beforehand. This book may not be sold, resold, hired out or otherwise disposed of by way of trade in any form of binding or cover other than that with which it is published, without the prior consent of all relevant publishers. The contents of this publication are believed correct at the time of printing. Nevertheless, the publishers cannot be held responsible for any errors or omissions or for any changes in the details given in this guide or for the consequences of any reliance on the information provided by the same. This does not affect your statutory rights.

AA Media Limited strives to ensure accuracy of the information in this guide at the time of printing. Due to the constantly evolving nature of the subject matter the information is subject to change. AA Media Limited will gratefully receive any advice from our readers of any necessary updated information.

Web site addresses are included in some entries and specified by the respective establishment. Such web sites are not under the control of AA Media Limited and as such AA Media Limited has no control over them and will not accept any responsibility or liability in respect of any and all matters whatsoever relating to such web sites including access, content, material and functionality. By including the addresses of third party Web Sites the AA does not intend to solicit business or offer any security to any person in any country, directly or indirectly.

Typeset/Repro:AA Media Limited
Printed and bound by Graficas Estella, Spain

Fanum House, Basing View, Basingstoke, Hampshire RG21 4EA. Registered number 06112600

A CIP catalogue record for this book is available from the British Library

ISBN: 978-0-7495-6639-5
and 978-0-7495-7046-0 (SS)

A04547

With thanks to The Tea Guild and The United Kingdom Tea Council

This product includes mapping data licensed from Ordnance Survey® with the permission of the Controller of Her Majesty's Stationery Office.
© Crown copyright 2011.
All rights reserved. Licence number 100021153.

Perfect places for
Afternoon Tea

Contents

The Tea Guild

The Tea Guild is a prestigious organisation that encourages excellence in tea brewing, reflects the importance of taking tea as an enjoyable social ritual, and recognises and rewards tea rooms, tea shops and hotels that offer the highest standards of tea service. A division of The United Kingdom Tea Council (UKTC), an independent, non-profit making organisation representing the interests of the tea industry, The Tea Guild was founded in 1985 to provide recognition for those outlets that succeeded in meeting the high standards for serving tea set by The UK Tea Council.

Tea Guild Members

Membership of The Tea Guild is strictly by invitation only. Tea rooms are visited by an incognito tea inspector who will judge whether the tea room complies with The Tea Council's high standards.

If it does, it is invited to become a member of The Tea Guild. Once an establishment has been invited to join, The Tea Guild keeps a watching brief and conducts further incognito inspections throughout the year to ensure that standards of excellence are maintained.

Benefits of membership

Tea Guild members benefit from the expertise and reputation of The UK Tea Council, and in addition benefits include:

- Automatic entry on The Tea Guild member pages of The UK Tea Council website (www.tea.co.uk) that enjoys 3,000 hits every day.

- Automatic entry in the latest edition of The Tea Guild guidebook.

- The Tea Guild plaque to display in your tea lounge

- Increased exposure through The Tea Guild's links with local and national press

- Automatic entry into the annual competition for the Top Tea Place of the Year, Top London Tea Place, or Top City and Country Hotel.

- Regular issues of *Guild News*.

- Automatic invitation to all Tea Guild events, such as conferences.

The Tea Council

The ideal tea room
The standards set by The UKTC focus on tea. Establishments serving tea must cater for all tastes and offer a wide selection of good quality teas, which are both brewed and served well. The atmosphere should be welcoming and comfortable, and customers should be treated with care and courtesy.

Serving tea
The teapots, cups and saucers, general crockery and cutlery should reflect the overall style, theme and atmosphere of the venue. A top quality tea room may offer different brewing and drinking vessels according to the different types of tea they serve.

Teapots
Not all materials are suitable for the successful brewing of tea. The best teapots are made from porcelain, bone china, glazed stoneware, unglazed Chinese red earthenware, silver and glass. They lose heat slowly from the outside and maintain a good temperature inside.

Cups and saucers
Porcelain and bone china make the best teacups. They keep the tea hot and are more elegant and easier to lift and use.

Cups, mugs or bowls?
For traditional British tea drinking, cups and saucers are best but, for oriental teas, little bowls or tall, straight-sided cups with no handles are culturally correct and add an interesting and colourful element to the tea drinking experience.

Tea Guild Members in this Guide
You can identify members of The Tea Guild by looking for the Tea Guild logo which appears in their entry.

The United Kingdom Tea Council is a non-profit making organisation dedicated to raising awareness of the benefits and tradition of excellence in the UK.

Learn more about tea on
www.tea.co.uk

Contact :
The United Kingdom Tea Council Ltd
Suite 10, Fourth Floor, Crown House,
One Crown Square, Woking, GU21 6HR
Tel: 01483 750599

The Tea Guild Awards 2011

The Tea Guild's team of tea experts take tea in hotels and tearooms across Britain to find the finest places to enjoy afternoon tea. Visits are anonymous and the judges award points for the variety, flavour and knowledge of the teas offered, together with the quality of food, service, décor, ambience, and presentation. With 125 points to be lost or gained on the judge's scorecard, only those tea establishments achieving the very highest standards across a number of categories can make it to the top. Irene Gorman, Head of The Tea Guild, said "The standard of entrants this year was incredibly high, with many excellent entries from across the UK. The tradition of afternoon tea has never been stronger, with Tea Guild members busier than ever. More and more people are taking time out to enjoy afternoon tea - modern life can be very hectic and demanding and afternoon tea is the perfect way to slow down and relax."

The Tea Guild's
Top Tea Place 2011

Top Tea Place 2011 – Award Winner
Rocke Cottage Tearoom
Craven Arms, Abcott, Clungunford, Shropshire

Rocke Cottage Tearooms was praised by the judges for its pleasant surroundings, the warm and friendly welcome, and the "quietly efficient" service that guests enjoyed. The judges were impressed by the variety and amount of sandwiches, crumpets, scones and delicious cakes and were won over by the excellent selection of teas and the staff's exceptional knowledge. Owner Karin Clarke said: "We're very proud to be members of The Tea Guild and winning The Tea Guild's Top Tea Place 2011 Award is a huge honour - we're absolutely delighted. We aim to give our customers the very best afternoon tea experience possible and all our staff work tirelessly to make Rocke Cottage a great place to relax and enjoy the highest quality food and tea. We know just how important it is to get all aspects of afternoon tea exactly right."

Top London Tea Place 2011 – Award Winner
Claridge's
Brook Street, London W1

Claridge's hugely impressed Tea Guild judges with exceptional service, great quality tea and the extensive knowledge of the staff. This is the second time in recent years that Claridge's has been awarded this accolade, having also won in 2006. The Foyer gained a near perfect score, and the inspectors praised the tasteful art deco style and fine furnishings, as well as friendly and efficient staff and excellent selection of scones, sandwiches and cakes. When it came to the tea itself, once again Claridge's surpassed expectations with the selection of teas. Knowledgeable staff excel in both advising customers on the choice of tea blends on offer and then serving those teas perfectly. The judges concluded that Claridge's offered "a very enjoyable and relaxing tea experience in splendid surroundings." General Manager Thomas Kochs, said: "As a proud member of The Tea Guild we are delighted and honoured to receive this hugely prestigious award. All of our staff are passionate about creating a memorable guest experience and when it comes to serving the perfect afternoon tea, we strive to get every detail just right."

Top City & Country Hotel 2011 – Award Winner
The Angel Hotel
15 Cross Street, Abergavenny

The Angel Hotel was praised it for its smart and elegant surroundings, attentive and efficient service and tasty sandwiches, cakes and scones. The judges were also very impressed by the choice of teas on offer and the quality of tea served. The judges concluded that "it was a smooth operation from start to finish. Everyone was made to feel special." William Griffiths, owner and General Manager of The Angel Hotel said: "It's a fantastic honour for us to win this award and we are absolutely thrilled. The Angel Hotel are proud to be members of The Tea Guild and we place the highest value on the choice and quality of the tea we serve. Our customers demand the very best and we strive at all times to fulfil their expectations. It's a real team effort here and all our staff work tirelessly to create somewhere special, where the quality of food, relaxing atmosphere and the very best standards are paramount."

The Tea Guild Awards

Abbey Cottage Tea Rooms, New Abbey
Abbey Tea Rooms & Restaurant, Tewkesbury
Ashdown Park Hotel, Wych Cross
Athenaeum Hotel, London W1
The Balmoral Hotel, Edinburgh
Bettys Café Tea Rooms – Harrogate
Bettys Café Tea Rooms – Ilkley
Bettys Café Tea Rooms – Northallerton
Bettys Café Tea Rooms – York
Bettys at RHS Gardens Harlow Carr
Bingham, Richmond upon Thames
The Black Swan Hotel, Helmsley
The Bridge Tea Rooms, Bradford-on-Avon
Bullivant of York, York
Cemlyn Tea Shop, Harlech
Charlotte's Tea House, Truro
Cheristow Lavender Tea Rooms, Hartland
The Chesterfield Mayfair, London W1
Claris's, Biddenden
The Corn Dolly, South Molton
Cream Tea Room, Stow on the Wold
Dartmoor Tearooms & Café, Moretonhampstead
Derrick's Tea Room, Cheddar
De Wynn's Tea & Coffee House, Falmouth
The Dorchester, London W1
Elizabeth Botham & Sons, Whitby
The English Tea Rooms at Brown's Hotel, London W1
Espelette at The Connaught, London W1
Flying Fifteens, Lowestoft
Food for Thought, Westerham
Four Seasons Hotel Hampshire, Dogmersfield,
Gilbert White's Tea Parlour, Selborne
Gillam's Tea Room, Ulverston
Ginger & Pickles, Nantwich
The Goring, London SW1
The Grand Tea Lounge, Turnberry Resort, Turnberry
Hazelmere Café & Bakery, Grange-over-Sands

Juri's – The Olde Bakery Tea Shoppe, Winchcombe
King John's Hunting Lodge, Lacock
The Lanesborough, London SW1
Little Bettys, York
Loopy Lorna's Tea House, Edinburgh
The Lowry, Salford
The Manor House Hotel, Castle Combe
The Marshmallow Tearooms, Moreton in Marsh
The Milestone, London W8
Moggerhanger Park Tearooms, Moggerhanger
The Montagu Arms Hotel, Beaulieu
The Montagu at Hyatt Regency London
   – The Churchill, London W1
The Montague on the Gardens, London WC1
Muffins Tea Shop, Lostwithiel
Northern Tea Merchants, Chesterfield
The Old Stables Tea Rooms, Hay-on-Wye
Ollerton Watermill Tea Shop, Ollerton
Orange Pekoe, London SW13
The Park Room and Library at
   Grosvenor House, London W1
The Palm Court at The Langham, London W1
Peacocks, Ely
Pennyhill Park Hotel & Spa, Bagshot,
Rectory Farm Tearooms, Morwenstow, nr Bude
Regency Tea Rooms, Bath
The Ritz, London W1
The Savoy, London WC2
St Tudno Hotel, Llandudno
Searcy at the Pump Room, Bath
Sheraton Park Lane Hotel, London W1 NOTE NAME
Sofitel London St James, London SW1
Swinton Park, Masham
Tea on the Green, Danbury
The Tea Shop, Wadebridge
Tiffin Tea Rooms, Alresford
Tiny Tim's Tearoom, Canterbury

The Perfect Cup of Tea

Choose tea to suit your taste and the occasion. The most popular tea in the Western world is black tea, but green teas and special teas are gaining in popularity. Breakfast Tea is prefect to kick-start the day, Darjeeling is the more delicate partner to afternoon tea, and green tea is perfect for after meals.

How to make and enjoy the perfect brew

- Use good quality loose leaf tea or tea bags.
- Boil fresh water.
- Warm your favourite teapot and teacup.
- Allow a rounded teaspoon of loose tea for each cup.
- Pour freshly boiled water over the tea and stir once and twice while it is brewing.
- Timing is everything! Allow the tea to brew for the recommended number of minutes.
- Pour, add milk or lemon, put your feet up and enjoy!

Hints and tips

- Store tea in a air-tight container at room temperature.
- Always use fresh water - it has more oxygen which draws the full flavour out of the tea.
- Use fully boiled water for black and herbal teas, but green teas are best made with water that has been boiled and allowed to cool slightly.
- Reduce the taste of chlorinated water with a water filter.
- For best results, use loose tea, or good quality tea bags.
- A teapot makes the best tea. It allows the leaf to infuse and release a fuller flavour.
- An alternative to a teapot is a tea leaf infuser.

Stop Press!
Three further establishments joined The Tea Guild just as we went to press.
For more information visit www.tea.co.uk

Great Fosters Hotel
Egham, Surrey TW20 9UR
01784 433822
www.greatfosters.co.uk

Davenports Tea Room
Bridge Farm, Warrington Road
Bartington, Northwich, Cheshire CW8 4QU
01606 853241
www.davenportsfarmshop.co.uk

Mistletoe House Tearoom & Gallery
Combe, Presteigne, Powys LD8 2HL
01544 260035
www.mistletoehouse.co.uk

Types of Tea

Much like wine, the flavour and characteristics of tea change depending on the soil, altitude and climate where it's grown. Other factors include the tea making process and blending of teas from different growing areas. Learn more about processing on page 135.

Today it is estimated that there are 1,500 different varieties of tea, grown in some 36 countries. Tea can be divided into six main categories; black, green, oolong, white, compressed and flavoured teas.

CHINA – BLACK TEAS

Lapsang Souchong

Perhaps the most famous China tea, the best coming from the hills in north Fujian. It is a unique large leaf tea distinguished by its smoky aroma and flavour. The tarry taste is acquired through drying over pine wood fires.

Keemun

A popular black tea from Anhui Province, this is a 'gonfu' tea - it is made with disciplined skill to produce the thin tight strips of leaf without breaking the leaves. The tight black leaves give a rich brown liquor, which has a lightly scented nutty flavour and delicate aroma.

Yunnan

A black tea from the province of Yunnan in south west China. It has a rich, earthy, malty flavour similar to Assam teas and is best drunk with milk. It makes an excellent breakfast tea. Other recommended China black teas are Keemun Mao Feng (Hair Point) and Szechwan Imperial.

GREEN TEAS

Many green China teas are still traditionally made by hand using age-old methods. However, more and more teas are now made in mechanised factories. Green teas are totally unoxidised (compared to black teas which are fully oxidised).

The first stage of the manufacturing process is to kill any enzymes that would otherwise cause oxidation to take place. To de-enzyme them, the freshly plucked leaves are either steamed (to make 'sencha'-type teas) or tumbled quickly in a wok or panning machine (to make pan-fired teas) and are then rolled by hand or machine to give the leaf a particular appearance - some teas are twisted, some curved, some rolled into pellets, etc. To remove all but 2-3% of the remaining water, the tea is then dried in hot ovens or over charcoal stoves.

Gunpowder

Most Gunpowder tea is produced in Pingshui in Zheijian Province. After it has been pan-fired to de-enzyme it, the leaf is rolled into small pellets and then dried. The pellets look remarkably like lead shot or gunpowder, giving the tea its descriptive name. Gunpowder tea has a soft honey or coppery liquor with a herby smooth light taste.

Chun Mee

Chun Mee literally means 'precious eyebrows' and the shape of the leaves give this tea its name. The processing of 'eyebrow' teas demands great skill in order to hand roll and dry the leaves to the correct shape at the right temperature for the correct length of time. These long, fine jade leaves give a clear, pale yellow liquor with a smooth taste.

Other green teas from China include Longjing (Dragon's Well) from Zheijiang; Taiping Hon Kui (Monkey King) from Anhui; and Youngxi Huo Qing (Firegreen).

OOLONG

Traditionally from China's Fujian province and Taiwan, these are semi-oxidised teas that vary from greenish rolled oolongs (with a light, floral liquor reminiscent of lily of the valley, narcissus, orchid or hyacinth) to dark brown leafed oolongs (that yield liquors with deeper, earthier flavours and hints of peach and apricot).

These two distinct types of oolong are made by two very different processes. To manufacture the darker leafed oolongs, the freshly plucked leaf is withered, then shaken or 'rattled' in bamboo baskets or in a bamboo tumbling machine to lightly bruise parts of the leaf, then oxidised for a short time. When 60-70% oxidation has been reached, the leaf is dried.

To manufacture the greener oolongs, the leaf is withered and then wrapped inside a large cloth and rolled in a special machine. The bag is opened and the leaf is spread out briefly to oxidise lightly. The leaf is repeatedly wrapped, rolled and oxidised until approximately 30% oxidation has been achieved. The tea is then dried to remove all but 2-3% of the remaining water. The most famous of these greener, light, fragrant oolongs is Tie Kuan Yin. All oolongs are better drunk without milk.

Tie Kuan Yin

This is made in China's Fujian province and in Taiwan. The name means 'Tea of the Iron Goddess of Mercy' who is said to have appeared in a dream to a local tea farmer, telling him to look in a cave behind her temple. There he found a single tea shoot that he planted and cultivated. The bush he grew is said to have been the parent bush from which cuttings have been grown and leaf plucked over the centuries to make this very fragrant tea. It is today one of the most sought after oolongs around the world.

Other recommended China oolong teas are Fonghwang Tan-chung, Shui Hsien (Water Sprite), Oolong Sechung and Wuyi Liu Hsiang, Huan Jin Qui (Yellow Golden Flower), Da Hong Pao (Great Red Robe), Loui Gui (Meat Flower) and Wuyi Yan (Bohea Rock).

POUCHONG

Produced in China's Fujian province and Taiwan, pouchong teas are more lightly oxidised than oolongs. The name means 'the wrapped kind' which refers to the fact that the tea was traditionally wrapped in paper after the manufacturing process when the tea was ready for sale. Long, stylish black leaves brew a very mild cup with an amber infusion and a very smooth, sweet taste.

WHITE TEAS

White teas traditionally come from China's Fujian province and are made from leaf buds and leaves of the Da Bai (Big White) tea varietal by the simplest process of all teas. Very young new leaf buds and baby leaves are simply gathered and dried - often in the sun. The best known white teas are Pai Mu Tan (White Peony) and Yin Zhen (Silver Needles).

Pai Mu Tan Imperial

This rare white tea is made from very small buds and a few baby leaves that are picked in the early spring, and once they have been dried, they look like lots of tiny white blossoms with a few darker leaves surrounding the white bud - the reason for the name, 'White Peony'.

Yin Zhen

From Fujian province, this tea is made from tender new buds that are covered in silvery white hairs hence the name 'Silver Needles'.

PUERH TEAS

The official Chinese definition of Puerh tea is 'Products fermented from green tea of big leaves picked within Yunnan province'. Even Chinese specialists cannot agree on the true definition but, in general terms, Puerh teas are teas from Yunnan that are aged for up to 50 years in humidity- and temperature-controlled conditions to produce teas that have a typically earthy, mature, smooth flavour and aroma.

There are two types of Puerh tea made by two different methods of manufacture: Naturally Fermented Puerh tea (also known as Raw Tea or Sheng Tea) and Artificially Fermented Puerh tea (also known as Ripe Tea or Shou Tea).

To make Naturally Fermented Puerh tea, fresh leaves from the bush are withered, de-enzymed in a large wok, twisted and rolled by hand, dried in the sun, steamed to soften them and then left loose or compressed into flat cakes or blocks of various shapes. The tea is then stored in controlled conditions to age and acquire its typically earthy character.

To make Artificially Fermented Puerh tea, fresh tea leaves are withered, de-enzymed in a large wok, twisted and rolled by hand, dried in the sun and then mixed with a fixed quantity of water, piled, covered with large 'blankets' made from hide and left to ferment. The tea is stirred at intervals and the whole process takes several weeks. When the teas have fermented to a suitable level, they are steamed and then left loose or compressed in the same way as Naturally Fermented Puerh teas.

The teas are then stored in damp, cool conditions to age. Naturally Fermented Puerh teas are left for at least 15 and up to 50 years; Artificially Fermented Puerh teas are aged for only a few weeks or months. When ready, each cake of Puerh tea is wrapped in tissue paper or dried bamboo leaves.

Puerh tea is named after Puerh city in Yunnan province which was once the main trading centre for teas made in the area.

COMPRESSED TEAS

Tuancha

Tuancha, meaning 'tea balls', are made in differing sizes, the smallest is about half the size of a table tennis ball. These little balls are often made from Puerh aged tea and have an earthy flavour and aroma.

Tuocha

Originally from Yunnan province, Tuocha is usually a Puerh tea that has been compressed into a bird's nest shape and has a similar earthy, elemental taste.

FLAVOURED AND SCENTED TEAS

Jasmine

China tea which has been dried with Jasmine blossoms placed between the layers of tea. The tea therefore has a light, delicate Jasmine aroma and flavour.

Rose Congou

A large-leafed black tea scented with rose petals. The manufacture of 'gongfu' teas demand great skill in the handling of the leaves, the temperature control and the timing of each part of the process.

Earl Grey

Traditionally, a blend of black China teas treated with natural oils of the citrus Bergamot fruit which gives the tea its perfumed aroma and flavour. Earl Grey tea is said to have originally been blended for the second Earl Grey by a mandarin after Britain had completed a successful diplomatic mission to China.

Other teas in this category from China include Osmanthus, Magnolia, Orchid, Chloranthus and Lichee.

TEAS FROM INDIA AND SRI LANKA

India is one of the main tea growers, exporting more than 12% of the world's tea and with 523,000 hectares under cultivation. Although indigenous to the Assam region, the first commercially produced teas were raised from seeds brought from China. The plantations range from low-grown areas (sea level up to 2000ft) to high-grown (more than 4000 ft high). Generally plucked from March to October, each area produces teas of distinctive character. The Tea Board of India has endorsed several speciality blends so that their quality and consistency is assured. Although India produces mostly black teas, a small amount of green tea (1% of total production) is produced, mainly for the Afghan market.

Assam

Assam is a major growing area covering the Brahmaputra valley, stretching from the Himalayas down to the Bay of Bengal. There are 655 estates covering some 407,000 hectares. Assam tea has distinctive flecked brown and gold leaves known as "orange" when dried. In flavour it is robust, bright with a smooth, malt pungency and is perfect as the first cup of tea of the day. Such teas are used in everyday popular blends because of the full-bodied richness. There is also an Assam Green tea with an unusual light, almost sweet liquor.

First Flush Assam

Assam tea bushes start growing in March and the first flush is picked for 8 to 10 weeks, first flush Assams e.g. Bamonpookri, an excellent quality tea with a strong fresh flavour; are rarely marketed in the Europe, unlike first flush Darjeelings.

Second Flush Assam

The plucking of the second flush begins in June with most of the production taking place from July to September. The second flush Assam is the best of the season and when brewed gives a rich aroma, a clear dark read liquor and a strong malty taste. Good examples of second flush Assams are Napuk, displaying all the qualities of a well made Assam and Thowra, which has a strong spicy liquor and lots of body.

Darjeeling

Regarded as the "Champagne of Teas", Darjeeling is grown on 100 estates on the foothills of the Himalayas, on over 18,000 hectares at about 7000 ft. Light and delicate in flavour and aroma, and with undertones of muscatel, Darjeeling is an ideal complement to dinner or afternoon tea. The first "flushes"

(pluckings) are thought to produce the best Darjeeling vintage but all crops are of very high quality. Darjeeling Green is rare tea similar to Japanese Sencha with an exquisite aroma and delicate taste.

First Flush Darjeeling

The Darjeeling bushes' first new shoots - the first flush - are picked in April. These first teas of the season are the finest and are much in demand, fetching incredibly high prices at auction. Castleton First Flush has a perfect green-brown leaf and is from one of the most prestigious gardens in the area. It gives an exquisite perfume and taste of green muscatel. Bloomfield First Flush is again from a recognised garden and its subtle astringent flavour is typical of Darjeeling first flush.

Second flush Darjeelings

These are picked between May and June and produce excellent quality teas that are considered by some to be better than the first flush as they have a fruitier, less astringent flavour than the earlier teas. The leaves are darker brown and contain plenty of silvery tip. Good examples of second flush Darjeelings are Puttabong, which has a discernible muscatel flavour, and Namring, a fruity balanced taste perfect for afternoon tea.

Nilgiri

The Nilgiri region, situated in southern India, forms a high hilly plateau at the conjunction of the Eastern and Western Ghat mountains. More than 20,000 smallholders grow and pluck tea with some 90,000 hectares under cultivation. Most Nilgiri teas are used for blending, but there is a rapidly growing demand for the speciality tea of the area. Nilgiri has a bright amber colour and a refreshing, bright and delicate taste. Nunsch is a typical Nilgiri tea, large-leafed, which gives a fruity, bright and flavourful brew.

India Tea

A blend of teas from all parts of India, this is often served as afternoon tea or after a meal. It is full-bodied, refreshing and with delicate hints of its regional origins.

TEA FROM SRI LANKA (CEYLON)

In 1972, the island then known as Ceylon reverted to the traditional name of Sri Lanka, but retained the name of Ceylon for the marketing of teas. Sri Lanka has over 188,0000 hectares under tea cultivation yielding about 298,000 tonnes of "made" tea, and accounting for over 19% of world exports. Tea from Sri Lanka falls into three categories: low-grown (on estates up to 2000 ft high); medium grown (between 2000 and 4000 ft); and high grown (over 4000 ft). Each level produces teas of unique character. By blending teas from different areas of the island, Sri Lanka can offer a very wide range of flavour and colour. Some are full-bodied, others light and delicate, but all Ceylon blends will have brisk full flavours and bright golden colour. Because of the geographical location, tea can be plucked in Sri Lanka all year round: the west and east of the island are divided by central mountains so that as each region's season ends, the other begins.

Dimbula

Probably the most famous of Ceylon teas, Dimbula is cultivated on estates first planted with tea when their coffee crops failed in 1870. Grown 5000 ft above sea level, all Dimbula teas are light and bright in colour with a crisp strong flavour that leaves the mouth feeling fresh and clean. Today, it forms part of the high-grown zone of central Sri Lanka which includes Dickoya and Nuwarah Eliya.

Kenilworth

This tea has long wiry beautiful leaves that give an exquisite, almost oaky taste and good body and strength.

Uva

A fine flavoured tea grown at altitudes between 2,000ft and 4,000ft above sea level on the eastern slopes of the Central Mountains. It has a bright, deep amber colour when brewed, with the brisk and crisp, strong Ceylon flavour. These teas are also used in Ceylon blend and make an ideal morning drink or an after-lunch tea.

Saint James

This is a copper-coloured infusion with a very smooth, pronounced taste and a wonderful aroma. It is a perfect breakfast or daytime tea.

Nuwara Eliya

Nuwara teas are light and delicate in character, bright in colour and with a fragrant flavour. Their flavour is heightened when taken with lemon rather than milk.

Nuwara Eliya Estate

This tea has a bright brisk flavour and a wonderful perfume, good to drink at any time of day with just a little milk

Ceylon Blend

Ceylon teas span the entire spectrum of tea production, from low to high grown teas. By blending teas from different areas of the island, Sri Lanka is able to offer a very wide choice of flavour and characteristics.

TEA FROM JAPAN

The Japanese have always been known to produce high quality green tea. The worldwide export of Japanese tea has dwindled over the past few decades, almost entirely due to price considerations, land and labour costs in Japan are comparatively more expensive than other tea growing regions in the world. Japan has 50,000 hectares planted with tea.

Sencha

The most commonly drunk tea in Japan. The dark green flat needles give a pale yellow infusion that has a light delicate flavour.

Gyokuro

Gyokuro, which means Precious Dew, is the very best of Japan's teas and is the one chosen to serve to visitors and for special occasions. The leaves are beautiful, flat and pointed emerald needles that give a smooth taste and a subtle perfume, it is a very refined tea.

TEAS FROM KENYA, MALAWI AND ZIMBABWE

African countries have been able to build on the experience of other producers. As a result, Africa is now a major force in world tea, producing teas of high quality and good bright colour which are used for blending all over the world.

Kenya

One of the oldest of the African producers, Kenya has a history of tea dating back to 1903. Today, Kenya has 69000 hectares under cultivation by smallholders (shambas), under the protection of the Kenya Tea Development Authority, and tea producing companies in the public and private sector. Kenya exports over 349,000 tonnes of tea per year (22% of world exports). Kenya's equatorial climate allows tea growing all year round. The teas are very bright, colourful, with a reddish coppery tint and a pleasant brisk flavour. Kenya speciality tea is ideal as a drink for any time of day or night and is particularly ideal with beef and horseradish or ham sandwiches and rich chocolate cake. Kenya teas are also blended into many famous British brands.

Malawi

Malawi is the pioneer of tea growing in Africa, with production first starting commercially in the 1880s in Mulanje. Now exporting over 43,000 tonnes annually, Malawi has a 3% share of world exports and is mainly responsible for the spread of tea cultivation in Africa. Malawi was the first African country to adopt the cloning method of estate refurbishment. Although Malawi teas are not so well known as speciality teas, their superb colour and brightness means they are used in the blending of leading British tea brands.

Zimbabwe

Tea production in Zimbabwe could begin commercially only after the successful establishment of irrigated tea estates. With an average annual rainfall of not more than 26 inches per annum, as opposed to the 50 plus inches per annum usually required, irrigation is essential to continuous growth. Zimbabwe now exports over 15,000 tonnes of tea per year.

Today, tea is a "controlled" commodity in Zimbabwe so that its quality and industry growth are protected.

OTHER TEA PRODUCERS

Tanzania

Tea production in Tanzania is thought to be the legacy of German colonisation under the reign of Kaiser Wilhelm II, but its real development took place under British estate ownership between the two World Wars. Tanzania now exports over 22,000 tonnes of tea annually. The different altitudes result in distinct tea characteristics, but all Tanzanian teas are bright in colour with a brisk flavour that makes them ideal for use in blending.

South Africa

A black cut, torn and curled tea the tea factory and black tea manufacture from KwaZulu is the only South African tea to be exported for international consumption. The flavour is strong and lively and is best drunk with milk.

Indonesia

Tea has been part of the way of life in Indonesia for more than 200 years. Situated in the South China Sea and the Pacific Ocean, Indonesia forms an island chain stretching from Malaysia to Papua New Guinea. Java and Sumatra are the main growing areas. After World War II, the Indonesian tea estates were in very poor condition. By 1984, after a lot of hard work and investment, tea exports from Indonesia began to make their mark on the tea market. Improvement in tea production and replanting of old estates has continued, with the factories investing in new machinery. Now, Indonesia has some 142,000 hectares under tea cultivation, and in 2005 exported over 102,000 tonnes of tea, accounting for over 7% of world exports. Teas from Indonesia are light and flavoursome. Most are sold for blending purposes. In recent years, however, it has become possible to buy Indonesian tea as a speciality. It is extremely refreshing taken without milk: garnished with lemon, it makes an ideal drink for the figure-conscious.

England

Bedfordshire

Moggerhanger Park

The Tea Guild's Award of Excellence 2011

A Georgian house in wonderful parkland serving delicious home-made tea

Park Road, Moggerhanger,
BEDFORD, MK44 3RW
Tel 01767 641007
e-mail enquiries@moggerhangerpark.com
web www.moggerhangerpark.com

The house was built by Sir John Soane and the grounds were landscaped by Humphrey Repton, making this a place where you could spend all day. The house is open to visitors in the summer, while the extensive grounds contain walled gardens and an ice house. The tea rooms serve a good collection of teas as well as home-made scones, cakes and pastries. Produce from local suppliers is used whenever possible. Groups of 10 to 20 can use Mr Thornton's Library.

To eat Cream tea, sandwiches. Snacks

Open Daily 11am-4pm

Getting there
At Moggerhanger turn into Park Road and at left hand bend turn right into The Park.

What to see Shuttleworth Collection, Swiss Garden, Sandy RSPB Nature Reserve.

Berkshire

The Tutti Pole

Tradtional afternoon tea within easy reach of the Berkshire Downs

3 High Street,
HUNGERFORD, RG17 0DN
Tel 01488 682515

The name "Tutti" comes from the "Tithing" or "Tutti" men who still call in each year to collect a penny from all the Common Right Houses, and a kiss from the property occupants. The men (or women) carry a "Tutti Pole" which is a long staff decorated with flowers, an orange, and some blue ribbon. For many years, the staffs were made in the cottage where the tea shop is now located. The menu includes lunches, snacks, sandwiches, cakes and scones with home-made jam and cream accompanied by 13 blends of tea. Specialities include toasted teacakes and meringues. The picturesque Kennet Valley nearby offers keen walkers the chance to amble through green fertile meadows and birch and oakwoods.

To eat Afternoon tea.

Open Mon-Fri 9am-5:30pm, Sat & Sun 9am-6pm.

Getting there Hungerford is on the A4. Nearest motorway M4. Parking in the town.

What to see Antiques and collectors shops of Hungerford, Berkshire Downs and the Ridgeway Path, the Kennet Valley.

Barkham Tea Rooms

Comfortable tea rooms in which to spend a moment after browsing the antiques market

Barkham Antique Centre,
Barkham Street, Barkham,
WOKINGHAM, RG40 4PJ
Tel 0118 976 1355

Located within an 18th-century barn and stables, this tea room offers the visitor a comfortable place to relax after a leisurely browse through the huge Barkham Antique Centre, which sells a wide selection of items including furniture, general antiques and collectables. Light refreshments and cream teas are available and there is plenty of space for parking.

To eat Cream tea. Light refreshments.

Open Wed, Thu 11am-3pm, Fri-Sun 11am-4pm. Closed Mon, Tue.

Getting there Wokingham is on the A329, accessible from junction 10 of the M4.

What to see Barkham Antique Centre, Cantley Park, Elms Field, Dinton Pastures, Wokingham Town Hall, Look Out Discovery Centre.

Wokingham Town Hall

Bristol

Stern of ss Great Britain

Bristol Marriott Royal Hotel

Home-made pastries served in a luxurious hotel drawing room

College Green,
BRISTOL, BS1 5TA
Tel 0117 925 5100
e-mail bristol.royal@marriotthotels.co.uk
web www.marriott.co.uk/brsry

Splendid Victorian surroundings blend with stylish modern luxury to create an ideal setting for afternoon tea at this superb hotel. Easy to find, it stands next to the cathedral in the city centre. Inside, it's all polished mahogany, marble and glittering chandeliers. Tea is served in the lavish Club Lounge and the Drawing Room, and there are tables outside on warm afternoons. Home-made pastries and cakes created by the award-winning kitchen's speciality chef are served at teatime, and there's also a choice of sandwiches and wraps.

To eat Set teas.

Open Daily. Tea served 12-5pm.

Getting there Next to cathedral.

What to see Bristol Industrial Museum, City Museum and Art Gallery, SS Great Britain, Maritime Heritage Centre, British Empire and Commonwealth Museum.

Buckinghamshire

Chenies Manor

An architectually splendid manor house set in beautiful gardens

CHENIES, WD3 6ER
Tel 01494 762888
e-mail macleodmatthews@btinternet.com
web www.cheniesmanorhouse.co.uk

Chenies Manor is celebrated as a visitor attraction for the beauty of its gardens, which include imaginative plantings in the sunken, white, rose and physic gardens as well as the parterre with its yew maze. Tunnels run underneath the lawns and there is an ancient well. The Manor house was the original home of the Russells – Earls and Dukes of Bedford – and was visited by Henry VIII and Elizabeth I on numerous occasions. Home-made teas are served in the Garden Room.

To eat Set teas. Light refreshments.

Open Apr-Oct, Wed-Thu and Bank Holiday Mondays 2-5pm.

Getting there Chenies Manor is off the A404 between Rickmansworth and Amersham. Nearest motorway M25, Jnct 18. Own car park.

What to see The church at Chenies Manor (special permission required to visit the chapel); Milton's Cottage, Chalfont St Giles; Hughenden Manor, High Wycombe; Garden of the Rose, St Albans.

Compleat Angler Hotel

Afternoon tea at this hotel with wonderful view of the Thames and the Marlow Weir

Marlow Bridge,
MARLOW, SL7 1RG
Tel 0844 879 9128
e-mail bowaters.compleatangler@macdonald-hotels.co.uk
web www.macdonaldhotels.co.uk

The Compleat Angler Hotel takes its name from the famous book of the same name by Izaak Walton, written here in 1653. Nowadays the river scene is more to do with pleasure boats than solitary fishermen. An afternoon tea at this picturesque Thames-side hotel offers the additional pleasure of sweeping river views. Food offered includes a light lunch, snacks, sandwiches, cakes, and scones with jam and cream, and there is a choice of seven teas. Cakes are served with afternoon tea. Booking is advised.

To eat Afternoon tea.

Open Mon-Fri 3:30-5:30pm, Sat, Sun and Bank Holidays 4-5:30pm.

Getting there Marlow is on the A4155, nearest motorway M4, M40 and the M25. There is parking in the hotel car park.

What to see Mary Shelley's house in West Street (where Frankenstein was written), Marlow Regatta (mid-June), Chiltern Hills.

Danesfield House Hotel and Spa

Victorian mansion house with a large estate overlooking the Thames

Henley Road, MARLOW, SL7 2EY
Tel 01628 891010
e-mail sales@danesfieldhouse.co.uk
web www.danesfieldhouse.co.uk

Spectacular views across the River Thames are afforded from this country house hotel, which is set in rolling grounds high up in the Chiltern Hills. There are three set teas to choose from: the cream tea, afternoon tea (using a selection of some of the world's finest teas) or Champagne tea. The most lavish option comprises finger sandwiches, scones with jam and clotted cream, rich fruit cake, shortbread, dainty cakes and pastries, along with a glass of Laurent Perrier Champagne cocktail. Interesting sandwich fillings include tuna with pickled ginger and wasabi. Booking is recommended at weekends.

To eat Afternoon tea, Cream tea, Champagne tea.

Open Daily. Tea served 3-6pm. Closed 25-26 Dec.

Getting there M4 junct 8/9 or M40 junct 40, A404, A4155 Marlow, follow Henley signs, under footbridge, hotel on left.

What to see Windsor Castle, Hell Fire Caves, Dashwood Estate, Blue Max Museum.

Claydon House

An extraordinary house with mementoes of Florence Nightingale and offering a variety of teas

MIDDLE CLAYDON, (near Buckingham),
MK18 2EY
Tel 01296 730349

Claydon House (National Trust) has been the home of the Verney family for hundreds of years and the mainly 18th-century house contains a series of fine Rococo state apartments and an unusual Chinese room. A suite of rooms, once occupied by Florence Nightingale, is now a museum. The gardens opened for the first time recently. Food served in a privately run café includes a light lunch, snacks, sandwiches, cakes, and scones with jam and cream.

To eat Afternoon tea.

Open 12 Mar-2 Nov (2011), Sat-Wed 11-5pm (last admissions 4:30pm).

Getting there Middle Claydon is signposted off the A41 A413 roads. The nearest motorway is the M40. Claydon has its own car park.

What to see Chiltern Hills, Vale of Aylesbury, Stowe Landscape Gardens (National Trust), Bicester, Buckinghamshire Railway Centre.

Windsor Castle

Swanbourne Cottage Tea Rooms

Former bakery turned tea rooms offering several varieties of tea and light lunch

26-28 Winslow Road,
SWANBOURNE, MK17 0SW
Tel 01296 720516

The 16th-century Tea Rooms and Garden are situated in the rural village of Swanbourne, owned by the lord of the manor. The Cottage used to be the village bakery, and older patrons may still remember running down the lane for a warm penny loaf! Inside the cottage is a cosy tea room with all kinds of small treasures and mementoes, such as pictures and memorabilia. Home-made lunches, snacks, cakes and cream teas are served as well as traditional Sunday roast (booking only).

To eat Afternoon tea. Light lunches.

Open Sat-Tue 10am-4pm.

Getting there Swanbourne is East of Winslow on the B4032. Parking is permitted in the village.

What to see Swanbourne village, Aylesbury, Catherine of Aragon's house at Long Crendon, Claydon House (National Trust), Ascot House (National Trust).

Statue of John Hampden, Aylesbury

Catherine of Aragon's house at Long Crendon

Cambridgeshire

Peacocks

The Tea Guild's Award
of Excellence 2011

A friendly and welcoming tea shop with a considerable range of teas located close to the Cathedral

65 Waterside,
ELY, CB7 4AU
Tel 01353 661100
e-mail tea@thepeacocks.co.uk
web www.peacockstearoom.co.uk

The owners of Peacocks add a little extra to the traditional tea room experience with their home-made specialities. Light meals such as Norfolk ham salad and cakes are available all day, with both soup and a dish of the day offered. A definite treat are the scones baked by the owner, served with Cornish clotted cream. The choice of teas is truly remarkable, with 70 listed, from the well known blends to many more unusual varieties. Try something different – maybe the Chocolate Imperial from Paris if you have a taste for chocolate, or a jasmine blossom green tea. The Special Afternoon Tea includes finger sandwiches, scones with a choice of jam: strawberry or raspberry, and a selection from the cakes available.

To eat Cream tea and full afternoon tea. Lunches.

Open Wed-Sun 10:30am-4:30pm. Tea served all day; Closed one month during winter (usually Jan).

Getting there Downhill from cathedral, overlooking River Great Ouse and Slipway, between Waterside Antiques Centre and Babylon Gallery.

What to see Ely Cathedral, Waterside Antiques Centre, River Great Ouse walks and boat trips, Oliver Cromwell's House, Ely Museum.

River Tea Rooms

Cream tea and cakes by the river

1 & 2 Manor Mews, Bridge Street, ST IVES PE27 5U
Tel 01480 464921
e-mail info@rivertearooms.co.uk
web www.rivertearooms.co.uk

Set in a pretty Grade II* manor house, one of the oldest buildings in town, the River Tea Rooms enjoy a fantastic riverside setting beside the historic Chapel Bridge which spans the River Great Ouse. In summer, sit and relax on the riverside terraces and watch the boats and wildlife on the river. Suzy Dell has run the tea rooms since 2006 when she spotted a gap in the market for quality tea and cakes in this charming market town. On offer are a wide variety of loose-leaf teas, and a homemade cake selection that includes fantastic Victoria sponges as well as lemon drizzle, coffee and walnut, and chocolate. Scones are also freshly baked each morning on the premises. Choose from the selection of sandwiches, toasties and paninis, all made fresh to order and with local ingredients whenever possible. Jacket potatoes, quiche and ploughman's lunches are all available, or you can try the Cambridgeshire Cream Tea or St Ives High Tea. There's a 'Tiddlers Menu' for children and the tea rooms will accommodate special dietary requirements where possible. They sometimes arrange group events; maybe combining a riverboat trip with a cream tea, or breakfasts with early morning bird watching cruises.

To eat Lunches, Teas

Open 9am-5pm Mon-Sat, 10am-4pm Sun

Getting there Cross Chapel Bridge and left into Manor Mews. Parking at the Dolphin Hotel

What to do River Great Ouse walks and cruises, St Ives Norris Museum, Houghton Mill (National Trust), Cambridge and Ely.

The Orchard Tea Garden

More famous people have taken tea here than anywhere else in the world

45-47 Mill Way,
GRANTCHESTER, CB3 9ND
Tel 01223 847 788
e-mail otg@callan.co.uk
web www.orchard-granchester.com

This Tea Garden must be unique. It has been running since 1897 and has served tea to such luminaries as Bertrand Russell, Virginia Woolf and, of course, Rupert Brooke, who lived in Grantchester. It is a relaxed, casual meadow, with deck chairs everywhere, as likely as not, filled with students and their laptops. But they know all about afternoon tea and have a wide selection of cakes, freshly made scones and tray bakes, together with a good selection of teas, fruit teas, coffee and soft drinks, as well as Champagne for that special occasion. In the winter, delicious 'winter teas' are served in the atmospheric setting of The Pavilion, which has been standing for nearly 100 years.

To eat Afternoon Tea. Light lunches.

Open Daily. Dec-Feb 9:30am-4:30pm, Mar-May 9:30am-5:30pm, Jun-Aug 9:30am-7pm, Sep-Nov 9:30am-5:30pm.

Getting there On Mill Way just below Granchester Church. Or walk or cycle from Cambridge along Grantchester Meadows

What to see Cambridge colleges, Fitzwilliam Museum, Imperial War Museum, Duxford

Trinity College, Cambridge

Cheshire

The Chester Grosvenor & Spa

Luxurious listed building in the heart of this historic city

Eastgate, CHESTER, CH1 1LT
Tel 01244 324024
e-mail hotel@chestergrosvenor.com
web www.chestergrosvenor.com

Behind the traditional black and white timber frontage of this Grade II listed building, dating back to 1865, is a luxuriously elegant and stylish interior. Tea is taken in the Arkle Bar and Lounge, where you can relax on sofas in an intimate, comfortable atmosphere. The Grosvenor Tea features a selection of finger sandwiches, freshly-made fruit and plain scones with clotted cream and fruit jams, followed by French pastries and fancies; the "Indulgent" version adds strawberries and Taittinger Champagne. Booking is advisable.

To eat Grosvenor Tea, Indulgent Grosvenor Tea.

Open Daily. Tea served 12-5pm. Closed 25-26 Dec.

Getting there On Eastgate in the city centre.

What to see Roman walls and amphitheatre, Deva Roman Experience, Cathedral, Zoo, Military Museum, Visitor Centre.

Crewe Hall

This magnificent former stately home is the perfect place to stop for tea

Weston Road, CREWE, CW1 6UZ
Tel 01270 253333
e-mail crewehall@qhotels.co.uk
web www.qhotels.co.uk

Set in extensive grounds, and once the seat of the Earl of Crewe, the Hall has some breathtaking features, and guided historic tours are available. A Victorian architect extended the original Jacobean pile, and the Grade I listed building offers gracious reception rooms that are the epitome of the afternoon tea venue. In the ornate Sheridan Lounge you can try the light tea of sandwiches and loose black or green tea, or coffee; the high tea – sandwiches, cakes, warm scones with clotted cream and jam; the full Crewe tea and even the Champagne tea. Booking is recommended.

To eat High tea, Cream tea, Champagne tea.

Open Daily. Tea served 2-5:30pm (from 3pm Sun).

Getting there M6 junction 16, A500 to Crewe, last exit at roundabout onto A5020, 1st exit at roundabout then it's a short distance on the right.

What to see Little Moreton Hall (NT), Stapeley Water Gardens, The Potteries.

Little Moreton Hall

Roses Tea Rooms

An appealing and award-winning modern incarnation of the traditional tea room

Ness Botanic Gardens,
Neston Road, NESS,
South Wirral,CH64 4AY
Tel 0151 353 0123 ex. 220
e-mail info@rosestearooms.co.uk
web www.rosestearooms.co.uk

Originally located in Heswall, Roses has relocated to Ness Botanic Gardens. The move has enhanced its already excellent reputation for top class service, great food and freshly baked cakes. Summer visitors will be able to pick up a picnic full of delectable treats including the famous buttermilk scones flavoured with natural ingredients such as rose petals and lavender. A full breakfast menu, light lunches, daily hot specials, freshly baked cakes, scones and puddings and of course afternoon tea, are all on offer. Children have their own menu with healthy choices as well as nursery tea. Beverages include a wide selection of loose leaf teas, freshly ground coffees, artisan hot chocolates, ice cream milkshakes and British juices. For the ultimate treat indulge in a vintage afternoon tea complete with vintage china, linen tablecloths, and accessories.

To eat Breakfasts, meals, light snacks, afternoon tea, nursery tea, childrens menu, cream teas, cakes.

Open Mon-Sun 9.30am-5pm including Bank Holidays. Closed 25-26 Dec.

Getting there Off the A540, between Little Neston and Burton.

What to see Ness Gardens, Warships Birkenhead, Lady Lever Gallery, Port Sunlight, Blue Planet, Chester Zoo.

Ginger and Pickles

The Tea Guild's Award of Excellence 2011

A child-friendly tea shop with delicious treats

3A Mill Street,
NANTWICH, CW5 5ST
Tel 01270 610329
e-mail andyozard@btopenworld.com

This charming little tea room provides delicious, high quality food, using local produce, and offers exceptional service. It is equally popular with both adults and children, attracting customers both locally and from much further afield. The warm and friendly staff serve an excellent selection of delightful home-made savouries and cakes as well as a selection of freshly made and deliciously filled assorted sandwiches. The Cream Tea consists of a large scone accompanied by clotted cream and preserve and served with a pot of tea. The carefully chosen tea varieties include English Breakfast, Darjeeling, Earl Grey, Lady Grey, Ceylon, Assam, Lapsang Souchong and Green Tea. The afternoon teas can be accompanied by a glass of Champagne.

To eat Afternoon Tea, Cream Tea.

Open Mon-Fri 9am-5pm, Sat 9am-6pm, Sun 10am-4pm.

Getting there In town centre, off Water Lode

What to see St Mary's Church, Battle of Nantwich re-enactment, Nantwich Museum.

Cornwall

de Wynn's

 The Tea Guild's Award of Excellence 2011

Gas lights add to the ambience of this traditional tea shop

55 Church Street,
FALMOUTH, TR11 3DS
Tel 01326 319259

After a stroll along the picturesque Falmouth waterfront stop for tea at this traditional tea shop with bow windows and atmospheric gas lighting. It is attractively furnished with simple wooden settles and benches, enhanced by the interesting antique pieces and unusual objects dotted around the place. You can choose from eight different varieties of tea to accompany the tempting selection of sandwiches, cakes and scones with jam and cream, and light lunches and snacks are also on offer. Specialities include Granny Nunn's bread pudding. This place is justifiably popular, and booking is essential.

To eat Cornish cream tea. Light lunches and snacks.

Open Mon-Sat 10am-5pm.

Getting there Falmouth is on the A39, A394 roads. Nearest motorway M5. Town car parks.

What to see The Church of King Charles the Martyr, Pendennis Castle, boat trips around the Fal estuary, National Maritime Museum.

Muffins Tea Shop

The Tea Guild's Award of Excellence 2011

An award-winning tea shop serving varied meals and teas

32 Fore Street,
LOSTWITHIEL, PL22 0BN
Tel 01208 872278
e-mail info@muffinsdeli.co.uk
web www.muffinsdeli.co.uk

In summer Muffins' lovely walled cottage garden is just the place for afternoon tea. At other times the light and spacious tea shop, with its pretty tablecloths and pine furniture, is a magnet for tourists. Reservations are taken, though, so there's no danger of missing out on this treat. Parts of Lostwithiel date from the late 13th century, but Muffins has moved with the times and serves a variety of tasty meals throughout the day, based where possible on fresh local produce. The Cornish Cream Teas are hard to beat, with their delicious Trewithen clotted cream and strawberry jam, or you can try the famous home-made muffins, all to be enjoyed with a pot of top quality tea from the wide choice on offer. You can buy a wide range of local food from the deli area.

To eat Breakfast, Cream tea, full English tea, Cornish tea.

Open Tue-Sat 10am-5pm, plus Mon Jul-Aug. Tea served all day.

Getting there Off A390, on main street, behind the church.

What to see The Eden Project, Lanhydrock (National Trust), Restormel Castle (English Heritage).

Island Café

An enticing location at one of Cornwall's most picturesque attractions

The Harbour,
St Michael's Mount,
MARAZION, TR17 0HS
Tel 01736 710748

Walking down through Marazion, the splendid St Michael's Mount beckons from its location just offshore – even more so when this excellent tea room, in a converted laundry, figures as part of your destination. At high tide take the ferry; at low tide walk across the cobbled causeway. The setting is unusual, the service is cheery and welcoming and, best of all, the menu offers a mouthwatering array of treats and six varieties of tea. As well as traditional teas, there are light lunches and snacks, with local Cornish pasties as a speciality.

To eat Cream tea. Light lunches and snacks.

Open Apr-early Nov, Sun-Fri 10:30am-5pm. Closed Sat.

Getting there St Michael's Mount is approached from the town of Marazion on the A394. Town car parks.

What to see St Michael's Mount, Penzance, Trengwainton Gardens, Chysauster Ancient Village; Trevarno Estate Gardens and Museum of Gardening.

St Michael's Mount

Headland Hotel

Simply stunning coastal setting and incredible views of Fistral Beach

Fistral Beach,
NEWQUAY, TR7 1EW
Tel 01637 872211
e-mail reception@headlandhotel.co.uk
web www.headlandhotel.co.uk

With the Atlantic Ocean on three sides, this is a magnificent Victorian hotel in a dramatic location, making it a popular choice as a film location; movies set here include Roald Dahl's *The Witches*. Staff are very friendly and welcoming, and high standards are set throughout the hotel. You can take tea in The Terrace, one of the many lounges or outside (with more great views) when it's warm. As well as traditional Cornish Cream Tea, there is a selection of freshly prepared sandwiches, cookies and delicious home-made cakes. A glass of Champagne makes this even more of a treat. On weekend evenings a pianist plays in the Lounge. Group bookings are available.

To eat Cornish cream tea, afternoon tea, full afternoon lounge tea, Champagne tea.

Open Daily. Tea served 10am-6pm. Closed 25-26 Dec.

Getting there From A30, follow signs for Newquay via A3058/A3059/A392. On edge of Newquay, follow signs for Fistral Beach. Hotel at end of headland on right.

What to see Fistral Beach surfing, Eden Project, National Maritime Museum, Tate St Ives, Cornish gardens.

Trevathan Farm Tea Room

Stunning views, superb teas and a quality farm shop

St Endellion,
Near PORT ISAAC, PL29 3TT
Tel 01208 880164

This charming tearoom stands on a hillside on the edge of St Endellion village, and is part of a working farm that has been farmed by the Symons family since 1850. A range of teas can be enjoyed in the tearoom or its elegant conservatory. Home-made cakes, hot and cold snacks, and, of course, the famous Cornish cream tea are all available (booking is advisable). The farm shop is well stocked with tempting local goodies, including the farm's own fresh meat, jams and chutneys.

To eat Cream tea. Hot and cold snacks.

Open Mid-Mar to Sep, daily 9:30am-5pm, Oct 10am-4:30pm.

Getting there Port Isaac is north of Wadebridge on the B3314. Parking on site.

What to see Port Isaac, surfing and sailing in Polzeath and Rock, the Camel cycle trail, St Enodoc or Bowood Golf course.

Trelissick Gardens

One of Cornwall's most glorious gardens

Feock,
TRURO, TR3 6QL
Tel 01872 863486
web www.nationaltrust.org.uk/main/w-trelissickgarden

The beautiful gardens and deciduous woods, which run down to the River Fal, make a delightful place to work up a healthy appetite for, or to walk off the indulgence of one of the excellent afternoon teas served here. The traditional spread of sandwiches, cakes and scones might include the speciality – Trelissick fruit slice – and there are 20 varieties of tea to choose from. Light lunches are also available. Booking is advisable for Sunday lunch and for anyone with any special requirements. There is an entrance fee to the gardens; the mansion is not open to the public.

To eat Cream tea. Light lunches and snacks.

Open See website for details of opening times.

Getting there Trelissick is south of Truro on the B3289. There is an on-site car park with a charge.

What to see Truro's fine Georgian buildings, Truro Cathedral, St Mawes.

Fishing boats, Port Isaac

Darjeeling

Many people think the delicate flavour and exquisite floral aroma make Darjeeling the ultimate afternoon tea.

Tea was first grown in the Darjeeling district in 1841. Each estate produces a distinctive flavoured tea with special characteristics, and tea menus often contain single estate teas (using tea from one garden alone) for the best, purest flavour. Darjeeling's unique taste is the result of a combination of factors. Most Indian tea comes from the large leaved Assam plant, but Darjeeling plants comprise a variety of small-leaved Chinese bushes. Here in the West Bengal region of North-East India climate, altitude and soil combine to create the perfect tea. The steep mountain terrain means the tea bushes get 50 inches of rain a year, essential for good growth. Then there's bright sunshine, humidity, and rich soil. Last but not least, only the best leaves are picked, with the growers favour quality over quantity.

Technically the tea is often created by a hard withering process, which makes many Darjeelings an oolong, rather than a black tea, as the oxidation process is often incomplete. Green, and a few rare white Darjeelings are available too. Different grades of Darjeeling are picked throughout the year. The tea bushes are dormant in winter, and, in March and April, tender new leaves appear and are picked to create *First Flush* teas. Plucked after the spring rains, these teas have a gentle flavour, light coloured liquor, floral aroma and mild astringency. This is also known as the *Easter or Spring Flush* and is considered the finest, commanding high prices at auction. From May the succulent summer leaves result in the *Second Flush*. These teas have amber coloured liquor, a mellower, fruitier, more full-bodied taste than the First Flush and Darjeeling's renowned muscatel flavour becomes more pronounced. Sometimes this is described as the *Summer Flush*. Harvests during the rainy monsoon season (called *Monsoon Teas*) result in stronger, darker teas, perfect for inclusion in breakfast blends and Masala Chai. Finally, after the rainy season, the *Autumnal Flush* - a full bodied, darker Darjeeling with a more robust flavour and less spiciness than earlier flushes. The liquor is light copper in colour with a sweet, fresh scent and sparkling character.

The Darjeeling logo, introduced in 1983, protects the tea's designated area of origin. This means that the tea plantation has been certified by the Tea Board of India and your brew contains 100% pure Darjeeling which has been processed in the region too.

Charlotte's Tea House

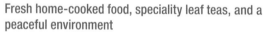
The Tea Guild's Award
of Excellence 2011

Fresh home-cooked food, speciality leaf teas, and a peaceful environment

Coinage Hall, 1 Boscawen Street, TRURO, TR1 2QU
Tel 01872 263706
e-mail teahouse@btconnect.com

The present Grade II listed building was built in 1848 and has been lovingly restored with a Victorian theme. It is on the site of the old Coinage Hall that has a history going back to 1302 and the days of Cornish tin mining. The tea house is on the first floor and presents a sanctuary of Victorian tranquillity just a few steps from the busy main street below. A large selection of well-chosen leaf teas is available, including the local tea from the Tregothnan Estate and a variety of herbal infusions. An extensive range of home-made cakes is available as well as scones, quiches, soups and light lunches, freshly prepared using local ingredients where possible.

To eat Cream tea, high tea.

Open Mon-Sat 10am-5pm.

Getting there Truro city centre, next to War Memorial.

What to see Falmouth Maritime Museum, The Eden Project, Trelissick Garden, Trewithen Garden, Cornish Mines and Engines at Pool.

The Edgcumbe

Varied lunch and teatime fare in a delightful riverside location

Cotehele,
SALTASH, PL12 6TA
Tel 01579 352 717

Set in Cotehele Bay, the Edgcumbe is where you'll find tables set in an intimate room nestling beside the river and a hearty Cornish cream tea. There are no less than nine different varieties of tea to accompany your sandwiches, cakes and scones with jam and cream (or perhaps a light lunch). Could anything be more heavenly? Booking is advisable for large lunch parties.

To eat Set cream tea. Light lunches.

Open Daily Jan 8-Dec 31 11am-5pm, evening opening Thu-Sat from 7pm, closed Dec 25-26.

Getting there Cotehele is located off the A388 A390 roads. Nearest motorway is M5. Parking is on site.

What to see Cotehele House, Morwellham Quay, Plymouth, Antony House at Torpoint, Dartmoor National Park.

Morwellham Quay

Rectory Farm Tearooms

The Tea Guild's Award of Excellence 2011

A 13th-century farmhouse just ten minutes from spectacular Cornish cliffs

Rectory Farm, Morwenstow,
Near BUDE, EX23 9SR
Tel 01288 331251
web www.rectory-tearooms.co.uk

This 13th-century working farmhouse is full of atmosphere. Heavy oak beams, salvaged from wrecked ships, ancient flagstone floors worn by countless feet and large, open fireplaces, all help to make a memorable visit. Food is locally sourced where possible, with a varied menu specialising in home-made scones, cakes, quiches, chutneys and delicious soups.
There are also proper Cornish pasties, cheeses, jams, fish (freshly caught locally) and their own beef and lamb as available. Fruit and vegetables come from local suppliers and their own kitchen garden. Specialist menus are available as well as healthy options for children. A large range of teas is available, including their own house blend (Smuggler's Choice)

To eat Cornish Cream tea, Afternoon Tea, Savoury Tea.

Open Easter-Oct, tea served daily 11am-5pm. Contact for winter opening times.

Getting there Turn off A39 at sign to Morwenstow and follow signs.

What to see Cornish Coastal Path, Church of St John the Baptist, Hartland Abbey.

The Tea Shop

 The Tea Guild's Award of Excellence 2011

Charming tea rooms serving all home-made food

6 Polmorla Road,
WADEBRIDGE, PL27 7ND
Tel 01208 813331

Fresh local produce takes pride of place on the menu at this bright and cosy tea shop, and everything served here is home-made. This proud boast comes from owner Nicky Ryland, whose support of the town is amply repaid by the regular customers attracted by her delicious food. A choice of 40 teas, including a selection of Cornish Tregothnan Estate leaf teas, makes her a winner with visitors to the area too, as do around 30 cakes including boiled fruit cake, strawberry pavlova and apple and almond cake always available. Ice creams are another favourite, and there are light lunches such as jacket potatoes, salads and fresh local crab sandwiches for those whose intentions are less frivolous. The Tea Shop is child-friendly, with a highchair available, and there is pushchair and wheelchair access. Reservations available. Next door is a take-away tea shop for those in a hurry.

To eat Cream tea. Light lunches.

Open Mon-Sat 10am-4pm. Closed Bank Holidays, Christmas.

Getting there From The Platt, turn into Polmorla Road (pub on left); tea shop is half way down on right.

What to see Camel Trail for walking and cycling, Coastal walks, Pencarrow House.

Quarterdeck at the Nare

Spectacular coastal views from this luxurious and comfortable hotel

Carne Beach, Veryan-in-Roseland,
TRURO, TR2 5PF
Tel 01872 501111
e-mail manager@narehotel.co.uk
web www.narehotel.co.uk

The magnificent location and sub-tropical climate make The Quarterdeck at The Nare a great place in which to enjoy afternoon tea. When the weather is nice, tea is served outside on the terrace so guests are able to fully enjoy the wonderful sea views across Gerrans Bay. The Traditional Afternoon Tea, which comprises a selection of finger sandwiches filled with delicacies such as locally-caught crab and lobster, homemade cakes and biscuits, and scones with Cornish clotted cream and jam, is served with Tregothnan Tea. A variety of teas are available, ranging from Darjeeling to Green Tea.

To eat Afternoon Tea

Open Daily 2:30-5:30pm.

Getting there From Tregony follow A3078 for approx 1.5miles. Turn left at Veryan sign, through village towards sea and hotel.

What to see Trelissick Gardens, The Lost Gardens of Heligan, St Mawes Castle.

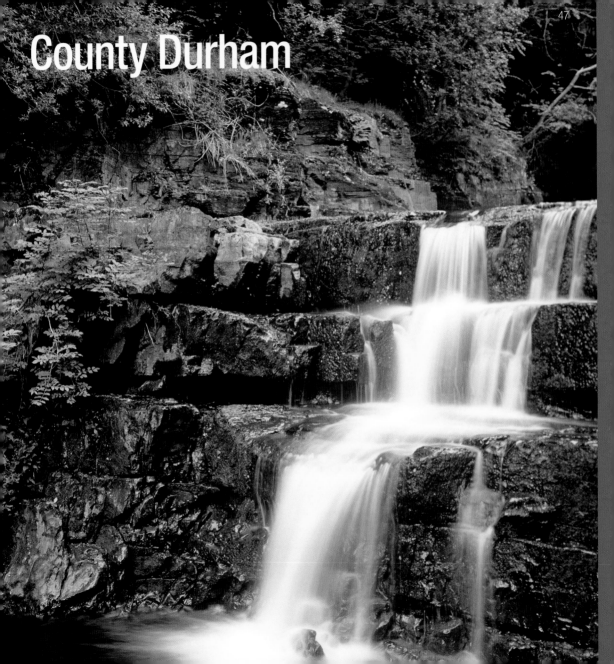

County Durham

The Market Place Tea Shop

Tasty teas at reasonable prices in a building
that's full of character

29 Market Place,
BARNARD CASTLE, DL12 8NE
Tel 01833 690110

This charming tea shop, with 17th-century flagstones, bare stone walls and an open fireplace, was in previous incarnations a pub, and for a time a gentleman's outfitters, kitting out the local farm workers. Despite the rustic surroundings, fine tea is served in silver teapots by uniformed waitresses, and is accompanied by a tempting list of goodies – meringues filled with cream and strawberries, Yorkshire curd cheesecake, fruit tarts and scones might appear on the daily-changing menu. Savoury dishes include home-made steak pie with vegetables and prices are reasonable. The upstairs Artisan shop sells china, glassware, prints and original paintings.

To eat Set tea.

Open Mar-Oct, Mon-Sat 10am-5:30pm. Closed 24 Dec to 7 Jan.

Getting there Barnard Castle is on the A67 west of Darlington. Nearest motorway A1(M).

What to see The Bowes Museum, Raby Castle, Barnard Castle, High Force waterfall.

Raby Castle

Cumbria

Rothay Manor

A secluded and peaceful retreat from the lakeland tourist hotspots

Rothay Bridge,
AMBLESIDE, LA22 0EH
Tel 01539 433605

On a hot summer afternoon, when the world seems to have congregated in Ambleside, this is the sort of place we all want to seek out – a traditional stylish country house hotel with a beautiful garden and a friendly welcome. Afternoon Tea is served as a buffet, which includes savouries - such as Scotch egg, pork pie, savoury frittata and sausage rolls - as well as a selection of sandwiches, and a variety of scones, tea breads and cream cakes. A choice of a dozen blends of tea is available. Booking is advisable.

To eat Buffet Afternoon Tea.

Open Daily 3:30-5pm.

Getting there Ambleside is on the A591 road. Nearest motorway M6.

What to see The Armitt Museum, Beatrix Potter Gallery at Hawkshead, Townend at Troutbeck, Windermere, Coniston Water, Brantwood.

Sheila's Cottage

Delightful cottage tea room in the heart of literary Lakeland

The Slack,
AMBLESIDE, LA22 9DQ
Tel 01539 433079

This charming 17th-century Lakeland cottage and adjoining barn, both built of local stone, is always busy with a mixture of visitors to the lakes and regular local customers.
The setting, wonderful home-baked food and the friendly atmosphere make it a real treat. A choice of four blends of tea is on offer and, as well as the delicious cream teas, there is a light lunch menu that specialises in club and open sandwiches.

To eat Cream tea. Light lunches and snacks.

Open Daily 12-5pm.

Getting there Ambleside is north of Windermere on the A591. Parking is in the town.

What to see The Armitt Museum, Beatrix Potter Gallery at Hawkshead, Townend at Troutbeck, Windermere, Coniston Water, Brantwood.

Ambleside from Latterbarrow, Lake Windermere

Walk

Dent – Adam Sedgwick's land

From his birthplace through the countryside that inspired geologist Adam Sedgwick

Start/finish: Grid ref SD 704871

Parking: Pay-and-display car park at west end of Dent

Distance: 6 miles/9.7km

Level of difficulty: ● ● ●

Suggested map: OS Explorer OL2 Yorkshire Dales – Southern & Western

Walk directions

1 Leaving car park, go up lane almost opposite, **L** of Memorial Hall. Pass green and keep straight on at 'Flinter Gill' signpost. Lane becomes stony track climbing through trees alongside Flinter Gill. Slowly gradient eases and trees peter out. Finally reach gate beside seat high on fellside. Go through gate to T-junction of tracks.

2 Turn **R**, signed 'Keldishaw'. Follow walled track, eroded by 4x4 traffic, for 1.5 miles (2.4km), keeping straight ahead at junction. Reaching tarmac road, turn **R** for 0.25 mile

(400m) to crest of rise and signpost on **L**.

3 Go through gate and follow grassy track past shakeholes to ladder stile. Continue along dilapidated wall to track. This trends **R** below slope scattered with trees, then contours round with great views, descending through yard of restored farmhouse.

4 Follow access track winding downhill, crossing 2 tumbledown walls before marker posts on **L** lead you away from track. Meet stream, go **L** along bank for few paces, then cross simple bridge of 2 stones. Climb bank beyond and go ahead through farmyard.

5 Continue down farm track until it almost levels out alongside trees. Turn sharp **L** by large oak, through waymarked gate. Walk diagonally down field towards ruined farmhouse smothered in elder trees. Pass to its **R** and continue down, soon joining clearer track. Follow this downhill to drive and go **R** few paces to lane.

6 Turn **L** along lane. Follow it round to **R**, then back **L** as it levels out in valley bottom. Watch for ladder stile by barn on **L**. Don't use this, but look for signpost on **R**, about 50 paces on, with plank bridge and stile just below it. From stile cross field to riverbank. Go **R**, following river (and Dales Way) upstream for 0.75 mile

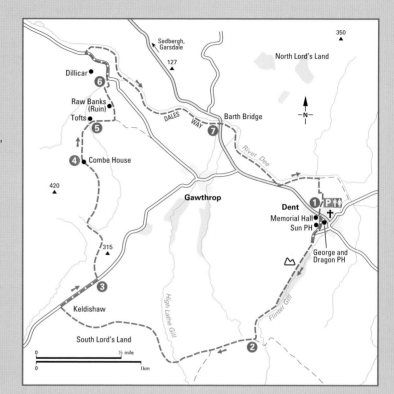

(1.2km) to steps leading to squeeze stile onto stone bridge.

7 Go straight across road and down steps to continue along riverside path, until it meets road. Turn **L**; path soon leaves road again. Follow riverbank through 2 more fields, then turn **R** on obvious path. Go through 2 fields; at top of 2nd turn **L**, then go **R** on track back into car park.

John Watt & Son

Victorian tea and coffee shop serving fine teas and coffees

11 Bank Street,
CARLISLE, CA3 8HG
Tel 01228 521545
e-mail info@victoriancoffeeshop.co.uk
web www.victoriancoffeeshop.co.uk

A long tradition of serving first class tea and coffee is maintained in this period tea room with its many artefacts and items of equipment on display. Established in 1865, they have been blending tea and roasting coffee for over 140 years. Over 50 types of loose tea are available as well as over 20 different coffees. Their specialities are freshly baked scones and home-made soup, but there are also delicious teacakes, crumpets and home-made cakes. Their shop also sells local specialities, preserves and groceries.

To eat Set tea. Lunches. Breakfasts

Open Daily 8:30am-4:30pm

Getting there In Carlisle city centre, in street opposite Marks and Spencer.

What to see Carlisle Cathedral, Carlisle Castle, Tullie House Museum

Stone Close

A real gem, located amid the wild country on the western edge of the Yorkshire Dales National Park

Main Street,
DENT, LA10 5QL
Tel 01539 625231
e-mail stoneclose@btconnect.com

Stone Close is popular with locals, writers, walkers, talkers – in fact, with everyone who chances upon this convivial 17th-century cottage, with its cast-iron range and flagstone floor. Some people plan their walk in the dales with lunch here, and return in time for tea because it's all so tasty and wholesome. Some stay the night to enjoy the excellent breakfast.The delicious afternoon spread,with a range of organic leaf and herbal teas, or Fairtrade coffees comes with a sumptuous array of home-made cakes. For High Tea, there is a selection of freshly made sandwiches and toasties, followed by a cream tea, fruit teacakes, scones and a wide range of cakes.

To eat Cream Tea, seasonal meals.

Open 10am-5pm Wed-Sun & BHs.

Getting there Dent is off the A683 and A684 roads. Nearest motorway M6. Parking in the village.

What to see The Yorkshire Dales National Park, Dentdale Heritage Centre, Dales Countryside Museum Centre.

Carlisle Castle

Hazelmere Café and Bakery

The Tea Guild's Award of Excellence 2011

A tea-lover's heaven, with delicious food to match

1 Yewbarrow Terrace,
GRANGE-OVER-SANDS, LA11 6ED
Tel 01539 532972
e-mail hazelmeregrange@yahoo.co.uk

Expect at least 28 types of tea from all around the world at this award-winning tea shop. Praise has been heaped upon owner Dorothy Stubley for the variety and quality of the excellent teas she offers, as well as the range of freshly-made and locally-sourced meals and snacks that are served here. Bread, cakes, chutneys, pâtés and preserves are all baked on the premises, and offered alongside local pheasant burgers, Cumbria lamb tattie pot, and Stalker's casserole. Teatime specialities include Cumberland Rum Nicky, vanilla slices, and scones made with apricot and yoghurt, and the large gracious tea room with its open fire or summer verandah can be found in a handsome Victorian arcade. Winner of The Tea Guild's Top Tea Place Award 2006.

To eat Hazelmere afternoon tea, Cumbrian cream tea. Meals and snacks.

Open Winter 10am-4:30pm; summer 10am-5pm. Cream tea served all day, Hazelmere afternoon tea served 2-4pm. Closed 25-26 Dec, 1 Jan.

Getting there From A590 take B5277 into Grange-over-Sands. Pass station, then 1st left at mini-rdbt. Hazelmere is on right.

What to see Priory Gatehouse (NT), Lakeside & Haverthwaite Railway, Lakeland Motor Museum.

The Wild Strawberry

A lovely tea room that, it is claimed, serves the best scones in the area

54 Main Street,
KESWICK, CA12 5JS
Tel 01768 774399

This cheery, unpretentious tea room has a traditional feel, with its old beams, stone walls and flagstone floors. It takes its name not from the fruit but from the attractive porcelain used, which has a colourful strawberry motif. The scones are definitely a highlight, especially when topped with jam and cream and accompanied by one of the 11 varieties of tea. For a savoury palate, there's a light lunch menu of snacks and sandwiches. Local produce is used whenever possible.

To eat Cream tea. Light lunches and snacks.

Open Daily 9:30am-5pm. Closed for 2 weeks Dec. Open weekends only in Jan.

Getting there Keswick is on the A66 and A591 roads. Nearest motorway M6. Pay and display car parks in town.

What to see Keswick Museum and Gallery, Cumberland Pencil Museum, Mirehouse, Castlerigg Stone Circle, Skiddaw, Honister Slate Mine in Borrowdale. New Village Tea Rooms

Castlerigg Stone Circle

Cumberland Pencil Museum

Lakeside Hotel

A relaxing lakeside conservatory is the setting for an interesting range of hot and cold snacks and a choice of afternoon teas

Lake Windermere,
NEWBY BRIDGE, LA12 8AT
Tel 015395 30001
e-mail sales@lakesidehotel.co.uk
web www.lakesidehotel.co.uk

This impressive hotel, richly decorated and sumptuously furnished, started out in the 17th century as a coaching inn. A full afternoon tea here is a feast of sandwiches, cakes, toasted fruit bread, strawberries, scones and fresh cream, with speciality teas, coffees or hot chocolate. You can also choose a more modest selection of cakes and pastries, or there's a menu of open sandwiches, hot dishes (hot brasserie dishes of the day, three cheese tortellini) and desserts (Tiramisu mousse with coffee granité and mascapone ice cream and traditional bread and butter pudding). Booking recommended.

To eat Afternoon tea. Meals and snacks.

Open Daily. Afternoon tea served 3-5pm.

Getting there M6 junction 35, join A590 to Barrow, follow signs for Newby Bridge. Turn right over bridge and continue to the hotel on right — or follow Lakeside Steamers signs from M6 junction 36.

What to see Windermere Lake Cruises, Lakeside and Haverthwaite Steam Railway, Aquarium of the Lakes.

Lakeside and Haverthwaite Steam Railway

Walk

Keswick – above Derwent Water

Wonderful panoramas, a lake and sylvan splendour are the delights of this walk

Start/finish: Grid ref NY 265229

Parking: Derwent Head pay-and-display car park

Distance: 5.25 miles/8.4km

Level of difficulty: ● ● ●

Suggested map: OS Explorer OL4 The English Lakes (NW)

Walk directions

❶ Proceed down road to Derwent Bay. Go **L** opposite landing stages, past toilets, to take track through Cockshot Wood. Exit wood on to fenced lane across field to Borrowdale road. Cross road and climb stone steps to enter Castlehead Wood. Take path that trends **L** to ascend shoulder. In little way steeper path climbs **R**, to rocky summit of Castle Head and fine viewpoint.

2 Descend by same route to shoulder then bear **R** to locate kissing gate into enclosed lane. Follow this to Springs Road and turn **R**. At Springs Farm, cross bridge and take track up through Springs Wood. Bear **R** at junction and follow edge of wood up past TV mast. Ignore turning on **R** and continue to footbridge **L** to join Castlerigg Road. Turn **R** along road and walk up past Rakefoot to another footbridge on **R**.

3 Cross footbridge over stream and follow path, ascending by wall. Go through gate, and walk out on to open shoulder of fell, ascending steep grassy nose. The going levels until gate on **R**, through wall, leads to path which follows edge of crag. Caution – steep unfenced drop. To stay away from cliff edge take higher stile. Follow path across head of gully, to climb on to the polished rock cap of Walla Crag where views are superb.

4 Continue along main ridge path down to stile over wall. Cross and go **R**, down hill following grassy path which becomes increasingly steep and stepped into gorge of Cat Gill. Entering Great Wood continue steeply down, passing bridge before leaving beck to head into wood. Bear **L** down hill, across wooded car park and on, to find wall gap on Borrowdale Road. Cross to wall gap opposite and

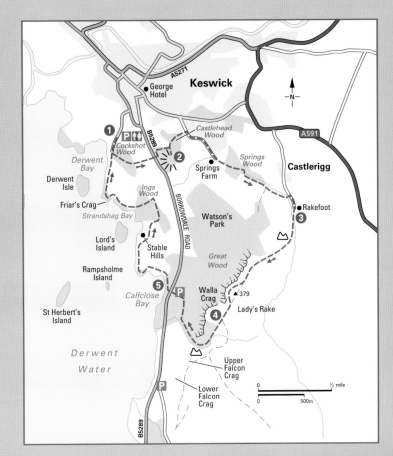

continue to lakeshore.

5 Bear **R**, following around Calfclose Bay, by Stable Hills, around Ings Wood and Strandshag Bay to Scots pine on Friar's Crag. Continue easily back to Derwent Bay and take footpath along road to car park.

Gillam's Tea Room

The Tea Guild's Award
of Excellence 2011

Organic and locally produced delicacies in an 18th-century tea room

64 Market Street,
ULVERSTON, LA12 7LT
Tel 01229 587564
e-mail douglasgillam@btconnect.com
web www.gillams-tearoom.co.uk

The Gillam family has been trading tea and coffee since 1892 and Gillam's Tea Room opened in this quaint 18th-century shop in July 2006. The period façade, the cosy log fire burning in the open hearth in cooler months and the soothing classical music create an old world charm that everyone will enjoy. The menu is all organic and vegetarian; all the loose leaf teas and herbals are organic and the menu includes very good special dishes every day including sandwiches filled with mushroom paté and cucumber, houmous or organic egg mayonnaise, and the excellent cakes are home-made. The organic teas include specialities such as Darjeeling First Flush, Oolong and Green Tea. There is now also a Gillam's Grocers as part of the operation.

To eat Afternoon Tea.

Open Mon-Sat 9am-5pm, Sun 10am-4pm.

Getting there In town centre, car parking 30 metres away.

What to see Laurel and Hardy Museum, Barrow Monument, Lakeside and Haverthwaite Railway.

Derbyshire

Northern Tea Merchants

The Tea Guild's Award of Excellence 2011

Excellent teas to sample with the traditional afternoon accompaniments, or to buy from a wide specialist range

Crown House, 193
Chatsworth Road,
Brampton,
CHESTERFIELD, S40 2BA.
Tel 01246 232600
e-mail enquiries@northern-tea.com **web** www.northern-tea.com

This tea and coffee tasting shop is owned and run by an old established family company of tea merchants – it doesn't get much more specialist than this! A family firm of tea blenders and tea bag manufacturers, which supplies stately homes and restaurants with their favourite brew, offers casual visitors the chance to sample the same quality fare. From Formosa Oolong to Russian Caravan and a range of flavoured teas, each one is clearly described, and served on its own or with a traditional afternoon accompaniment like cucumber sandwiches, home-made cake, or scone with jam and cream. The less exotic teas and a choice of five house blends are also listed. Light meals and snacks, such as filled jacket potatoes, ploughman's lunch, salads and sandwiches are served throughout the day. Tours of the premises and tea tastings can be arranged, and there's a shop selling tea caddies, teapots and, of course, tea.

To eat Set tea. Sandwiches and cakes.

Open Mon-Sat 9am-5pm. Tea served all day. Closed 25 Dec, 1 Jan, Easter Mon.

Getting there M1 junct 29, A617 Chesterfield; from rdbt at end of A617, follow signs for A619 Baslow. At rdbt at end of short dual carriageway take 2nd exit between B&Q and Wickes, to Chatsworth Rd. Tea shop on right.

What to see Crooked Spire of St Mary and All Saints Church, the Peak District National Park, Chatsworth House.

Chatsworth

Tea rooms found at Chatsworth's
beautiful, historic house

BAKEWELL, DE45 1PP
Tel 01246 565366
e-mail www.chatsworth.org

Hundred of thousands of visitors come to see Chatsworth House, its gardens and its park every year – and of course the wonderful tea room. It was formed from the old stables, and has been refurbished by the Duchess of Devonshire, with a luxurious new look and equine theme. There is a wide choice of teas, including their own house blend. The menu lists afternoon teas, freshly baked cakes and desserts, and home-made hot meals. It is now possible to book for Afternoon Tea online.

To eat Afternoon Tea, cakes, hot meals.

Open Mar-end Dec, Daily 11am-4pm.

Getting there Chatsworth is north of Matlock off the B6012. Ample parking on site.

What to see Hob Hurst's House, Longshaw Estate, Eyam Moor, Bakewell, Shepherd Wheel, Bakewell.

Gingerbread Shop

Try delicious gingerbread men made from an
original recipe

26 St John Street,
ASHBOURNE, DE6 1GH
Tel 01335 346753

A great favourite with locals and visitors alike, this cheerful combination of tea room and bakery in the centre of town offers remarkable cakes, tarts and, of course, gingerbread men. It is a unique example of a late 15th-century timber built building, which has been in continuous use as a bakery since 1805. Four different varieties of tea are served, as well as a tasty range of snacks, sandwiches, cakes, scones and biscuits.

To eat No set teas. Light lunches.

Open Mon-Sat 8:30am-5pm (5:30 on Thu).

Getting there Ashbourne is on the A52, A515 and A517 roads. Nearest motorway M1. Town car parks.

What to see Chatsworth House, Dovedale and Thorpe Cloud, Ilam Hall and park, Tissington Hall.

Dovedale

Walk

Stanton Moor – sacred worship

Circular walk across the mysterious Stanton Moor

Start/finish: Grid ref SJ 938697

Parking: Roadside parking on Main Street, Birchover

Distance: 4 miles/6.4km

Level of difficulty: ● ● ●

Suggested map: OS Explorer OL24 White Peak

Walk directions

1 From Druid Inn at end of Main Street take signposted footpath on bend opposite. Follow this up along wooded ridge above village. Where it ends at quarry car park go **L** on to road. After 0.25 miles (400m) turn **R** for signposted path on to moor.

2 Go over stile and veer **L** at Cork Stone for wide path across middle of heather moor. Stay on main path as it enters silver birch scrub, then swing **R** on wide grassy track, with fence over **L**, until you reach Nine Ladies.

3 At Nine Ladies, walk to interpretation panel and turn **L** on main path. In 50 yds (46m) fork **R** for path through gorse and heather. Go over stile and turn **R** on to path along high wooded edge of moor to Earl Grey Tower. Continue on this open path to stile in fence on **R**.

4 Cross over stile and at junction of tracks turn **L**. At crossroads of routes turn **L** again, downhill, to reach road. Turn **R** and walk along this for 50yds (46m) and go **L** on footpath.

5 Follow this well-signposted route along **L-H** edge of camping field, and then around buildings and ahead on rough farm track along **R-H** edge of 2 successive fields.

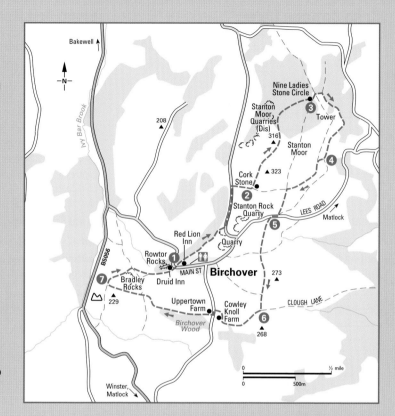

When you meet unsurfaced Clough Lane turn **R**.

6 Walk along lane to its end, at Cowley Knoll Farm. Turn **L** on to surfaced lane and almost immediately turn **R**, by Uppertown Farm, for gated path through fields. After hugging wall on **R** path continues past cottage and begins huge loop around hilly outcrop of Bradley Rocks. At far end go

through gate to reach path junction.

7 Ignore path downhill to **L** and continue with level track as it swings back east towards Birchover. Joining gravel drive on bend, take lower route and at crossroads of lanes go straight on past church to return to Birchover village and Main Street. To explore Rowtor Rocks look for narrow path on **L** just before Druid Inn.

Rose Cottage Cafe

A lovely place to rest after a walk in Hope Valley

Cross Street,
CASTLETON, S33 8WH
Tel 01433 620472

A friendly welcome awaits you at the Rose Cottage Café in the picturesque Hope Valley. They are used to hungry walkers and climbers dropping in and provide all kinds of delicious home-cooking to sample inside or to take into the pretty rustic garden. There are ten different varieties of tea alongside a light lunch menu of snacks, sandwiches and set teas. Specialities include a Rose Cottage sandwich.

To eat Cream tea. Snacks.

Open Sat-Thu, 10am-5pm. Closed Jan.

Getting there Off the A6187.

What to see Peveril Castle, Mam Tor, Blue John Cavern, Speedwell Cavern, Treak Cliff Cavern, Peak Cavern.

Eyam Tea Rooms

The enchanting village of Eyam is home to charismatic tea rooms

The Square,
EYAM, Hope Valley, S32 5RB
Tel 01433 631274

In one of Derbyshire's most famous villages – in 1665 the inhabitants stayed within the parish confines and so prevented the plague from spreading elsewhere – is a very friendly and popular tea room. There are various teas and coffees on offer, breakfasts until 11.30am, light lunch, traditonal Sunday lunch, assorted freshly baked cakes, and cream teas.

To eat Set tea. Snacks and light meals available.

Open Tue-Sun 10am-4pm. Closed Christmas day.

Getting there Eyam is signposted off the A623 road. Nearest motorway M1. Parking in the village.

What to see Eyam Museum, Eyam Walk, Mompesson Well, The Parish Church of St Lawrence, Eyam Hall, Plague Cottage.

Walkers on Mam Tor

Village green, Eyam

Caudwell's Mill

Pleasant surroundings and an excellent reputation for food

ROWSLEY (near Bakewell),
Matlock, DE4 2EB
Tel 01629 733185

Caudwell's Mill, built in the 19th century, is a complex of craft workshops and a working water-powered mill where you can take tea while enjoying the lovely view. Everything is made on the premises using freshly milled flour. They offer ten different varieties of tea with a light lunch menu including vegetarian choices, snacks, sandwiches and cakes.

To eat Set tea. Light snacks.

Open Daily 10am-5pm. Closed 24-26 Dec.

Getting there Rowsley is on the A6. Nearest motorway M1. Parking on site.

What to see Haddon Hall, Nine Ladies, Peak Railway, Magpie Mine, Chatsworth, Hob Hurst's House, Bakewell.

Chatsworth

Bakewell

Devon

Saunton Sands Hotel

Popular hotel with superb sea views for enjoying afternoon tea to the full

Saunton,
BRAUNTON, EX33 1LQ
Tel 01271 890212
e-mail reservations@sauntonsands.com
web www.brend-hotels.co.uk/TheSauntonSands

This luxury hotel stands high on a cliff looking down on five miles of golden sands and great seas for surfing. You have a choice of places to take tea. The Terrace Lounge serves a delicious Devon Cream Tea every afternoon, and here you can enjoy the wonderful views the hotel has to offer. But if you want to get nearer to the beach, the Sands Café is just a short stroll away, but has a real beach-side atmosphere. Here, they serve tea nearly all day, as well as other snacks. Local West country produce is used wherever possible.

To eat Devon Cream Tea.

Open Daily. 3:30-5:30 in Terrace Lounge, all day in Sands Café .

Getting there Off A361 at Braunton, signed Croyde B3231, hotel 2miles on left

What to see Braunton Burrows Reserve, Watermouth Castle, Eden Project.

Northcote Manor

Experience country-house living in this 18th-century manor house

BURRINGTON, EX37 9LZ
Tel 01769 560501
e-mail rest@northcotemanor.co.uk
web www.northcotemanor.co.uk

At the end of a winding, wooded driveway, this stone-built manor, dating from 1716, is set in 20 acres of gardens and grounds, with dramatic views over the Taw Valley. Take your tea by an open log fire in the hotel lounge or Oak Room, or enjoy fine weather on the sun terrace overlooking the water garden. The menu offers lunches as well as traditional cream teas with lashings of clotted cream and full afternoon teas, including sandwiches and a selection of home-made cakes and biscuits. Booking is advisable at weekends. Dogs welcome.

To eat Set tea, Devon cream tea, Strawberries and Bubbles.

Open Daily. Tea served 2:30-6pm. Closed when guests reserve exclusive use.

Getting there Just off the A377 outside Burrington village.

What to see Exmoor National Park, RHS Rosemoor, Dartington Crystal.

Exmoor National Park

Walk

Morwenstow – the parson poet

A walk in the footsteps of the eccentric Victorian poet, Robert Stephen Hawker

Start/finish: Grid ref SS 206154

Parking: Small free car park by Morwenstow Church and Rectory Farm and Tea Rooms

Distance: 7 miles/11.3km

Level of difficulty: ● ● ●

Suggested map: OS Explorer 126 Clovelly & Hartland

Walk directions

❶ Follow signposted track from car park and church to coast path; turn **L**. Reach Hawker's Hut in about 100yds (91m). Continue along coast path to Duckpool.

❷ Reach inlet of Duckpool, walk up road along the bottom of valley to T-junction. Turn **L**. Turn **R** at next junction to cross bridge beside ford. Follow lane round **L** for 150yds (137m), then bear **L** on broad track through woodland.

3 After 1 mile (1.6km), cross stile on **L**, cross wooden footbridge, climb slope, then turn **R** and up track. Turn **L** at T-junction, keep ahead at next junction. In 40yds (37m) go **R** through metal gate.

4 Follow signed field track to lane at Woodford. Turn **L**, go downhill past Shears Farm then round **R** and uphill to junction with road. Turn **L** past bus shelter.

5 After 100yds (91m), turn **L** along path between cottages to kissing gate. Turn **R**, immediately **L** and follow edge of field to stile on **L**. Cross stile, then cross next field to hedge opposite.

6 Cross 2 stiles; go straight up next field (often muddy) to hedge corner. Go alongside wall and over stile to hedged track and on to junction with lane.

7 Go through gate opposite; turn **R** through gap. Bear **L** across field to stile. Keep straight across next field to top left-hand corner; go through gate up to Stanbury House. Turn **R** to reach surfaced lane.

8 Go **L** along lane (few paces) then over narrow stile on **R**. Go straight across next 2 fields to kissing gate into farm lane behind Tonacombe House.

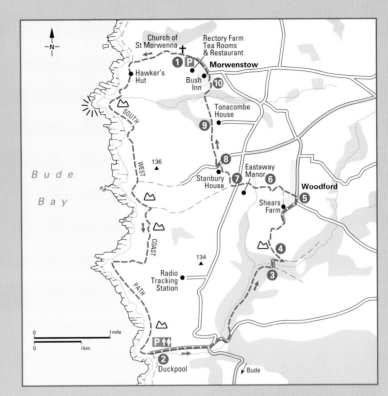

9 Keep ahead through kissing gate, then along muddy track and through another. Cross 2 fields; descend into wooded valley. Keep **R**, cross stream, go **R** and up steeply to kissing gate.

10 Cross fields to garden behind Bush Inn. Go down the **L-H** side of buildings, then up to road. Turn **L** for Morwenstow Church and car park.

Cheristow Lavender Tea Rooms

The Tea Guild's Award
of Excellence 2011

Lavender is the key at these delightful tea rooms

Higher Cheristow, HARTLAND EX39 6DA
Tel 01237 440101
e-mail cheristow@btinternet.com
web www.cheristow.co.uk

Set in an Area of Outstanding Natural Beauty, Cheristow Lavender Farm is a delightful setting for these Tea Rooms. The menu reflects the owners' commitment to providing homegrown and locally sourced produce. They use their own free range eggs, beef from their herd of Ruby Red Cattle, and lamb from their sheep. Pickles, chutneys and preserves are all made on the premises, as are the award-winning cakes and scones. An exclusive selection of loose teas are blended by Kamelia Budd of North Devon, which include Cheristow Blue with lavender, (their version of Lady Grey), and Gingery Lemon and Lavender. Tea and cakes are available every day, but if you want to sample the special afternoon tea please note it is only available on Sundays, and you need to book in advance as Michelle makes all mini cakes and scones to order. More than big enough to share, it includes finger rolls with a variety of fillings, as well as a selection of five mini cakes, two mini lavender scones with strawberry and lavender conserve and fresh Cornish clotted cream. Please ring at least the day before if you have special dietary requirements - they usually have at least one gluten and dairy free cake on display, but cakes for vegans are made to order.

To eat Light lunches, teas

Open Sun-Thu 11-5.30 (Mar-Oct). Lunch 12-2.30. Sun afternoon tea 3-5.30

Getting there From Hartland take road towards Stoke & Hartland Quay. Right at sign for Tea Room. At top of hill (Berry Cross), turn right, continue for 0.5 mile. Right again, also signed for Tea Room. Farm entrance 70 yards down lane. Route NOT SUITABLE FOR CARAVANS/COACHES – see website for alternative.

What to see Hartland Peninsula; Hartland Abbey and gardens.

Dartmoor Tearooms & Café

The Tea Guild's Award of Excellence 2011

Haven of good food on beautiful Dartmoor

3 Cross Street,
MORETONHAMPSTEAD,
TQ13 8NL
Tel 01647 441116
e-mail darmoortearooms@aol.com
web www.dartmoortearooms.co.uk

After a walk across the superb scenery that is Dartmoor, this cosy 17th-century tearoom is a little haven not to be missed. Inside it is decorated with antique maps and memorabilia and furnished with lovely oak settles. The attraction, of course, is the food and drink, with home made scones, cakes and teacakes being especially good. In addition, snacks and more substantial meals are also available, including hot filled baguettes, and Dartmoor Rarebit, made to their own recipe. Afternoon Tea is, naturally, accompanied by Devonshire clotted cream. An impressive list of local producers supply most of the ingredients used, including free range chicken, eggs and meat. A huge choice of over 40 loose leaf teas is on offer, as well as wine, cider and beer from Devon.

To eat Afternoon cream tea, snacks, lunches

Open Wed-Sun 10-5pm. Closed Mon, Tue. Open Bank Holidays.

Getting there In Moretonhampstead, at crossroads of B3212 and A382; opposite Lloyds Bank.

What to see Castle Drogo, Dartmoor National Park, Miniature Pony Centre, North Bovey.

Walk

Grimspound – 3,500 years on Dartmoor

From Bronze Age to the Golden Dagger tin mine

Start/finish: Grid ref SX 680816

Parking: Bennett's Cross car park on B3212

Distance: 6 miles/9.7km

Level of difficulty: ● ● ●

Suggested map: OS Explorer OL28 Dartmoor

Walk directions

1 Walk to Bennett's Cross; at cross turn **R** on narrow path which bears **L** uphill. At hilltop turn **R** by cairn and follow narrow twisting path to reach Birch Tor.

2 Small path leads straight on from tor downhill to meet gritty path at **R** angles. Turn **L** towards Headland Warren Farm in valley ahead. Follow granite wall (**R**) to signpost.

3 Go straight on uphill to cross road. Take small path leading off R, up to Grimspound. Walk to **R** and then through 'entrance' in perimeter wall.

4 At centre of enclosure turn **R** and climb steeply uphill to gain Hameldown Tor at 1,735ft (529m). Obvious path on ridge top leads to Broad Burrow and Two Burrows; where you reach wall running ahead and downhill **R**.

5 Turn **R** to follow wall down valley side. Wall gives way to line of small beech trees and there are superb views towards Soussons Forest and Warren House Inn. Cross stock fence via stile to join permissive path, and over another stile on to road. Turn **R** until you reach drive to Challacombe Farm.

6 Turn **L** down concrete drive. At

T-junction turn **L** to pass farm and go through small gate. Keep **R** through next gateway (signs to Bennett's Cross) and along field edge.

7 Next gate takes you into edge of Soussons Forest. After few paces reach fascinating remains of Golden Dagger tin mine with information board. Follow main track. When it bears **L** continue ahead on smaller bridleway signed 'Bennett's Cross' and proceed up valley through gate back on to low-lying yet open moorland, through masses of mining remains.

8 When you reach junction of tracks either turn **L** over stream, crossing by ruined building and ascending to Warren House Inn, or go straight on, keeping **R** where path forks after few paces. Follow narrow and indistinct path uphill to grassy gully. Climb out at top, bear **L** and then **R** up to Bennett's Cross car park.

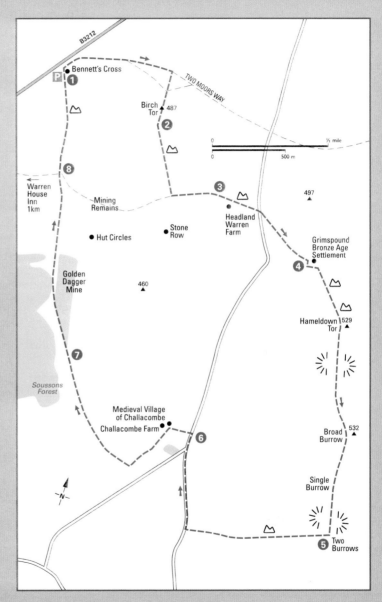

Hotel Riviera

A hospitable seaside hotel where tea is taken very seriously

The Esplanade,
SIDMOUTH, EX10 8AY
Tel 01395 515201
e-mail enquiries@hotelriviera.co.uk
web www.hotelriviera.co.uk

Old-fashioned service and modern comforts share a prominent place on the agenda of this delightful Regency hotel. In a town once patronised by royalty, it comes as no surprise to find that taking afternoon tea in sumptuous surroundings remains a revered and celebrated custom. Afternoons here are accompanied by the delicate tinkling of silver on bone china in the lounge and foyer, and on the patio in fine weather. There's a choice of set teas, with one of six speciality infusions prepared expertly to suit your mood. Reservations taken.

To eat Devon cream tea, strawberry cream tea, traditional afternoon tea.

Open Daily. Tea served 3-5:30pm.

Getting there In centre of Esplanade.

What to see Bicton Gardens, Exeter Cathedral, Crealy Adventure Park.

Thurlestone Hotel

Long-established family-run hotel overlooking National Trust coastline

THURLESTONE, TQ7 3NN
Tel 01548 560382
e-mail enquiries@thurlestone.co.uk
web www.thurlestone.co.uk

For over a century guests have been welcomed to this handsome hotel, owned by the Grose family since 1896. Tea is served in the lounge, the landscaped garden or on the terrace overlooking the bay. Guests help themselves from the afternoon buffet, advising lounge staff of their choice of set teas. There are three options: the cream tea with plain or fruit scones, strawberry jam and Devonshire clotted cream; tea or ground coffee with a choice of cake; or the traditional tea with both scones and cake. There is also a range of freshly cut sandwiches including Devonshire beef, ham and Salcombe white crab meat.

To eat Set teas.

Open Daily. Tea served 3-5:30pm.

Getting there Get to Kingsbridge on the A381 or A379, then take an unclassified road southwest to Thurlestone.

What to see Overbecks (NT), Walks on South West Coast Path, Cookworthy Museum of Rural Life, Kingsbridge.

Exeter Cathedral

Four and Twenty Blackbirds

Eclectic furniture and reading matter enhance the experience here

43 Gold Street,
TIVERTON, EX16 6QB
Tel 01884 257055

Old tables and chairs of different shapes and sizes – some more antique than others – make the adjoining beamed rooms both individual and inviting. There are fresh flowers on the tables and current issues of local and national magazines are there for you to browse. There are seven varieties of tea available, including the speciality Blackbird Tea, alongside a light lunch menu with snacks, sandwiches, cakes and a Devonshire cream tea with scones and jam.

To eat Devonshire cream tea.

Open Mon-Sat 9:30am-5:30pm.

Getting there Tiverton is on the A361 and the A396 roads. Nearest motorway M5. Public car parks.

What to see Tiverton Castle, Tiverton Museum of Mid Devon Life, Knightshayes Court.

Georgian Tea Rooms

Enjoyable food at reasonable prices in unpretentious surroundings

35 High Street,
TOPSHAM, EX3 0ED
Tel 01392 873465
web www.broadwayhouse.com

The atmosphere at the Georgian Tea Rooms is much like having tea at a favourite aunt's house. Tables are covered with attractive embroidered cloths and plants are dotted about the place. It's unlikely, though, that even a favourite aunt would be able to offer you the Georgian's choice of 12 varieties of tea to go with your scones with jam and cream. Light lunches and snacks are also available. The West Country Platters are particularly appetising. Booking is preferable.

To eat Full cream tea, mini cream tea. Light lunches and snacks.

Open Tue-Sat 8:30am-4:45pm.

Getting there Topsham is on the A376. Nearest motorway M5. Parking in the town.

What to see World of Country Life (Exmouth), Bicton Park Botanical Gardens, Exeter Cathedral, Quay House Visitor Centre and Royal Albert Memorial Museum in Exeter.

Grand Western Canal, Tiverton

The Corn Dolly

The Tea Guild's Award
of Excellence 2011

A wide choice of sweet and savoury teas, with old favourites for children

115a East Street, SOUTH MOLTON, EX36 3DB
Tel 01769 574249
e-mail info@corndollyteashop.co.uk
web www.corndollyteashop.co.uk

This is a real tea shop, with a serious approach to the national drink, and the quality of the product served here. This relaxed and friendly tea shop, a popular meeting place for locals and a magnet for Devon's summer visitors, provides a delicious range of meals and snacks throughout the day. For lunch there are salads, filled jacket potatoes, sandwiches and tasty things on toast. Children will enjoy the Humpty Dumpty Tea of boiled egg and soldiers, or Tigger Tea of beans on toast. For adults there's a range of tea choices, like Gamekeeper's Tea – venison, duck and pheasant pâté with toast – or perhaps the Queen's Ransom of toasted crumpets with Stilton. The Corn Dolly Tea of scones, clotted cream and jam, and the Apple Pie Tea – a hearty slice with clotted cream – are sweeter versions, but all are served with a refreshing pot of loose leaf tea from an impressive choice.

To eat Selection of set teas.

Open Mon-Sat 9:30am-5pm, Sun 11am-5pm. Tea served all day. Closed 25, 26 Dec and 1 Jan.

Getting there South Molton is just off the A361 North Devon Link Road.

What to see Quince Honey Farm, RHS Rosemoor, Dartington Crystal, Exmoor National Park.

Tea Blending

Approximately 90% of the tea drunk in Britain is one of the leading blends made by the popular brands - the type of tea that you can buy anywhere.

These blends contain up to 35 different teas. How do they remain constant in quality, character and flavour? Each popular blend has its own secret recipe. It is the job of the tea blender – an experienced tea taster - to ensure that his company blend meets all the criteria. To do this, the blenders and buyers - all tea tasters - taste the teas bought at auction when they arrive at the tea-packaging factory. This is to check that they haven't been contaminated or damaged while in storage or transit. During the course of a day, a blender can sample between 200-1000 teas, adjusting the recipe to ensure that the company's brand remains constant. The blender's findings are fed into a computer which calculates the correct amount of the different teas, which are then added to a large blending drum. This rotates, mixing all the teas together. When the blending is complete, the blend is ready for packaging into packets or tea bags.

It takes at least five years to train as a tea taster and it continues to be a learning process. In order to prepare teas for tasting the (carefully weighed) dry leaves are laid out in containers on the tasting bench. Boiling water is poured and on and the brewing is carefully timed for 5 -6 minutes. The brewed tea is then poured into tasting bowls, and the infused leaf is tipped onto the lid of the brewing mug. The taster slurps the tea much as a wine taster does, then rolls the liquid around his mouth to assess the flavour before spitting it out into a spittoon. The taster also takes into account the appearance of the dry leaf, the infused leaf and the colour and quality of the liquor.

Dorset

Wheelwrights

You'll be spoiled for choice if you have a sweet tooth!

14 Rodden Row,
ABBOTSBURY, DT3 4JL
Tel 01305 871800
e-mail suenigel@wheelwrights.co.uk
web www.wheelwrights.co.uk

This little tea cottage has a relaxing atmosphere as cool as the Parisian jazz background music. The delightful garden creates a series of open-air rooms for dining out in summer, and even winter, complete with pretty views over the village and the surrounding hills. There's a huge variety of teas to choose from – all loose-leaf – and Wheelwrights' famous home-made scones, cakes and hot sweets. While you are there you can choose from a selection of stylish and contemporary gifts for the home.

To eat Cream tea. Light lunches, coffee and cakes.

Open Sat-Wed 1pm-5pm. Closed 25-26 Dec.

Getting there Abbotsbury is off the A35, on the B3157. Parking available in the village.

What to see Chesil Beach, St Catherine's Chapel, The Swannery and Sub-Tropical Gardens, Children's Barn, Smuggler's Barn, art galleries and craft sudios in the village.

The Sticky Bun Tea Room

A charming tea room offering a true flavour of Dorset

Wolvercroft World of Plants, Fordingbridge Road,
ALDERHOLT, SP6 3BE
Tel 01425 652437
e-mail gardens@wolvercroft.co.uk
web www.wolvercroft.co.uk

There's a wide selection of home-made cakes and a select variety of teas to choose from here. Try a famous Dorset Knob, handmade to a recipe first created in 1860, or treat yourself to a Dorset clotted cream tea. There are also plenty of savoury snacks. In warm weather, you can enjoy your cup of tea outside on a pretty patio. An extensive range of traditional Dorset souvenirs is for sale, such as puzzles, fudge, jams, greeting cards and House of Dorchester chocolates.

To eat Cream tea. Snacks. Lunches

Open Summer Mon-Sat 10am-4:45pm, Sun 10am-4pm. Winter daily 10am-4pm.

Getting there Alderholt is on the B3078, southwest of Fordingbridge.

What to see The New Forest, Cranborne Chase, Alderholt Mill, Rockbourne Roman Villa, Avon Valley Path.

New Forest ponies

Mortons House Hotel

Enjoy a break in a 16th-century Elizabethan manor house

East Street,
CORFE CASTLE, BH20 5EE
Tel 01929 480988
e-mail stay@mortonshouse.co.uk
web www.mortonshouse.co.uk

Mortons is one of Dorset's undiscovered jewels, standing under the watchful eye of Corfe Castle, to which it is linked by underground tunnels. Enjoy a refreshing stop for an afternoon, a night or a week. Those who have tasted the style, flavour and character of the hotel once, invariably return. Large parties should pre-book.

To eat Traditional cream tea.

Open Daily 2pm-5.30pm in summer.

Getting there On the A351. Nearest motorways M3 and M27. Parking in the village.

What to see the Castle, Durdle Door, Kimmeridge, Lulworth, Studland, Swanage.

The Horse with the Red Umbrella

A warm, cosy atmosphere in an unusually named tea shop

10 High West Street,
DORCHESTER, DT1 1UJ
Tel 01305 262019

Who thought up this oddly delightful name? Nobody really seems to know! The Horse with the Red Umbrella describes itself as "just a friendly place to eat". That it certainly is, offering snacks, sandwiches, cream teas and a choice of 12 types of tea. It is just a warm, unpretentious place hung with baskets, mugs and assorted what-nots.

To eat Cream tea. Light lunches. Lunch specials. Breakfasts.

Open Mon-Sat 8am-4:30pm.

Getting there Dorchester is on the A35, A37 and A354. Limited parking in the town. Free parking on Sundays.

What to see Max Gate, built by Thomas Hardy, Higher Bockhampton, Judge Jeffreys' lodgings, the Old Crown Court, Dorset County Museum.

Durdle Door

The T Shop

A family-run tea shop that also caters for special dietary requirements

11a Trinity Street,
The Harbourside,
WEYMOUTH, DT4 8TW
Tel 01305 788052

Set in a converted 18th-century stable block, the T Shop is well known for its scrumptious selection of cakes and tasty afternoon tea favourites; don't leave without trying a traditional sultana scone or a delicious wedge of Dorset apple cake. Dorset afternoon teas complete the appeal of this pleasant little tea shop. Coeliac and diabetic dietary needs are catered for here. Weymouth is renowned for its sunshine, so sit outside overlooking the harbour and enjoy a cup of Earl Grey, Darjeeling or one of their many fruit teas. A selection of local produce is also for sale.

To eat Afternoon tea.

Open Spring, Tue-Sun 10am-5pm; summer, daily 9:30am-6pm; winter, Thu-Sun 10:30am-3:30pm.

Getting there Weymouth is on the A353 and A354.

What to see The Deep Sea Adventure, Brewer's Quay, Sea Life Park, Portland, Lulworth, the Jurassic Coast.

Lulworth Cove

Essex

Tea on the Green

The Tea Guild's Award of Excellence 2011

Tea shop on the village green with superb cakes and savouries

3 Eves Corner,
DANBURY, CM3 4QF
Tel 01245 226616
e-mail micktog@btinternet.com

Teapots of all shapes and sizes and a collection of books on tea and coffee to peruse leave customers in no doubt about the function of the large pink building that houses Tea on the Green. Overlooking Danbury village green on National Trust land, it has tables outside for summer weather, and a bright and spacious interior, where fine white bone china and three-tiered cake stands sit on floral tablecloths. There is plenty to eat, from breakfast and light lunch choices such as filled pitta bread to a broad range of tea items: hot-buttered crumpets, muffins and cinnamon toast, finger sandwiches, scones and cakes and a choice of speciality teas. Booking is possible for lunch.

To eat Afternoon tea. Light lunches. Sandwiches, wraps, ciabatta.

Open Mon-Fri 8:30am-4:30pm, Sat 10am–5pm, Sun 11am-5pm (winter closes 4pm). Tea served all day. Closed 25-26 Dec, 1 Jan.

Getting there M25 then A12 to Colchester, A414 to Maldon and Danbury.

What to see Danbury Country Park and Lakes, Blakes Wood, Maldon Estuary, Chelmsford, Royal Horticultural Society Garden Hyde Hall.

The Garden Tea Rooms

Quaint tea rooms in a beautiful location on the edge of Chelmsford

Lordship Road, Writtle,
CHELMSFORD, CM1 3RR
Tel 01245 422600
e-mail info@gardentearooms.co.uk
web www.gardentearooms.co.uk

Set in one of the most attractive villages in Essex, these old fashioned tea rooms retain a deep sense of tradition with their original beams and friendly service, and provide a pleasant view over the pretty Writtle College Garden centre. The owners are tea merchants too, and so their large variety of loose-leaf teas is sourced directly. Among many home-made cakes, the rich, moist hand made cake is well worth a taste. You might like to take home a Chatsford teapot and a bag of their speciality tea so you can enjoy a good quality cuppa in the comfort of your own home. Wednesday lunchtimes are enlivened by music from the resident pianist. Booking is not required.

To eat No set teas.

Open Tue-Fri 10am-4:30pm, Sat-Sun 10am-4pm.

Getting there Writtle is on the A414 on the west side of Chelmsford. Parking available.

What to see Hylands House, Battlesbridge, Marsh Farm Country Park, Cressing Temple and Blake Hall.

The Essex Rose Tea House

Welcoming tea house in the heart of Constable country

High Street,
DEDHAM, C07 6DE
Tel 01206 323101
e-mail dedham@trooms.com

Picturesque Dedham is, of course, celebrated for its long term resident, the landscape painter John Constable. It has many interesting and well-preserved historic buildings and it is the unspoilt pink exterior of The Essex Rose Tea House that brings its instant appeal. Inside, the interior is welcoming and also very traditional. Tables are set close together on the wooden floors, and pictures and paintings cover the walls. It's a lively, bustling spot, the meeting place for local people as well as visitors. The light lunch menu includes snacks, sandwiches, home-made cakes and scones with Tiptree jam and cream, and there are nine varieties of tea. You'll also discover a wealth of gift items to buy.

To eat Cream tea. Lunches and snacks.

Open daily 10am-5:30pm (winter closes at 4:30pm).

Getting there Dedham is on the B1029 northeast of Colchester. Designated parking in the village.

What to see The Valley of the River Stour, Flatford Mill and Cottage (National Trust).

Philpott's Tea Rooms

An olde-worlde experience in a small Waltham Abbey tea rooms

Lychgate House, Church Street,
WALTHAM ABBEY, EN9 1DX
Tel 01992 767641

Not far from the town centre of Waltham Abbey, this small 15th-century house looks over the abbey and churchyard. The interior is more or less as it has been for the last 400 years – oak cross beams, small windows and an inglenook fireplace. The Tea Rooms serve a light lunch with snacks, sandwiches, cakes and scones with jam and cream and five blends of tea are available.

To eat No set teas.

Open Daily 10am-4pm. Closed 25 Dec.

Getting there Waltham Abbey is to the northeast of London and can be approached via the M25, A121. Parking is possible on the side streets in the town.

What to see Abbey Church, the local museum in Sun Street, Epping Forest, Lee Valley Park, Forty Hall.

Lee Valley Park

Parish Church, Waltham Abbey

Gloucestershire

The Mad Hatter

An Alice in Wonderland tea party overlooking the River Windrush

Riverside,
BOURTON-ON-THE-WATER, GL54 2BX
Tel 01451 821508
e-mail admin@the-mad-hatter-tearoom.co.uk
web www.the-mad-hatter-tearoom.co.uk

An afternoon spent here will transport you back to a bygone era with its olde worlde atmosphere, brought to life by exposed wooden beams and an inglenook fireplace. This Grade II listed 18th-century building looks out onto the River Windrush in the lovely village of Bourton-on-the-Water. This scene is best experienced outside in the tea room gardens with a Cotswold Cream Tea just begging to be devoured. In colder temperatures, their home-cooked lunches will really hit the spot. Booking is recommended.

To eat Set teas. Full lunches.

Open Daily 10am-6pm.

Getting there Off the A436. Large car park nearby.

What to see The Cotswolds, Bird Land, National Trust gardens, The Model Village, The Dragonfly Maze.

Buckland Manor

Grand 13th-century manor house surrounded by beautiful gardens

BUCKLAND, WR12 7LY
Tel 01386 852626
e-mail buckland-manor-uk@msn.com
web www.bucklandmanor.com

Everything at Buckland Manor is geared towards the rest and relaxation of its guests. Spacious public areas are furnished with high quality pieces and decorated in an appropriately manorial style. Guest lounges are wonderfully comfortable, with crackling log fires in the cooler months. In summer, tea can be taken outside on the garden patio. A good choice of teas is offered, including decaffeinated and herbal alternatives, and your cuppa can be accompanied by sandwiches, home-made biscuits, fruit cake, or hot scones with Cornish clotted cream and strawberry jam. For the ultimate in luxury, you can add a glass of champagne to your order.

To eat Set tea. Sandwiches, cakes and scones.

Open Daily. Tea served Mon-Sat 2-5:30pm, Sun 4-5:30pm.

Getting there South of Broadway on B4632. 30 parking spaces available.

What to see Hidcote Manor Garden, Snowshill Manor, Sudeley Castle & Gardens.

Snowshill Manor gardens

Walk

Arlingham – seeking the Severn Bore at Arlingham

A long but fairly level walk along the river where Britain's regular tidal wave rushes in

Start/finish: Grid ref ST 708109

Parking: Arlingham village

Distance: 7.5 miles/12.1km 3hrs 30min Ascent 85ft/25m G1

Level of difficulty: ● ● ●

Suggested map: OS Explorer OL14 Wye Valley & Forest of Dean

Walk directions

1 From village centre, with The Red Lion Inn at your back, walk along 'No Through Road'. Pass church and continue along road. It becomes track which brings you to kissing gate. Go to top of bank.

2 With River Severn on **R**, turn **L** through kissing gate. Continue along this route, passing through kissing gates where they arise, until you see Hock Cliff ahead. Pass into field that begins to slope up towards cliff.

3 Turn sharp **L** to walk down bank and along **L** side of field. Cross bridge into next field. When field edge swings **R** go ahead and **L** to

footpath sign beyond farm track. Follow this path running between hedges.

4 Cross road and enter 'No Through Road' ahead. Follow it towards houses. Just before gateway turn **L** through 2 kissing gates into field. Follow its **R-H** side to stile and then continue on same line. Just beyond 2 big houses on **R** and about 100yds (91m) before farm buildings, turn **R** over stile into field. Crossing this diagonally brings you to kissing gate and lane.

5 Turn **L** and follow lane through Overton for just over 0.5 mile (800m). Where road goes sharply **R** beside long house, turn **L** to rejoin Severn Way. Path will lead away from river briefly, among trees, to emerge at stile beside meadow. Continue walking ahead, maintaining direction, passing through gates, always with River Severn on **R** and again ignoring any paths leading inland.

6 Footpath will soon take form of raised bank, or dyke. It reaches its northernmost point then swings to south, just after passing farm – town of Newnham should now be clearly visible on opposite bank. Continue to pub, The Old Passage Inn, on **L**.

7 Beyond inn take long, straight lane on **L**, which leads across flood plain back to Arlingham.

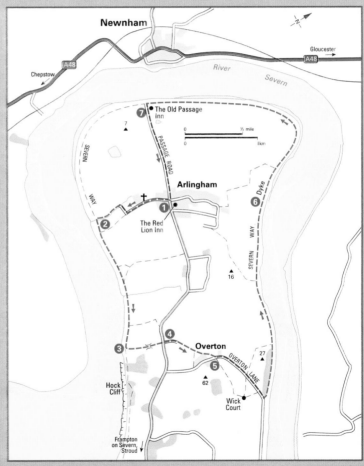

The Queen's

Tea remains an institution at this famous Cheltenham building

The Promenade,
CHELTENHAM, GL50 1NN
Tel 0870 400 8107
e-mail H6632@accor.com
web www.mercure.co.uk/cheltenham

A landmark hotel spectacularly located at the top of Cheltenham's main promenade. Afternoon tea can be taken in the comfortable hotel lounge or the garden in summer. Several classic teas are offered to accompany the Cotswold Cream Tea – scones with clotted cream and jam, and fruit or Madeira cake – or the Queen's Full Afternoon Tea that comprises a selection of finger sandwiches, scones and cream, and cream cakes and pastries. Other full and light meals and sandwiches are served, accompanied by an extensive wine list.

To eat Set tea. Sandwiches and cakes.

Open Daily. Tea served 10am-6pm. Closed 24-25 Dec.

Getting there In the centre of Cheltenham, signposted from all major routes. 60 parking spaces available.

What to see The Cotswolds, Broadway, Bourton-on-the-Water, Cirencester.

The Bantam Tea Rooms

Charismatic tea rooms in the historic town of Chipping Campden

High Street,
CHIPPING CAMPDEN, GL55 6HB
Tel 01386 840386

Nestled in the centre of the market town of Chipping Campden, this traditional, family-run tea room is situated amongst the wonderfully preserved buildings of golden Cotswold stone, many of which date back to the 14th and 17th centuries. The welcoming feel to this tea room will not fail to be draw you in to try one of their mouth watering, freshly-baked cakes or even a Bantam Afternoon Tea, choosing from a cup of traditional, fruit or herbal tea. However, if you cannot spare the time to stay longer, you can take some home with you, as all of their tasty treats are available to take away.

To eat Set teas and cakes.

Open Mon-Sat 10am-5pm, Sun 10:30am-5pm.

Getting there Between the B4081 and the B4035. Parking available.

What to see The Silk Mill, The Woolstaplers Hall, The Market Hall.

Recommended walk See pages 90 and 91.

Cirencester

The Dean Heritage Centre Teashop

Enjoy an afternoon tea with views overlooking the Forest of Dean

Soudley,
CINDERFORD, GL14 7UG
Tel 01594 822170

The Dean Heritage Centre is surrounded by the magnificent woodlands and natural treasures of the Forest of Dean, one of England's few remaining ancient forests. The teashop is crammed with tasty home-made delights, including their famous giant cream scones. Savoury snacks make the most of local produce, such as locally smoked fish and Gloucester Old Spot sausages, and there is a large variety of tea on offer to wash it all down with. The centre exhibits arts and crafts of the Forest of Dean's history.

To eat Set tea. Hot and cold lunches.

Open Daily 10am-5pm Mar-Oct, Daily 10am-4pm Nov-Feb.

Getting there Off the B4226 and the A4151. Parking available.

What to see The Forest of Dean Mechanical Organ Museum, The Great Western Railway Museum, Clearwell Caves Ancient Iron Mines.

Tollgate Tea Shop

A cosy tea shop with a traditional feel

Oldfield Gatehouse,
DYRHAM PARK, SN14 8LF
Tel 01225 891585
web www.tollgateteashop.co.uk

Tollgate Tea Shop is to be discovered in a distinctive stone building with arched windows and wooden floors. You can indulge in a delicious cream tea, for which vouchers can be bought, to the sound of peaceful, classical music and the wonderful scent of a fragrant wood-burning stove. Their use of traditional blue and white willow-pattern china perfects this teatime experience, where the atmosphere will leave you feeling completely relaxed. There is a nice selection of ten teas to choose from as well.

To eat Set tea. Cakes and snacks.

Open Tue-Sun 9:30am-5pm, Sat-Sun Summer 9:30am-6pm.

Getting there Off the A46. Parking available.

What to see Dyrham Park, Sir Bevil Grenville's Monument, Beckford's Tower, Avon Valley Railway.

Dyrham Park

The Marshmallow

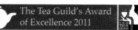

The Tea Guild's Award of Excellence 2011

Refreshment for energetic antiques-shop browsers

High Street,
MORETON-IN-MARSH, GL56 0AT
Tel 01608 651536

Blending with the numerous high-quality art and antiques shops in the High Street, The Marshmallow is a popular venue for tourists and locals alike. Tuesday is a particularly busy day, when the traders' market comes to this delightful Cotswold town. The tea shop is distinguished by its attractive frontage clad in colourful Virginia creeper; behind is a stone-flagged courtyard with tables and hanging baskets, where customers can take tea in the warmer months. The cake trolley is laden with tempting specialities including lemon meringue pie, roulades, Bakewell Tart, Victoria sponge and pecan Danish pastries. There is also a light lunch menu of sandwiches and savoury snacks and a variety of different teas to choose from, including a house blend.

To eat Cream tea. Lunches. Snacks.

Open Tue 10am-4pm; Wed, Thur 10am-8pm; Fri, Sat 10am-8:30pm; Sun, Mon 10am-early evening.

Getting there On A429 between Stratford-upon-Avon and Stow-on-the-Wold. Tea shop at north end of main street. Public car park and on street parking.

What to see Walking on Thames Path, Cotswold Water Park, Buscot Park.

The Cream Tea Rooms

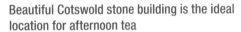

The Tea Guild's Award
of Excellence 2011

Beautiful Cotswold stone building is the ideal location for afternoon tea

Sheep Street, STOW-ON-THE-WOLD GL54 1AA
Tel 07814 249437
e-mail creamtearoom@hotmail.co.uk

This small family-run tea room in the idyllic market town of Stow-on-the-Wold is located on Sheet Street, the main road to Oxford. Built of beautiful honey-coloured Cotswold stone this is the perfect place to enjoy a cream tea after a day spent exploring this charming town with its many antique and independent shops. The Cream Tea Room offers an amazing range of over 90 loose leaf teas and tisanes, from the classic English Breakfast to the more contemporary Redespresso, all carefully kept, prepared and presented. The tea room offers an extensive selection of homemade scones served with homemade jam and clotted cream, seasonal cakes, (including dairy and gluten free) and light bites. A selection of teas is available to purchase and enjoy at home. For set teas they offer a traditional cream tea, the savoury Gardener's Tea which comes with a homemade cheese scone and cake, the Hearthside tea which features hot crumpets followed by cake, and the Stow tea, which includes a sandwich as well as a scone with cream and jam. The Deluxe afternoon tea offers a selection of sandwiches, along with a scone with cream and jam and homemade cake. All are served with your choice of tea from their large selection, and are very reasonably priced.

To eat Light lunches, teas

Open 10am-5pm (Thu-Tue in summer, Fri-Tue in winter, and every day in August)

Getting there A436 to Stow on the Wold. Tea room is opposite Tourist Information Centre.

What to do Explore the Cotswolds; Cotswolds Farm Park; Batsford Arboretum; Hidcote Manor Gardens.

Abbey Tea Rooms & Restaurant

The Tea Guild's Award of Excellence 2011

Traditional treats in a beautiful medieval building

59, Church Street,
TEWKESBURY GL20 5R
Tel 1684 292215
e-mail abbeytearoomsandrestaurant@btconnect.com
web www.abbeytearoomsandrestaurant.co.uk

Twewkesbury, set at the junction of the Rivers Severn and Avon, is one of Britain's best-preserved medieval towns. The fine medieval townscape includes many Tudor timber-framed buildings, overhanging upper stories and ornately carved doorways. The Abbey Tea Rooms itself serves traditional homemade fare in a superb medieval building which is over 500 years old and has many original features, including the best example of wattle and daub in Tewkesbury. Often asked if there are any ghosts here, the owners say "if there are they are they are clearly friendly, as Abbey Tea Rooms is the nicest place we have ever worked and lived" which is surely a great recommendation! Over 50 types of tea are available to accompany the set teas, which include the Cream Tea – with scones freshly baked in-house (plain or fruited) with Cornish clotted cream, fresh strawberries (when available), strawberry jam and a pot of English tea. Or try the High Tea - based on two sharing, this includes a selection of sandwiches, sakes, clotted cream tea and a pot of any tea.

To eat Hot and cold lunches, afternoon teas and a traditional Sunday lunch.

Open: Wed-Thu 10.30-4.30 Fri 10.30-3 Sat 10.30-5 Sun noon-4 Closed Mon-Tue (ex Bank Holidays)

Getting there M5 junct 9, follow signs for Tewkesbury, at first rdbt (which is the centre of town approx 1.5m from the motorway) go straight on into Church St, the tea rooms are 400yds on right, opposite main entrance to Abbey.

What to see Tewkesbury Abbey, Merchant's House, John Moore Countryside Museum and Roses Theatre.

Juri's - The Olde Bakery Tea Shoppe

 The Tea Guild's Award of Excellence 2011

A traditional tea room with a hint of Japanese influence

High Street,
WINCHCOMBE, (near Cheltenham), GL54 5LJ
Tel 01242 602469.
e-mail miyawaki@ma.kew.net
web www.juris-tearoom.co.uk

Juri's family-run tea room is found in an original Cotswold stone building with beautifully decorated interiors, and a conservatory and garden patio that look out over the magnificent Cotswold hills. They have 17 different types of speciality tea, including many herbal teas, fruit infusions and three Japanese green teas, one of which is Matcha, particularly used in traditional Japanese tea ceremonies. Juri Miyawaki is a graduate from "Le Cordon Bleu", the world renowned cookery school, and uses French and Japanese influences to inspire extraordinary recipes combined with a sense of traditional Englishness. All dishes are both home-made and handmade on the premises and there is a large selection of specials, freshly made each day to the highest of standards. All of their traditional English dishes are made from original recipes and are very popular. Booking is essential for full afternoon tea.

To eat Set teas. Full lunch menu.

Open Thu-Fri 10am-5pm, Sat 10:30-5pm, Sun 11am-5pm. Open Bank Holiday Mondays.

Getting there On the B4632. No designated parking available.

What to see Cheltenham Racecourse, Pittville Pump Room, St Mary's Church, Cheltenham Art Gallery and Museum.

Walk

Painswick – Painswick's traditions
Through the Washpool Valley

Start/finish: Grid ref SO 865095

Parking: Car park (fee) near library, just off main road, Painswick

Distance: 7.5 miles/12.1km

Level of difficulty: ● ● ●

Suggested map: OS Explorer 179 Gloucester, Cheltenham & Stroud

Walk directions

❶ Turn **R** from car park and **R** again. Turn **L** along Gloucester Street, join another road; continue uphill. Go **R** onto Golf Course Road. Bear **L** on track, joining Cotswold Way, through car park, turn **L** into lane; after 50 paces go **L** into woodland and across fairway.

❷ Keep **L** of cemetery; cross another fairway to path. Continue to road. After 50 paces turn **R**, leaving track after 60 paces. Walk along **L** edge of golf course to top, passing **R** of trig point. Descend other side and turn **L** down path. At track go **L** to road, aiming for gap in trees.

❸ Turn **R** to bus stop. Here cross to path amid trees. Beyond gate turn **L** down track to Spoonbed Farm, and descend bearing **R** at track junction. Pass farm to gate, then take path to field. In 2nd field keep **L** of ash tree to stile. Through new copse, after another stile cross field to **R** of Upper Holcombe Farm to stile.

❹ Turn **L** onto lane for 0.5 mile (800m) to Holcombe Farm. Continue straight on along track, passing gates at bend on **L**. Continue and at stile go **L** into next field. Cross stile and bear **R** to next stile. Cross; turn **R** into green lane which leads to footbridge with stile at each end. Bear **R** alongside stream and soon bear **L** uphill to stile. Over this follow **L-H** field margin uphill to stile.

5 Turn **L** towards Edge Farm; fork **R** at farm buildings to gate. Over stile cross 2 fields to gate onto road. Bear **R** at Y-junction. Opposite house turn **L** over stile, bear half **R** to next stile and onto path to enter Edge.

6 Turn **L**, then sharp **R** at postbox; pass village hall. Before farmhouse turn **L** over stile, then another; descend along field edge to footbridge. Cross; climb field to stile in opposite hedge, then head for gate at track, to **R** of farm. Enter gate and one opposite; walk field edge to kissing gate on to lane. Turn **L** and, after 30 paces, turn **R** via gate on to track. Track becomes path to stile. Cross fields on same line, then stile and go quarter **L** to field gate and another, passing **R** by house to road.

7 Turn **L**; cross A46. Go along Pincot Lane. At Primrose Cottage turn **L** over stile; cross to stile. Drop to cross footbridge, climb; cross field to gate, **L** of Sheephouse. Walk on drive, where it forks go **L** to King's Mill. Bear **R** through gate, over weir, then stile. Walk beside stream to lane, via 2 stiles. Turn **L** to Painswick.

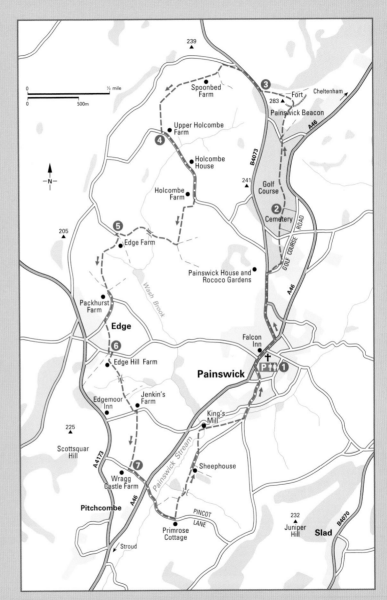

The Café Above (Walkers the Bakers)

Try a variety of teas in this traditional tea shop

1 Threadneedle Street,
STROUD, GL5 1AF
Tel 01453 762441

Just a few steps from the High Street, the Café Above is an independent, family-run café that serves tea, coffee, hot chocolate and other drinks all day. As well as light snacks there are also home-made mail meals available, using fresh and local ingredients wherever posssible.

To eat Cakes, light snacks, main meals.

Open Mon-Sat 9:30am-3:30pm.

Getting there Stroud is on the A46 and A419. Nearest motorway M5. Public car parks.

What to see Stratford Park, The Subscription Rooms, Stroud House Gallery, Made in Stroud, Cotswold Playhouse.

Lords of the Manor

Wonderfully welcoming 17th-century manor house

UPPER SLAUGHTER, GL54 2JD
Tel 01451 820243
e-mail reservations@lordsofthemanor.com
web www.lordsofthemanor.com

Formerly a rectory, this fine country house hotel stands in eight acres of gardens and parkland surrounded by Cotswold countryside. Stylish public rooms are warmed by open fires in winter, and in summer French windows open onto the terrace. Tea is served in the drawing room, library and bar, and outside too when the weather permits. The afternoon tea menu offers a cream tea, tea and biscuits; traditional full afternoon tea with finger sandwiches, scones and cakes, and the luxurious 'Gourmet Afternoon Tea' which includes potted shrimp and Cotswold cheeses.

To eat Cream tea, full afternoon tea, gourmet afternoon tea.

Open Daily. Tea served Mon-Sat 12-5:30pm, Sun 3-5:30pm.

Getting there Off the A429, through Lower Slaughter, into Upper Slaughter. 60 parking spaces available.

What to see Bourton-on-the-Water, Hidcote Manor Gardens, Stratford-upon-Avon.

Westonbirt Arboretum

Hidcote Manor Gardens

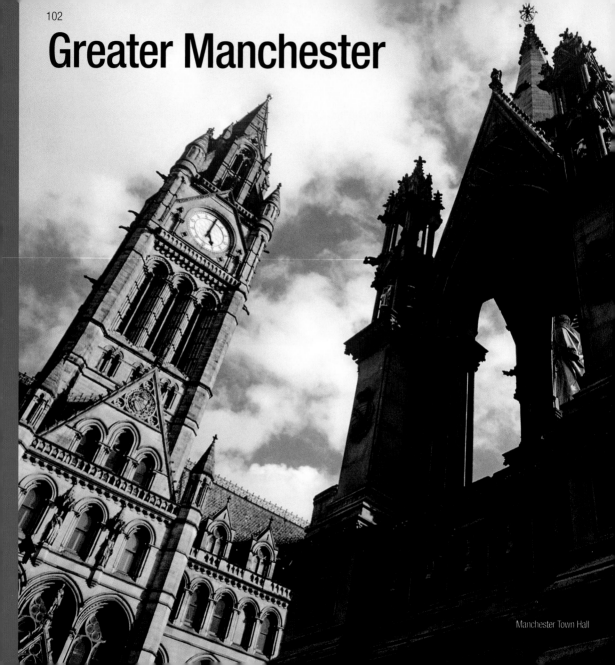

Greater Manchester

Manchester Town Hall

River Bar and Restaurant, The Lowry Hotel Manchester

The Tea Guild's Award of Excellence 2011

Traditional afternoon tea in a stylish, modern hotel

50 Dearmans Place,
Chapel Wharf,
MANCHESTER, M3 5LH
Tel 0161 827 4000
e-mail reservations.lowry@roccofortecollection.com
web www.roccofortecollection.com

Manchester is a vibrant, lively city, and this is reflected in the contemporary style of the Lowry Hotel. The River Bar has an attractive outlook over the River Irwell and is a very chic place for tea. The scones, pastries and cakes are all freshly baked in the hotel, and can be enjoyed with one of over twenty teas, or with a glass of Champagne. The presentation of the cakes or savouries is a work of art and adds to the pleasure of eating here. The traditional afternoon tea includes freshly-cut finger sandwiches, followed by fruit and plain scones with clotted cream and strawberry preserve. The excellent tea menu includes Earl Grey, Morning Blend, Afternoon Blend, and Organic Downy Tip Green Mao Jian. Booking is recommended.

To eat Afternoon tea. Light lunches.

Open Daily 3-5:30pm

Getting there In city centre, beside River Irwell

What to see Lowry Art Gallery, Manchester Town Hall, Urbis

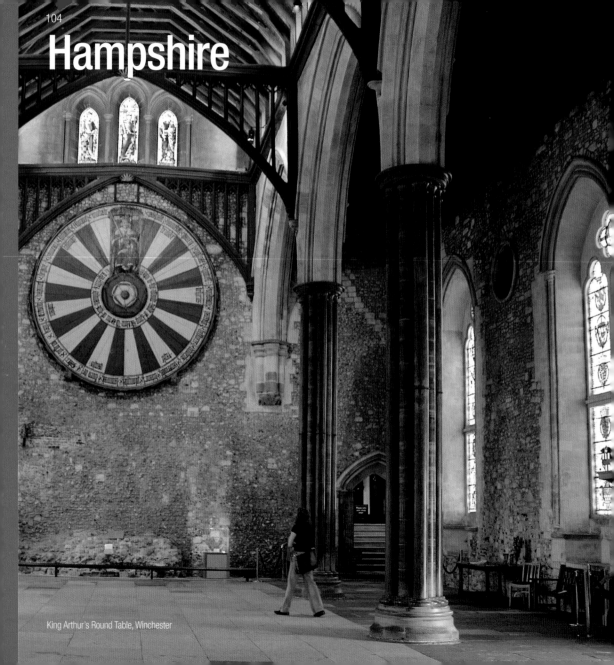

Hampshire

King Arthur's Round Table, Winchester

Tiffin Tearooms

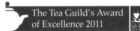

The Tea Guild's Award of Excellence 2011

A traditional tea room serving speciality teas.

50 West Street,
ALRESFORD, SO24 9AU
Tel 01962 734394
e-mail tiffintearooms@hotmail.co.uk

Located in Alresford's West Street and owned by Christopher and Sharon Pendlebury who take great pride in offering friendly and knowledgeable service, this is a traditional English, family run tearoom with a particularly pretty garden where, in summer, customers can enjoy the Pendleburys' carefully selected speciality teas and delicious home-baked cakes and food. They serve 24 different types of loose leaf tea, and many of the 15 different cakes are made from family recipes. The lemonade is also home-made.

To eat Classic Cream Tea, Savoury Tea, Watercress Tea, Afternoon Tea. Light lunches.

Open Summer Mon-Fri 10am-5:30pm, Sat 9:30am-5:30pm, Sun 2-5pm. Winter Mon-Fri 10am-4pm, Sat 10am-5pm

Getting there Alresford is to the north of the A31 between Alton and Winchester.

What to see Watercress Line, Avington Park, Hinton Ampner

Montagu Arms Hotel

The Tea Guild's Award
of Excellence 2011

**Historic 16th-century hotel on the Beaulieu estate,
with a character and charm that make visiting a delight**

Palace Lane,
BEAULIEU, SO42 7ZL
Tel 01590 612324
e-mail reservations@montaguarmshotel.co.uk
web www.montaguarmshotel.co.uk

Hospitality is top of the bill at this olde-worlde retreat. On a cool day, the blazing log fires in the lounge encourage a relaxing doze on the comfortable sofas, and the conservatory, which looks out onto the terrace and gardens, is another cosy spot. Here you can enjoy a traditional afternoon tea, including finger sandwiches, cakes, scones, cream tea fancies, shortbread, local jams, and strawberries accompanied by a choice of speciality loose leaf teas such as Russian Caravan. Booking required for full afternoon tea.

To eat Afternoon tea, cream tea, lunch, dinner.

Open Open daily. Tea served 3:30pm-5:30pm.

Getting there Beaulieu is on the B3054 and B3056, southeast of Lyndhurst.

What to see National Motor Museum, Buckler's Hard, New Forest Visitor Centre at Lyndhurst, Hurst Castle, Otter and Owl Centre.

Old Farm House

Enjoy the atmosphere of an old-fashioned country tea room of 40 or 50 years ago

The Cross, Ringwood Road,
BURLEY, BH24 4AB
Tel 01425 402218
web www.oldfarmhouseinburley.co.uk

Push open the front door of this thatched former farmhouse and discover a place full of beams, log fires, nooks and crannies. Its all rather seductive and captivating and proves you can have your cake and eat it. There's also a range of tasty snacks and sandwiches on offer, plus 10 varieties of tea. Booking is advisable, but not essential.

To eat Cream tea. Light lunches.

Open Daily 9am–5pm (Fri-Sat also 7-9pm).

Getting there Burley is on the Ringwood Road; nearest routes A338, A31 and the M3. Own car park.

What to see Romsey, The New Forest, Salisbury, Winchester, Bournemouth, Isle of Wight.

Cassandra's Cup

Take tea in the village where Jane Austen once lived

The Hollies,
CHAWTON (near Alton), GU34 1SB
Tel 01420 83144

Across the road from Jane Austen's House, in an idyllic village setting, you will discover a small and friendly tea room. Choose one of the varieties of tea to accompany your cakes or sandwiches, or have a delicious Jersey ice-cream, then browse in the two rooms for small gifts and old china items.

To eat Cream tea. Light lunches. Snacks

Open May-Sep, Wed-Sun; Mar-Nov, Thur-Sun 10:30am-4:30pm. Closed Jan-Feb.

Getting there Chawton is off the A31, southwest of Alton. Nearest motorway M3. Parking in the village.

What to see Jane Austen's House, Watercress Line (Mid Hants Railway), Gilbert White's House and the Oates Museum at Selborne.

Fallow deer, New Forest

Watercress Line, (Mid Hants Railway)

Four Seasons Hotel Hampshire

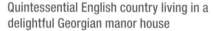

Quintessential English country living in a delightful Georgian manor house

Dogmersfield Park, Chalky Lane, Dogmersfield, HOOK RG27 8TD
Tel 01252 853000
web www.fourseasons.com/hampshire/

Set in acres of rolling countryside and listed gardens, The Four Seasons Hampshire is built around a Grade I listed 18th century manor house at the heart of the Dogmersfield estate. Built on the site of a medieval palace that played host to Henry VI on many occasions, this was where the future Henry VIII first met Catherine of Aragon. The Library, restored to its former glory, is an elegant, beautifully appointed residents' lounge and the setting for afternoon tea. Decorated in warm earth tones, it boasts an abundance of comfy armchairs and supple sofas. Traditional afternoon tea features a selection of sandwiches including garlic and nettle cheese with homemade piccalilli; smoked trout with horseradish cream; gammon and radish salad with honey mustard; ricotta with mint and cucumber; and organic egg and asparagus salad. There is a selection of scones, too – traditional, apricot and black tea, served with strawberry and rhubarb jam and clotted cream, and delicious French pastries which include lemon meringue tartlet; rhubarb and white chocolate macaroon; almond moelleux; strawberry cheesecake; and chocolate toffee bar. The tea menu features an excellent selection of well-described varieties, and booking is recommended (especially at weekends).

The Tea Guild's Award of Excellence 2011

To eat Traditional Afternoon Tea; Champagne Tea

Open All week 3-5

Getting there Exit M3 at Junction 5. Follow signs to Farnham A287. Continue over two rdbts, following A287/Farnham signs. Stay on A287 for approx 3m. On left sign for Dogmersfield. Left onto Chalky Lane, after approximately 1m turn left for Four Seasons (signed).

What to see Jane Austen's House at Chawton; The Vyne (NT); Winchester.

Courtyard Tea Rooms

A fine selection of 20 different teas

49 The Hundred,
ROMSEY, SO51 8GE
Tel 01794 516434

It is worth making a trip to Romsey for afternoon tea at this cosy, beamed tea room with a charming walled garden. On offer are all sorts of goodies, including tea cakes, cheese scones, salads, toasted sandwiches, sandwiches, omelettes and cakes. A Courtyard cream tea and a Courtyard savoury tea are available, and the atmosphere is most welcoming.

To eat Cream tea. Light lunches.

Open Tue-Fri 10am-3.30pm, Sat 10am-5pm. Closed Christmas.

Getting there Romsey is on the A31 and A3057. Nearest motorways M3 and M27.

What to see Broadlands, Mottisfont Abbey, Breamore House and Garden, Paultons Park, Winchester, Southampton.

Tylney Hall Hotel

A Victorian country house set in fabulous grounds

ROTHERWICK (near Hook), RG27 9AZ
Tel 01256 764881
e-mail sales@tylneyhall.com
web www.tylneyhall.com

Afternoon tea and light meals are served in the Italian Lounge by the log fire in winter or out on the garden terrace in summer. You can choose to enhance your Tylney Hall tea with a glass of Champagne. Otherwise the set tea comprises a selection of sandwiches, home-made pastries, and scones with clotted cream and preserves. Reservations for tea are advisable for non-residents; parking is available.

To eat Full afternoon tea.

Open Daily. Tea served 3:30-5:30pm.

Getting there M3 junction 5, take A287 towards Basingstoke. Follow signs for Newnham/Rotherwick.

What to see Milestones Museum, Basingstoke, West Green House Gardens, Hartley Wintney, Silchester Roman Wall, Wellington Country Park, Jane Austen's House, Chawton.

Antony Gormley's *Sound II*, Winchester Cathedral

Gilbert White's House & Garden and The Oates Collection

The Tea Guild's Award of Excellence 2011

Restored home of the great naturalist Gilbert White

The Wakes,
SELBORNE, GU34 3JH
Tel 01420 511275
web www.gilbertwhiteshouse.org.uk

The quintessentially English, charming and elegant Tea Parlour at Gilbert White's House prides itself on offering an extensive range of speciality teas and delicious homemade cakes including date and walnut loaf, farmhouse fruit cake, and coffee sponge. Light lunches are served from midday and include homemade soup, freshly made sandwiches and Homity Pie. The house itself was home to famed 18th-century naturalist, Gilbert White, and has been restored as much as possible, to the way it was when he lived here. The house is also home to collections of artefacts relating to Captain Oates, and his Uncle, Frank, who was a natural historian and collector.

To eat Cream tea. Light lunches

Open Feb-Mar, Tue-Sun 10.30am-4:30pm. Tea served all day.

Getting there Selborne is on the B3006 Alton to A3 road.

What to see Gilbert White's House and The Oates Museum in Selborne, Jane Austen's House in Chawton, Watercress Line (Mid Hants Railway), Alton.

Lainston House Hotel

Historic country house hotel serving high quality meals

Sparsholt,
WINCHESTER, SO21 2LT
Tel 01962 863588
e-mail enquiries@lainstonhouse.com
web www.exclusivehotels.co.uk

Dating from the 17th century, Lainston House combines historic charm with contemporary elegance and serves tea in its peaceful drawing room looking out onto the beautiful, very English garden where roses, honeysuckle and clematis scramble over wrought iron pergolas and ancient stone walls. Afternoon tea offers plenty of home-baked bread, pastries and a selection of speciality teas including rare and unusual teas from China, India and Sri Lanka. Pastry Chef, Mark Tilling has been awarded the title of UK's Official Chocolate Master, so why not try one of his delightful creations?

To eat Afternoon Tea.
Open Daily 3:30-5:30pm.
Getting there two miles north west of Winchester, off B3049 towards Stockbridge.
What to see Winchester Cathedral, St Cross Almshouses, Broadlands.

Hertfordshire

Down Hall Country House Hotel

Splendid country house surroundings for a classic afternoon tea

Hatfield Heath,
BISHOP'S STORTFORD, CM22 7AS
Tel 01279 731441
e-mail reservations@downhall.co.uk
web www.downhall.co.uk

An imposing Victorian mansion house, Down Hall is set amid expansive parkland and gardens. The grand interior has lofty ceilings, panelled walls, large fireplaces and sparkling chandeliers. Afternoon tea is served in the delightful lounge. The set tea includes an assortment of finger sandwiches, scones, preserve and clotted cream, rich fruit cake and cream pastries. Down Hall Royal afternoon tea includes lobster and caviar mayonnaise sandwiches, but give 48 hours notice. Booking required for Sundays.

To eat Afternoon tea.

Open Daily. Tea served 2pm-5pm.

Getting there M11 junct 7. A414 towards Harlow. At 4th rdbt follow B183 towards Hatfield Heath. Later, the road bears right, signed for hotel. Ample parking is provided in the grounds.

What to see Hatfield Forest (National Trust), Gibberd Gardens, Cambridge City Centre.

The Old Swan Tea Shop

Lunch specialties and a large variety of tea

HARE STREET VILLAGE,
(near Buntingford), SG9 0DZ
Tel 01763 289265
web www.oldswanteashop.co.uk

Originally a village inn, The Old Swan was first granted a licence when Elizabeth I was on the throne, before that, however, the inn-keepers were frequently imprisoned for serving ale without one. Times have changed and the Old Swan now specialises in serving home-cooked food and country fare. Afternoon tea comes with a large choice of different teas to go with the home-made cakes and scones. The light lunch menu includes sandwiches, snacks and cakes. Specialities include pasties and steak and kidney pie.

To eat Afternoon tea. Breakfast. Lunch. Sunday roast.

Open 1st Sun of every month only, and for group bookings of 10+ at other times.

Getting there Hare Street Village is north of Puckeridge on the B1368.

What to see Great Hormead, the tiny Norman church at Little Normead, Hatfield House, Hertford Castle and Museum, Hertford.

East gardens, Hatfield House

Battler's Green Farm

Light lunch and tea on a working Hertfordshire farm

Common Lane,
RADLETT, WD7 8PH
Tel 01923 857505

Battler's Green prides itself that it is still a working farm, although it is now also home to a wealth of diverse shops and businesses. As well as farm produce you can also shop for an Aga, bathroom and home furniture, jewellery, flowers, picture frames, fresh fish and plenty more. The Bull Pen Tearoom is in a timbered barn where the pleasant aromas of home-baking waft through the door, and you can sample some of the eleven varieties of tea served here. The light lunch menu includes snacks, sandwiches, cakes and scones with jam and cream.

To eat Afternoon tea. Light lunches.

Open Daily. 8am-5pm (Mon 9am-4pm)

Getting there The A5143 runs through Radlett. Nearest motorway M25. Parking at the farm.

What to see Ayot St Lawrence (the last home of George Bernard Shaw), Hatfield Palace, Knebworth, Gardens of the Rose.

Marriott Hanbury Manor Hotel & Country Club

Tranquil Jacobean-style manor house close to London

WARE, SG12 0SD
Tel 01920 487722
e-mail guestrelations.hanburymanor@marriotthotels.co.uk
web www.marriott.co.uk/stngs

Built in 1890 and set in mature formal grounds and extensive parkland, Hanbury Manor is an impressive hotel and is well known for its championship golf course. Enjoy afternoon tea in the baronial Oak Hall. Five set teas range from the modest Cake Tea (a slice of cake and a pastry), to the lavish Champagne Tea (finger sandwiches, scones with jam and clotted cream, slices of cake and pastries). All the cakes, scones and pastries are produced by the hotel's pastry chef. Booking is required.

To eat Cream tea, afternoon tea, champagne tea.

Open Daily. Tea served 3:30-5:30pm.

Getting there M25 junct 25, then A10 north.

What to see Paradise Wildlife Park, Hatfield House, Duxford Imperial War Museum, Welwyn Viaduct, Scott's Grotto.

Knebworth House

Growing and Producing Tea

Tea grows best in regions which enjoy a warm, humid climate with a rainfall of at least 100 centimetres a year. Ideally, it likes deep, light, acidic and well-drained soil.

An evergreen tropical plant from the Camellia family, tea (Camellia sinensis) has green, shiny pointed leaves and was originally indigenous to both China and India.

Tea grows best in regions which enjoy a warm, humid climate with a rainfall of at least 100 centimetres a year. Ideally, it likes deep, light, acidic and well-drained soil. Given these conditions, tea will grow in areas from sea level up to altitudes as high as 2,100 metres above sea level. Tea is grown on estates or smallholdings. A smallholding is privately owned, and can be as small as 0.5 hectares. Where tea is grown on smallholdings, very often co-operatives are formed to build a tea-processing factory central to a group of smallholders. The smallholders then sell their plucked leaf to the factory for processing. By contrast, an estate is a self-contained unit, often hundreds of hectares in size, housing its own factory, tea growing area, schools, hospital, staff houses and gardens, places of worship, reservoir and guest house.

Bushes are grown from cuttings or clones which are carefully nurtured in nursery beds until ready for planting out. Young bushes are planted approximately 1.5 metres apart in rows with a distance of one metre between each row. In the higher altitudes these rows follow the contours of the hills or mountainsides and terraces may be built to avoid soil erosion.

The bushes are grown to a eight of around a metre, to make plucking easier, and trained into a fan shape, with a flat top, called a plucking plateau. This is about 1 x 1.5 metres in area and will take three to five years to come to maturity. (This is dependent on the altitude). Before the first plucking, the bushes are severely pruned by a method known as "lung" pruning.

Bushes are plucked, mostly by hand, every 7-14 days. A tea bush grown at sea level will replace itself more quickly than one growing at a higher altitude, where the air is often cooler. Only the top two leaves and a bud are plucked from the sprigs on the plucking plateau.

The plucked leaves are collected in a basket or bag carried on the back of the plucker. When full this is taken to a collection point and weighed before being taken to the factory for processing, or 'making'. On an estate, each plucker is credited with their own weights of tea for subsequent payment. A skilled plucker can gather up to between 30-35 kg of plucked leaf a day, sufficient to produce about 7.5 to 9 kg of processed black tea.

Kent

Claris's

The Tea Guild's Award of Excellence 2011

Beams, inglenook, lace tablecloths, and delicious food

1–3 High Street,
BIDDENDEN, TN27 8AL
Tel 01580 291025
e-mail info@collectablegifts.net
web www.collectablegifts.net

A 15th-century weaver's cottage in one of England's most unspoilt villages is the setting for a flourishing tea room and gift shop. Collectors of such diverse objects as fine pottery and Steiff teddy bears are drawn to this Aladdin's cave of treasures. Behind the windows, filled temptingly with Moorcroft pottery, lamps, glassware, enamels and soft toys, the tea shop itself exudes charm. The low oak beams and inglenook fireplace, and spacious tables covered in lace, are outdone in appeal only by the food. Huge light meringues are a house speciality, but equally irresistible are the wonderful walnut bread, lemon Madeira, and almond slice. Cream teas are served with a choice of carefully brewed teas, and there are also soups, sandwiches and snacks.

To eat Cream tea.

Open Thur-Sun 10:30am-5pm. Tea served all day.

Getting there M20 junct 8, B2163 south. Left onto A274 to Biddenden.

What to see Sissinghurst Castle Gardens (National Trust), Leeds Castle, Kent and East Sussex Railway, Tenterden.

Walk

Penshurst – through parkland

A fairly easy circular walk around the magnificent estate surrounding medieval Penshurst Place

Start/finish: Grid ref TQ 525439

Parking: On-street parking in Penshurst Road, and car park for Penshurst Place

Distance: 4 miles/6.4km

Level of difficulty: ● ● ●

Suggested map: OS Explorer 147 Sevenoaks & Tonbridge

Walk directions

❶ Walk up road away from village and take footpath **R** through gate. The house dates from 1341 and the Great Hall is a fabulous example of medieval architecture. It has a timber roof, a musicians' gallery and an open hearth. There have been some notable visitors to the house over the years: Elizabeth I danced here with Robert Edward Dudley; the Black Prince ate a Christmas dinner here, and the children of Charles I came here after their father was executed. Now bear **L** to gate, cross drive and bear

slightly **R** across parkland, keeping lone oak trees and lake **R**. Go through fence gap and bear **R** to pass lake to reach stile.

2 Path now veers to **L** and goes uphill. Go through squeeze stile, then walk up avenue of trees, bearing **R** at top. Path levels out with good views of Penshurst Place. You are following Eden Valley Walk, a 15-mile (24km) linear walk that traces route of Eden from Edenbridge to Tonbridge.

3 Cross stile and keep walking ahead along wide, grassy track

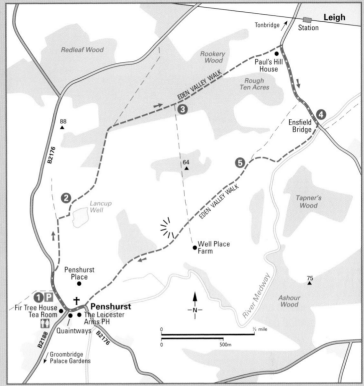

lined with trees. Exit trees and follow path to stile and gate, joining track leading to road beside Paul's Hill House. Turn **R** and follow road (care required) to bridge.

4 Go through squeeze stile and follow waymarked Eden Valley Walk through pasture, along side of River Medway which is on **L**. Walk by river for 0.25 mile (400m), then turn **R**, away from water, and head

across pasture to bridge. Follow footpath uphill to stile which takes you on to concrete track. Turn **R** and then **L** at junction.

5 Where track curves sharp **L**, keep ahead to stile, then bear **L** and walk down path from where there are lovely views of Penshurst Place. Rejoin concrete track and follow it under archway, then turn **R** and walk back into village.

The Secret Garden

Handmade cakes and seasonal produce at a
Victorian walled garden

Mersham Le Hatch, Hythe Road, Mersham, ASHFORD TN25 5NH
Tel 01233 501586
e-mail info@secretgardenkent.co.uk **web** www.secretgardenkent.co.uk

An award-winning country restaurant, The Secret Garden is set in an elegant converted 19th century coach house and offers a warm and friendly atmosphere, and excellent food from a varied seasonal menu. The main Coach House has lots of double doors which open onto a south-facing covered terrace, overlooking the Victorian walled gardens. These include a large kitchen garden, well kept lawns and a network of gravel paths and ancient espalier fruit trees. They make all their own cakes and the selection might include carrot and orange, lemon drizzle, apricot loaf cake and extra large scones. The choice of twelve teas are well kept and inlcude Pluckley Tea, Darjeeling, Jasmine and Earl Grey. Try the Cream Tea - extra large scones, strawberry jam, strawberries, clotted cream and a choice of teas – with refills – or local sparkling wine. Booking is essential if you want to sample the Afternoon Tea – dainty finger sandwiches, handmade crisps, selection of cakes, plus the scones, jam and clotted cream and plenty of tea or a glass of bubbly. The Secret Garden sells homemade cakes, pastries, bread and other items to take away with you, and it also has a cookery school which is open all year.

To eat Lunches, set teas, dinner

Open 10-5 and 7pm onwards Tue-Sat, 10-4 Sun-Mon

Getting there M20 junct 10, 2nd exit towards Sellindge, along A20, 2m on left beside cricket ground

What to see Deer Park Walk; Port Lymne Zoo; Cinque Port of Hythe

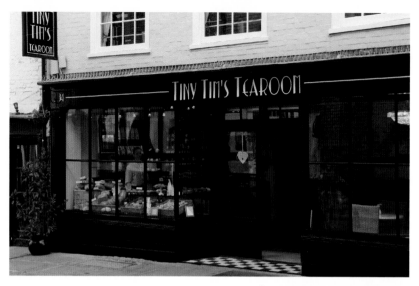

Tiny Tim's Tearoom

The Tea Guild's Award
of Excellence 2011

**Traditional tea rooms with a 1930s vibe in a
16th century building**

34 St Margaret's Street, CANTERBURY CT1 2TG
Tel 01227 450793
e-mail info@tinytimstearoom.co.uk **web** www.tinytimstearoom.co.uk

A charmingly English experience in the heart of Canterbury. Tiny Tim's is located in a 400 year old building, painstakingly restored after a devastating fire in the 1980s, and apparently haunted by the ghosts of three children. Sample one of the best afternoon teas in Kent in relaxing and luxurious surroundings, lit by crystal chandeliers. Local produce is widely used, and all of Tiny Tim's cakes and scones are freshly baked in house every morning, including Plump Pilgrims, a house speciality – fat, sweet, scone-like cakes with soft citrus pieces and currants, served warm with butter and jam. Tiny Tim's serves Kentish cream tea (scones with clotted cream and jam with a pot of tea) as well as High tea (poached egg on crumpets, scone with clotted cream and jam, and a selection of mini cakes and pastries). Afternoon tea is served on a three tier cake stand and offers finger sandwiches, scones with jam and clotted cream and a variety of mini cakes and pastries. There is also Gingerbread Tea for smaller visitors. The teas available are top quality and locally produced, including Lapsang Souchong, Ceylon and Assam, all fully described on the tea menu. Teas for special occasions are also available.

To eat Breakfast, lunches, afternoon tea, cream tea, high tea and celebration champagne tea

Open 9.30am-5pm Tue-Sat, 10.30-4 Sun

Getting there Opposite the entrance to the Marlowe Arcade, close to the Canterbury Tales visitor attraction

What to see Canterbury – the Cathedral, the castle, the museums and the shops.

The Moat Tea Rooms

Pleasant tea rooms within a short walk of the historic centre of Canterbury

67 Burgate,
CANTERBURY, CT1 2HJ
Tel 01227 784514
e-mail kelvin@moattearooms.co.uk
web www.moattearooms.co.uk

At the Moat Tea Rooms you'll find 16th-century surroundings with rich, dark wooden furniture, warm red walls, original fireplaces and two distinctive gargoyles at the front of the building. There is also an extensive selection of tea to choose from and a main speciality is the luxurious Champagne cream tea. Savoury snacks as well as cakes are also available. Booking is possible but not essential.

To eat Afternoon tea, Champagne cream tea. Light lunches

Open Mon-Sat 9am-6pm,
Sun 11am-5pm.

Getting there Parking available in a short-stay car park opposite the tea rooms.

What to see Canterbury Cathedral, Herne Bay, Whitstable, Bigbury Fort, Larkey Valley Wood, The Blean Woods National Nature Reserve.

The Oast House Tea Rooms

Tasty home-made fare and peaceful gardens full of colour

Beech Court Gardens,
CHALLOCK, (near Ashford), TN15 4BJ
Tel 01233 740735
e-mail info@beechcourtgardens. co.uk

Located on the North Downs in the gardens of Beech Court, The Oast House Tea Rooms are welcoming and attractive. Enjoy delicious home-baked scones, cakes, apple pies and locally baked bread, whether you choose to eat either in the Oast House, on the terrace or beside the pond, which enjoys a superb vista.

To eat Afternoon tea, cream tea. Light lunches.

Open Mon-Thu, Sat-Sun 10:30am-5:30pm.

Getting there Off the A252. Ample parking available.

What to see Challock Church Murals, Ashford Borough Museum, Kent and East Sussex Railway, Willesborough Windmill, Godinton House and Gardens.

Canterbury Cathedral

Shelly's Tea Rooms

Tea and a light lunch within easy reach of the beautiful Kent countryside

The Square,
CHILHAM, CT4 8BY
Tel 01227 730303

On one side of the square at Chilham stands Shelly's Tea Rooms. Inside, everything is in keeping with the style of the ancient house; low ceilings with wooden beams, small-paned windows and old brick fireplaces. Freshly-baked scones are served with cream teas, and a variety of cakes, sandwiches, snacks and baguettes are also available. Film fans may recognise Shelly's from a recent version of Jane Austen's *Emma*.

To eat Afternoon tea, light lunch.

Open Daily 10-5pm.

Getting there Chilham is five miles to the southwest of Canterbury on the A252. Parking is permitted in the village.

What to see The church of St Mary, Chilham Castle, Canterbury, Faversham, North Downs Way.

Fir Tree House Tea Rooms

A welcoming and traditional tea room in pretty surroundings

PENSHURST, TN11 8DB
Tel 01892 870382

Fir Tree House sits amongst a wealth of historic houses and half-timbered cottages in the pretty village of Penshurst. Inside the tea rooms the old stone walls, oak beams and working fireplaces give the place an atmosphere of charm and goodwill. There are 15 different varieties of tea, including the house blend of Smoky Earl Grey, sandwiches, cakes and a traditional afternoon tea with scones, jam and cream.

To eat Afternoon tea.

Open Wed-Sun 2:30-6pm.

Getting there Penshurst is five miles northeast of Tunbridge Wells on the B2176. Parking is possible in the village.

What to see Penshurst Place, medieval church at Penshurst, Spa Valley Railway, Tonbridge Castle, Hever Castle, Groombridge Place, Winnie the Pooh country.

Hever Castle

Quaintways Tea Room

Traditional tea rooms with a good selection of teas

High Street,
PENSHURST, TN11 8BT
Tel 01892 870272

Tea is served in these two attractive 16th-century cottages featuring original beams and artefacts; a Victorian oven still remains in one of the tea rooms as well as an old-fashioned polyphone. There is a wide selection of home-baked cakes and light refreshments on offer, all to be indulged within cosy surroundings with traditional blue and white crockery decorating the walls, as well as a choice of 12 types of tea. Tea can also be taken in the garden. An excellent selection of hand-made cards, bags, souvenirs, antiques, local apple juice and jams are all available to buy. No need to book.

To eat Afternoon tea.

Open Tue-Fri 10:30am-5pm, Sat, Sun 10am-5pm.

Getting there Penshurst is five miles northeast of Tunbridge Wells on the B2176. Parking available on the high street.

What to see Penshurst Place, Spa Valley Railway, Tonbridge Castle, Hever Castle, Groombridge Place, Winnie the Pooh country.

Peggoty's Tea Shoppe

A friendly and traditional shop for light snacks and tea

122 High Street,
TENTERDEN, TN30 6HT
Tel 01580 764393

This well-established tea shop is a good place to know for a light bite and a pot of tea when visiting the charming unspoilt market town of Tenterden, famous for its wide, tree-lined High Street. In good weather, tables trickle out onto the pavement, while inside tea is sipped beneath beamed ceilings in an olde-worlde atmosphere. Alternatively enjoy the delightful tea garden with its Italian fountain. This is simple tea fare, but there are more than 20 different varieties of tea and a light lunch menu that includes snacks, sandwiches, cakes and a cream tea with scones, jam and cream.

To eat Afternoon tea, cream tea. Light lunches.

Open Daily 10am-5pm.

Getting there Tenterden is situated on the main A28. Parking permitted up to two hours in designated spaces.

What to see St Mildred's Church, Tenterden and District Museum, Tenterden Vineyard Park, Kent and East Sussex Railway.

A A Milne plaque at Gills Lap

Food for Thought

The Tea Guild's Award
of Excellence 2011

Delicious homemade food and cheerful, friendly service

19-20 The Green, WESTERHAM, TN16 1EB
Tel 01959 563442
e-mail markandsamwork@yahoo.com
web www.foodforthought.eu

Ideally located in the heart of Westerham, overlooking the picturesque green with its statue of Winston Churchill, Food for Thought is run by chef and owner Mark Edwards, who has many years of experience in the catering industry, running all kinds of establishments from restaurants to cookery schools. All food is freshly made to order, and all cakes, scones and pastries are freshly baked in house, using locally sourced products where possible. The selection might feature Victoria sandwich, meringues, fresh lemon cake, ginger and lemon cake, carrot cake, coffee and walnut cake and chocolate cake or brownies, and they can cater for special diets, with gluten-free and wheat-free options. Mark works with Master tea blender Alex Probyn to provide suitable blends for his customers, including Earl Grey; Classic Green; Oolong; Lapsang Souchong; Classic Black; Darjeeling; Pai Mu Tan; and Jasmine Dragon Pearls as well as a selection of infusions. With the Cream tea you'll get a pot of tea served with two homemade scones, jam and clotted cream; or try the High tea - a pot of tea served with a sandwich followed by two scones, jam and clotted cream. Booking is advisable for lunch, when it gets very busy.

To eat breakfast, lunches, High Tea, Cream Tea, Afternoon Tea

Open 9am-6pm Sun-Fri, 8.30am-6pm Sat (closes an hour earlier in winter)

Getting there Situated between Oxted and Sevenoaks on the A25

To see Chartwell, Quebec House, Hever Castle

The Spa Hotel

18th century hotel in a peaceful parkland setting

Mount Ephraim,
TUNBRIDGE WELLS, TN4 8XJ
Tel 01892 520331
e-mail candb@spahotel.co.uk
web www.spahotel.co.uk

Surrounded by 14 acres of landscaped gardens, including three spring fed lakes, this is a warm and friendly hotel with professional staff. Tea is served in the comfortable lounge and in the beautiful new Orangery and consists of freshly made sandwiches, scones and cakes, accompanied by an extensive range of teas. Alternatively, enjoy a chilled glass of Champagne with your tea. Children are welcome. Booking recommended.

To eat Set tea.

Open Daily. Tea served 3-5:30pm.

Getting there From A21 take A26, follow signs to A264 East Grinstead, hotel on right.

What to see Hever Castle, Leeds Castle, Penshurst Place, Spa Valley Railway, Groombridge Place, Marle Place.

Chartwell

Sir Winston Churchill statue, Westerham

Lancashire

Forest of Bowland

Exchange Coffee Company

Victorian tea and coffee emporium

13-15 Fleming Square,
BLACKBURN, BB2 2DG
Tel 01254 54258

This old-fashioned café impresses with its display of traditional tins of exotic teas and coffees and its atmosphere of days gone by. They serve over 60 speciality teas and over 30 different coffees, so it is a place to escape the rush of daily life. Unusually, they believe that the best way to serve China tea is in a cafetiere, and it is certainly worth trying. One of their specialities is Caravan Tea, a blend of three teas recalling the tea that was taken from India to Russia by caravan. They make their cakes on the premises and also buy from local suppliers. All these delights and many more can be purchased from the shop on the premises.

To eat Afternoon Tea. Light lunches

Open Mon-Sat 9am-5:15pm.

Getting there In town centre across the road from the cathedral.

What to see Blackburn Cathedral, Blackburn Museum and Art Gallery, Samlesbury Hall.

Whitewell, Forest of Bowland

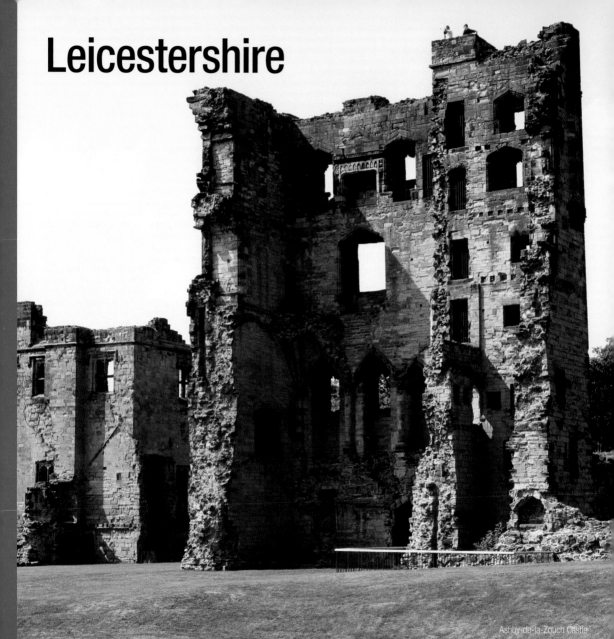

Leicestershire

Ashby-de-la-Zouch Castle

Miss B's Tea Rooms

Traditional treats in Grade II listed building

34A Market Place, MELTON MOWBRAY,
LE13 1XD

Tel 01664 481625
e-mail missbstearoomsmelton@gmail.com
web www.missbstearooms.co.uk

Miss B's Tea Rooms is set on the second floor of a Grade II listed building in the market town of Melton Mowbray, the self-styled 'Rural Capital of Food', famed for its Stilton cheese and pork pies. The heavy beams and uneven floors all add to the ambience in these traditional tea rooms. This sets the scene for a relaxing experience, where customer service is second to none and nothing is too much trouble. Tea is served from china pots into bone china tea cups, and the sugar with tongs and covered by crocheted doyley also helps to set the scene. A wide selection of homemade cakes and scones, all baked on the premises, and including gluten free versions, are available. The Afternoon Tea includes sandwiches, scones with jam and clotted cream and a slice of cake. A Cream Tea is also available, as is the Cottage Tea (crumpets, butter and preserve). You can choose from more than 20 different loose leaf teas, including Vanilla, Gunpowder and Roof of the World to name a few, and if you fancy something savoury they offer platters featuring those famous foods the town is renowned for.

To eat Lunches, afternoon tea.

Open Mon-Sat 9.30pm–4pm

Getting there in Melton Mowbray town centre. Head for the Market Square and look for the red teapot on the wall.

What to see Rutland Water, Belvoir Castle, Melton Cattle Market (Tuesdays), Twin Lakes Park.

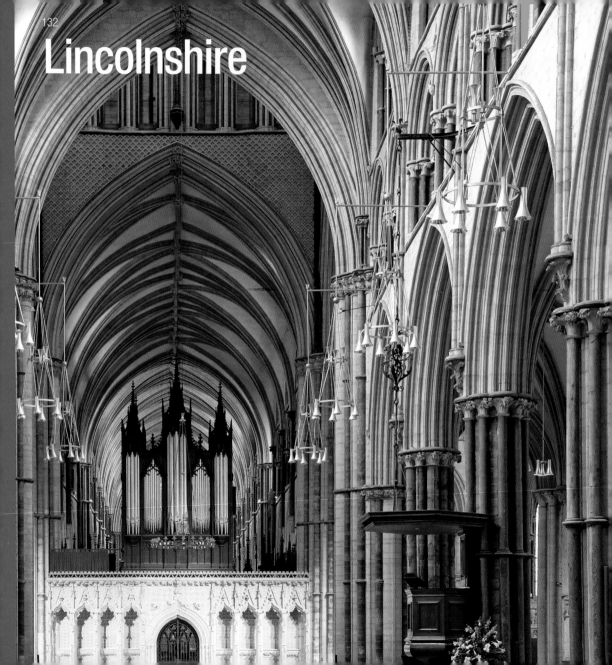

Lincolnshire

Sack Store Café

More than an award-winning café – a treasure trove of unusual household items

Redstone Industrial Estate,
Spalding Road, BOSTON, PE21 8EA
Tel 01205 310101
e-mail sales@sackstore.co.uk
web www.sackstore.co.uk

This huge building was once a store for farmers' sacks, waiting to go by train. It has been converted into an Aladdin's Cave with all kinds of furniture, tiles, stoves, and unusual items for the home. The café on the mezzanine floor serves freshly baked cakes and a variety of other snacks, which are all prepared in the open kitchen on view to all. The herbs used in the dishes come from their own kitchen garden and they strive to use locally grown organic ingredients. There is a bewildering choice of speciality teas and coffees. Allow plenty of time for any visit here so that you can properly explore all the nooks and crannies, either before or after your refreshing tea.

To eat Afternoon Tea. Snacks. Light lunches.

Open Mon-Sat 9am-5pm, Sun and Bank Holidays 11am-4pm.

Getting there Signposted off Spalding Road

What to see Boston Stump, Boston Guildhall, Sibsey Windmills.

Stokes

An afternoon tea with picturesque views of the River Witham

207 High Street,
LINCOLN, LN5 7AU
Tel 01522 512534
e-mail info@stokes-coffee.co.uk
web www.stokes-coffee.co.uk

This stunning black-and-white building is perched on a medieval bridge which spans the River Witham in the heart of Lincoln. The ground floor emporium sells teas and coffees whilst upstairs the snug rooms have low ceilings and traditional furniture. Through small leaded windows are views of the water, boats and the occasional swan. There are 10 different varieties of tea and a light lunch menu that includes snacks, sandwiches, cakes and an afternoon tea with scones, jam and cream.

To eat Afternoon tea. Cakes and savoury snacks.

Open Mon-Sat 9am-4:30pm, Sun 11:30am-4pm.

Getting there Lincoln is on the A15, A46 A158 roads. Nearest motorways M1 and M180. Restricted parking.

What to see Lincoln Castle, Lincoln Cathedral, Ellis Mill, Lincoln Jews Court, The Guildhall, St. Mary's Church, The Medieval Bishop's Place.

Lincoln Cathedral

Tealby Tea Rooms

Popular tea rooms with good old-fashioned standards

12 Front Street, TEALBY,
Market Rasen, LN8 3XU
Tel 01673 838261

In the heart of a most interesting village, this bright, bustling tea room is very popular with locals and visitors alike. A hundred years ago this was a meeting place for tea and the formula, then as now, remains the same: a pleasant ambience, good value, and a consistent standard of baking. People happily come for such delights as their Poachers Pasties and the homemade paté. Local honey can be bought in the village and there is also a well-stocked farm shop nearby. There are several varieties of tea served alongside a light lunch menu that consists of snacks, sandwiches, cakes and an afternoon tea with scones, jam and cream.

To eat Cream tea, Afternoon tea. Light lunches.

Open Mar-Oct, daily 11am-5:30pm.

Getting there Tealby is east of Market Rasen on the B1203. Parking in the village.

What to see Market Rasen Racecourse, Lincoln Castle, Museum of Lincolnshire Life.

Embroidered tapestry kneelers, All Saints Church, Tealby

How does the tea get from the plantation to your cup? It's quite a complex process.

The Tea Factory and Black Tea Processing

Once at the factory, the plucked leaf is spread on large trays or racks and left to wither in air at 25-30 degrees centigrade. The moisture in the leaf evaporates in the warm air, leaving the leaves flaccid. This process can take 10 - 16 hours, depending on the wetness of the leaf. Some factories will gently hasten the process with the aid of warm air fans. The withered leaf is broken by machine so that the natural juices, or enzymes, are released and on contact with the air will ferment, or oxidise. This breaking is done by two methods, know as Orthodox and Unorthodox – these terms are used to describe the machinery used.

The Orthodox machine rolls the leaf, which produces large leaf particles, known as grades, while the term Unorthodox covers teas broken by either a CTC (cut, tear and curl) or Rotovane machine.

Both chop the leaf into smaller particles than the Orthodox method. The smaller particles are more suited to modern market demands for a quicker brewing finished product. The broken leaf is laid out either on trays or in troughs in a cool, humid atmosphere for 3-4 hours to oxidise, and is gently turned every so often throughout the period until all the leaves turn a golden russet colour and oxidisation is complete.

After oxidisation, the leaf is dried or fired. The broken leaf is passed slowly through hot air chambers, all the moisture is evaporated, and the leaf turns dark brown or black. It is sorted into leaf particle sizes by being passed through a series of wire mesh sifts into containers, before being weighed and packed into chests or 'tea sacks' for loading onto pallets. Factory tea-tasters will taste the finished 'make' to ensure that no mistakes have been made during the manufacture and that the tea has not been contaminated by anything. Samples of the make are sent to selling brokers worldwide. All brokers will evaluate the tea for quality and price, reporting to the estate or co-operative, so the tea can be sold to the best advantage.

After each make the tea factory is washed from top to bottom to ensure that the next make of tea is not contaminated.

Green Tea processing

Green tea is not oxidised. The leaf is withered as for black tea (see page 10) and the withered leaf is steamed and rolled before drying or firing. This is done to prevent the veins in the leaf breaking and thus stopping any oxidisation of the leaf. When brewed, green tea has a very pale colour and the wet leaf is often left whole. Green tea is drunk mainly in China, Japan and some parts of South America.

Oolong tea processing

Oolong tea is a semi-green or semi-fermented tea. It follows the same process as black tea, but the oxidisation period is cut down to half the time, about 1-2 hours, before it is fired or dried. Such tea is a large leaf or Orthodox tea and is best drunk without milk, as it has a pale, bright liquor with a very delicate flavour.

White tea processing

White tea is carefully plucked before the new buds open, they are withered so that the natural moisture evaporates and then dried. The curled-up buds have a silvery appearance and are therefore sometimes referred to as Silver Tip.

London

The Landmark London

One of the last truly grand railway hotels

222 Marylebone Road,
LONDON, NW1 6JQ
Tel 020 7631 8000
e-mail reservations@thelandmark.co.uk
web www.landmarklondon.co.uk

Dating from 1899, when it opened as the Great Central Hotel, The Landmark combines a triumphant sense of scale and Victorian opulence with distinctive contemporary style. The Winter Garden Tea, taken in the opulent surroundings of the beautiful Winter Garden Restaurant atrium, comprises assorted tasty sandwiches, tea breads, fluffy light scones, delicious preserves and lashings of clotted cream, plus French pastries. Freshly brewed leaf tea can be chosen from a fine selection which includes Cornish-grown Tregothnan tea. The Landmark Tea adds a chilled glass of sparkling Champagne. Booking recommended.

To eat Afternoon tea, Champagne tea.

Open Mon-Fri Tea served 3-6pm. Sat-Sun Tea served 2:30pm-6:30pm

Getting there Nearest tube Marylebone, Baker Street.

What to see Madame Tussaud's, Regents Park, The Wallace Collection.

Burgh House

A welcome break in a Grade I listed Queen Anne house

New End Square, Hampstead,
LONDON, NW3 1LT
Tel 020 7431 0144
e-mail buttery@burghhouse.org.uk

Burgh House, with its many famous associations opens its stunning period rooms for concerts, exhibitions and events. A local history museum tells the story of Hampstead, and the Buttery Garden Café welcomes visitors all year round. Installed in the former kitchens and servants' quarters the newly refurbished Café serves mouth-watering breakfasts, lunches and afternoon teas. Visitors can also enjoy the cosy dining room and the award-winning garden.

To eat Afternoon tea, cream tea. Light lunches and snacks.

Open Wed-Sun 12-5pm.

Getting there Nearest tube Hampstead.

What to see Hampstead Heath, Keats House, Freud Museum, Kenwood House, Fenton House, 2 Willow Road (modern art collection).

Louis Patisserie

Savour a cup of your favourite brew at this intimate patisserie

32 Heath Street, Hampstead,
LONDON, NW3 6TE
Tel 020 7435 9908

This diminutive shop is on one of Hampstead's most lively village streets. Like taking a trip to old Vienna or Budapest, Louis Patisserie is sheer indulgence. All year round, the window tempts passers-by with marzipan confections, apple strudels, chocolate and cream delights and dark chocolate Linzertortes. They can all be sampled in the little tea salon at the back of the shop, along with a choice of seven blends of tea.

To eat Afternoon tea. Sandwiches, pastries and cakes.

Open Daily 9am-6pm.

Getting there Nearest tube Hampstead.

What to see Hampstead Heath, Keats House, Freud Museum, Kenwood House, Fenton House, 2 Willow Road (modern art collection).

The Hampstead Tea Rooms

You are bound to find a brew you like at this busy little tea room

9 Southend Road,
Hampstead,
LONDON, NW3 2PT
Tel 020 7435 9563

Can you jog or even walk past the Hampstead Tea Rooms without stopping to marvel at the endless rows of enticing pastries? Once you've paused you will soon find your way inside for a spot of tea – there's a choice of 20 different blends. There are three small, intimate seating areas, and in good weather you can sit outside and watch the busy Hampstead world pass by.

To eat Afternoon tea. Light lunches and snacks.

Open Daily 7:30am-7pm.

Getting there Nearest tube Belsize Park.

What to see Hampstead Heath, Keats House, Freud Museum, Kenwood House, Fenton House, 2 Willow Road (modern art collection)

The London Eye

Afternoon stroll, Hampstead Heath

The Goring

The Tea Guild's Award
of Excellence 2011

A highlight of a visit or stay – the Goring Tea

Beeston Place,
Grosvenor Gardens,
LONDON, SW1W 0JW
Tel 020 7396 9000
e-mail reception@thegoring.com
web www.thegoring.com

Ever since The Goring opened its doors in 1910 afternoon tea has been a constant feature. This icon of hospitality serves its classic set tea in the comfort of various reception rooms, including The Lounge and The Terrace. The menu is long and probably best enjoyed in the company of friends gathered for an enjoyable chat; start with a savoury, move on to a selection of sandwiches followed by home-made scones with clotted cream and jam and delicious pastries – don't forget to leave a little room for The Goring 'Not Quite a Trifle!' A wonderful range of well described teas, perfectly brewed and beautifully served, accompany the meal. For an extra special treat, have the Bollinger Tea. Booking is recommended

To eat Traditional Goring tea, Bollinger tea.

Open Daily. Tea served 3pm-5pm.

Getting there Nearest tube Victoria.

What to see Queen's Gallery, Buckingham Palace and Royal Mews, Westminster Abbey.

Mandarin Oriental Hyde Park, London

An elegant hotel in the heart of Knightsbridge

66 Knightsbridge,
LONDON, SW1X 7LA
Tel 020 7235 2000
e-mail molon-dine@mohg.com
web www.mandarinoriental.com/london

It's all change at one of London's grandest hotels, Mandarin Oriental Hyde Park, which was built in 1889 and enjoys a great location in Knightsbridge. The restaurants have undergone a complete refurbishment, and as we went to press afternoon tea was available in the brasserie-style Bar Boulud, London. This is a temporary measure, however, as the plan is that tea will be served in the new restaurant, Dinner by Heston Blumenthal. Designed by Adam D. Tihany, the restaurant has a subtle, elegant interior that is contemporary and innovative. Making use of natural materials, such as wood, leather and iron, in modern ways creates a rustic but refined atmosphere. There are uninterrupted views over Hyde Park, and floor-to-ceiling glass walls provide a glimpse into the open kitchen. During the summer months, a terrace overlooking Hyde Park provides guests with one of London's finest al fresco dining locations. Check the hotel website or telephone to find out the latest information - booking is recommended.

To eat Afternoon tea, Champagne afternoon tea.

Open Daily 3-6pm

Getting there Nearest tube Knightsbridge.

What to see Serpentine Gallery, Apsley House (Wellington Museum), Victoria and Albert Museum.

Walk

The Royal Parks – my kingdom for a park

A healthy linear walk from St James's Park to Kensington Gardens

Start/finish: Charing Cross tube station; High Street Kensington tube station

Distance: 4.25 miles/6.8km

Level of diifficulty: ● ● ●

Suggested map: AA Street by Street London

Walk directions

❶ From Charing Cross Station turn **L** into Strand and **L** again into Northumberland Street. Bear **L** along Northumberland Avenue and, after few paces, cross and turn **R** into Great Scotland Yard by Nigeria House.

❷ At end turn **L** into Whitehall, cross to other side and head for arch of Horse Guards Parade, where guards are on duty for an hour at a time. Continue through arch to gravel square used for Beating the Retreat ceremony in June.

❸ Enter St James's Park to **L** of Guards Monument and follow path that bears **L** around lake, taking the 1st **R-H** fork. Continue along this path, past weeping willow trees, to blue bridge.

❹ Cross bridge, stopping half-way across to enjoy views: westwards is Buckingham Palace and eastwards is Horse Guards Parade, where skyline looks almost fairytale-like. Turn **L**, past Nash Shrubberies, and leave park on **R**. Cross The Mall and enter Green Park from Constitution Hill.

❺ Take 2nd path on **L** and continue over next set of paths. At next junction take 2nd path on **L**. Where next paths cross, take **L-H**

path that inclines slightly to Hyde Park Corner.

6 Use pedestrian crossing to first reach central island and Wellington Arch, and then Hyde Park itself. Cross road, Rotten Row, and follow **L-H** path through rose garden with cherub fountain. Dogs are not allowed in Rose Garden. After 350yds (320m) follow path **R** of Dell Restaurant and continue beside Serpentine.

7 Walk under Serpentine Bridge and up steps on **R**. Cross bridge and enter Kensington Gardens. Take middle path and continue ahead, ignoring other paths to pass bandstand, then turn **R** at next opportunity.

8 At junction bear **L** along path that runs **L** of gates to Kensington Palace state apartments. At end turn **L** to reach Kensington Road. Pass Royal Garden Hotel, Kensington Church Street and cross Kensington High Street to tube station on **L**.

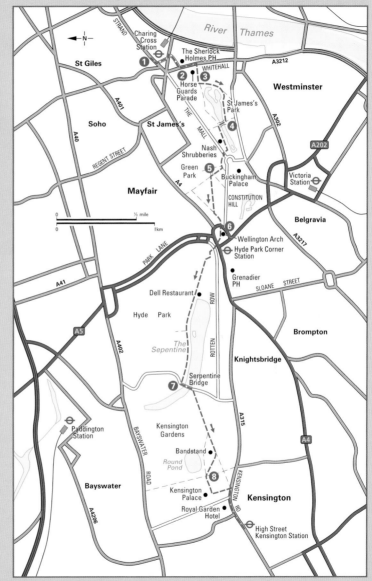

The Knightsbridge Lounge at The Sheraton Park Tower Hotel

Delightful choice of teas and an elegant ambience

101 Knightsbridge,
LONDON SW1X 7RN
Tel 020 72335 8050
e-mail pianobar.parktower@luxurycollection.com
web www.sheratonparktower.com

A splendid, discreetly opulent circular room at the heart of this impressive modern hotel, The Knightsbridge Lounge features an amazing 18-foot teardrop glass chandelier, beautiful *trompe l'oeil* wall decorations with the appearance of draped silk, and original artwork. Relax in a comfortable gilded chair at a glass topped table and peruse the menu. There is a delightful selection of light lunches and teas, including such delicacies as French rock oysters from Brittany, served with shallot vinegar and buttered bread. Alternatively enjoy a quintessentially English afternoon tea of delicious freshly baked scones with clotted cream and jam, finger sandwiches, fresh pastries and a fragrant selection of fifteen loose-leaf teas. Booking is essential!

To eat lunches; set teas – traditional British Afternoon Tea; Oriental, a fusion of Chinese and Japanese tea ceremonies; Tisane, an array of herbal and fruit infusions.

Open Tea served 3pm-6pm

Getting there
Knightsbridge tube station

What to see Knightsbridge shops - Harrods, Harvey Nichols

Sofitel St James London

The Tea Guild's Award of Excellence 2011

A thoroughbred tea taken to the resonant strains of a harp

6 Waterloo Place,
LONDON, SW1Y 4AN
Tel 020 7747 2222
e-mail H3144@accor-hotels.com
web www.sofitelstjames.com

Afternoon tea, so the menu of the Rose Lounge informs its visitors, first became fashionable in the 1840s. That it is now firmly established as a treasured national tradition is incontestable, although few establishments include a glass of Champagne cocktail in their set tea as does the Sofitel (a non-alcoholic version is also available). A harpist playing in the small lounge harks back to a more gracious era, and against this classy musical background the tea ritual itself is equally reassuring and refined. Healthy appetites are necessary for a list that includes a selection of finger sandwiches, followed by freshly baked warm scones and crumpets with Devonshire clotted cream and jam, English and French pastries, a variety of cakes, and a pot of tea from the excellent tea menu. The decadent 'Tea en Rose' includes rare vintage teas from China together with a Champagne cocktail and the hotel's rose macaroons.

To eat Afternoon tea, Le Tea en Rose.

Open Daily. Tea served 2:30-5:30pm.

Getting there Nearest tube Piccadilly Circus.

What to see London Eye, Cabinet War Rooms, National Gallery.

The Capital

Enjoy a British tradition at one of London's most delightful hotels

Basil Street, Knightsbridge,
LONDON, SW3 1AT
Tel 020 7589 5171
e-mail bar@capitalhotel.co.uk
web www.capitalhotel.co.uk

From the moment you're greeted by the uniformed doorman you'll know you're in one of Britain's smartest and most elegant hotels. The aim of The Capital's staff and management is to make you feel as though you're visiting a "well run and much loved home", and while most of us certainly don't live anywhere that remotely resembles this wonderful place, it really is relaxed and comfortable. Afternoon tea is served in the Sitting Room, and shows the same attention to detail that you'll find everywhere in the hotel. Everything from jam and preserves to chocolate and pastries is produced in the hotel's famous restaurant, and a selection of delicate sandwiches is followed by scones and pastries, with a good choice of well kept, top quality teas, including Jasmine Pearls, Rosebud Gong Fu, Darjeeling Second Flush, and Silver Needle White Tea. Booking recommended.

To eat Afternoon tea, Champagne tea.

Open Daily. Tea served 2:30-5.30pm.

Getting there Nearest tube Knightsbridge.

What to see Harrods, Harvey Nichols, Hyde Park, Royal Albert Hall, British Museum, Natural History Museum, Science Museum.

Dr Johnson's House, Gough Square, EC4

Science Museum

Blakes Hotel

Luxurious and indulgent setting for tea

33 Roland Gardens, LONDON SW7 3PF
Tel 0207 370 6701
e-mail blakes@blakeshotels.com
web www.blakeshotels.com

One of the world's first luxury boutique hotels, Blakes was created in 1978 by world famous design guru Anouska Hempel. Famous for its design and service (and the celebrities one might encounter there) the hotel has become a byword for glamour and sophistication. Inspired by Hempel's travels, you'll find Chinese, Indian, Thai, Cambodian and Italian themes amongst the abundant, luxurious furniture and accessories. Afternoon tea is served in two locations – the subterranean, sensuous splendour of the Chinese Room, wonderfully decorated with Chinese artefacts, sumptuous seating, candles and a profusion of exquisite candles, and in the beautiful and tranquil Japanese Garden. Delicate freshly prepared finger sandwiches include cucumber, smoked salmon and beef and chilli horseradish (served in a glass box) are accompanied by homemade 'light as air' scones served with fresh strawberries and cream, and a selection of mouth watering cakes – maybe Madeira or chocolate fudge. There is a good selection of teas to choose from - English breakfast, Lapsang Suchong, Darjeeling and Earl Grey as well as green tea and ginger tea. Booking is essential.

To eat Full Afternoon Tea, Champagne Afternoon Tea

Open every day 12-5.30

Getting there Off Old Brompton Road, 5 minutes from South Kensington or Gloucester Road tube stations

What to do Natural History Museum and Victoria & Albert Museum, Kensington shops

Millennium Bailey's Hotel London Kensington

A modernised Victorian hotel where, happily, some things never change

140 Gloucester Road,
LONDON, SW7 4QH
Tel 020 7373 6000
e-mail reservations@mill-cop.com
web www.millenniumhotels.com/baileys

Olive's Bar at Bailey's serves cool and contemporary cocktails, state-of-the-art sandwiches, tasty light bites and snacks from mid-morning to late. But if you turn up between 3 and 5pm, the chances are that you'll be heading for the afternoon tea menu. In the cosmopolitan atmosphere of Olive's, this institution is taken with reassuring seriousness. Expect a traditional tea stand bearing finger sandwiches, patisseries, scones with clotted cream and jam, and a refreshing choice of teas. Variations on the theme include the Champagne afternoon tea or a modest though delicious selection of pastries.

To eat Afternoon tea, Champagne tea.

Open Daily. Tea served 3-5pm.

Getting there Nearest tube Gloucester Road.

What to see Science Museum, Natural History Museum, Kensington Gardens.

Millennium Gloucester Hotel London Kensington

Ideally placed for hungry shoppers

4–18 Harrington Gardens,
LONDON, SW7 4LH
Tel 020 7373 6030
e-mail sales.gloucester@mill-cop.com
web www.millenniumhotels.com/gloucester

If you're worn out from too much shopping or exploring Kensington's museums, then head for the tranquil atmosphere of this elegant hotel. Marble floors, beautiful drapes and impressive flower arrangements all add to the luxurious ambience. Tea is served in Humphrey's Bar (named after Humphrey, Duke of Gloucester, who was brother to Henry V and fought with him at Agincourt). The menu for afternoon tea consists of finger sandwiches, French pastries and fruit scones. A wide range of coffee and tea is available, or, if you prefer, they'll make you a mug of hot chocolate with whipped cream.

To eat Traditional afternoon tea.

Open Daily. Tea served 3-6pm.

Getting there Nearest tube Gloucester Road.

What to see Harrods, Victoria and Albert Museum, Science Museum, Kensington Palace.

Kensington Palace Gardens

Orange Pekoe

The Tea Guild's Award of Excellence 2011

A haven for tea lovers near the River Thames

3 White Hart Lane, Barnes,
LONDON SW13 0PX
Tel 020 8876 6070
e-mail info@orangepekoeteas.com
web www.orangepekoeteas.com

For anyone interested in tea, this light and friendly tea room is the place to come. As you enter you see a collection of over 60 tea caddies each with a different type of tea or tisane. Order your tea and it will be perfectly brewed for you in a large filter which is removed from your pot (so that the tea does not stew) before being delivered to your table. Underneath the sparkling glass domes on the counter is a tempting display of cakes and scones, and you can buy packets of tea to take away together with books and other tea gifts. There are also tables outside for when the weather is fine.

To eat Afternoon tea. Breakfast. Lunches.

Open Mon-Fri 7:30am-5:30pm. Sat, Sun 9am-5:30pm

Getting there Off Mortlake High Street, near Barnes Bridge Rail Station

What to see Kew Gardens, London Wetland Centre, Richmond Park

Athenaeum Hotel

Scumptious afternoon treats in chic surroundings

116 Piccadilly,
LONDON, W1J 9JB
Tel 020 7499 3464
e-mail dining@athenaeumhotel.com
web www.athenaeumhotel.com

The Garden Room in this glamorous hotel is an intimate and very attractive setting for a choice of luxurious teas. The chef has designed a menu that begins with a selection of 13 different teas from across the world. Their popular Evergreen Tea (inspired by the Athenaeum's vertical garden) is a fusion of a traditional English afternoon tea with a breath of botanical, floral flavours. To accompany this a selection of delectable sandwiches are served, followed by mouth watering treats made with Regents Park honey, including honeycomb marquis, elegant honey macaroons and freshly baked scones served with Regents Park honey and rich Devonshire clotted cream.

To eat Honey Tea, Evergreen Tea

Open Daily 12:30pm-6pm

Getting there Nearest tube Green Park

What to see Buckingham Palace, Royal Academy, Green Park

Brown's Hotel –
The English Tea Room

The Tea Guild's Award
of Excellence 2011

Tea in one of the most historic hotels in London

Albemarle Street, Mayfair,
LONDON, W1S 4BP
Tel 020 7493 6020
e-mail reservations.browns@roccofortecollection.com
web www.brownshotel.com

Afternoon tea is synonymous with Brown's Hotel, which was established by James Brown for "genteel" folk over 170 years ago; sophistication and luxury are its hallmarks. A baby grand piano, crisp white linen and rich, dark wood all help to create its famous discreet and elegant setting that befits the romance of a true English afternoon tea. Make your visit memorable with a glass of Tattinger Rose Champagne to accompany your selection of finely cut sandwiches, freshly baked scones and delicate pastries. There is a choice of 17 different teas, including Brown's own special blend. A gift voucher for afternoon tea at Brown's is available via the website and is presented in tissue paper inside a stylish silver box.

To eat Afternoon tea, Champagne tea.

Open Mon-Fri, tea served 3-6pm. Sat, Sun, tea served 1pm-6pm.

Getting there Nearest tube Green Park.

What to see Knightsbridge, Bond Street, Royal Academy of Arts, Fortnum and Mason.

The Chesterfield Mayfair

The Tea Guild's Award of Excellence 2011

Enjoy a satisfying tea in an atmosphere of charm and character

35 Charles Street, Mayfair,
LONDON, W1J 5EB
Tel 020 7491 2622
e-mail bookch@rchmail.com
web www.chesterfieldmayfair.com

Located in the heart of prestigious Mayfair, the Chesterfield was once the home of its namesake, the Earl of Chesterfield, and with its wood panelling, oil paintings and leather armchairs it continues to reflect the charm and character of a bygone era. Afternoon tea is served in the light-filled conservatory and waiters deliver your selection of tea on an elegant trolley. In these sumptuous surroundings, the more adventurous may go for the Chocolate Lover's Tea or the Champagne tea, while traditionalists will be drawn to the Devonshire cream tea or the Chesterfield afternoon tea. The excellent selection of teas includes Afternoon blend, Lapsang Souchong, Green Sencha tea and Jasmine tea.

To eat Devonshire tea, traditional afternoon tea, chocolate afternoon tea, Champagne afternoon tea.

Open Daily. Tea served 3-5:30pm.

Getting there Nearest tube Green Park.

What to see Royal Academy of Art, St James' Park, Buckingham Palace and Royal Mews.

Espelette at The Connaught

The Tea Guild's Award
of Excellence 2011

Enjoy a choice of teas and some Mayfair elegance

Carlos Place. LONDON W1K 2AL
Tel 020 3147 7100
e-mail dining@the-connaught.co.uk
web www.the-connaught.co.uk

The Connaught sits at the heart of Mayfair Village. Elegant, handsome and charming, there is a new found "feel good" factor to the area, with its network of wide streets, pretty mews, hidden gardens, luxury stores and galleries. With sweeping views of Carlos Place and Mount Street, Espelette is the ideal place to sample one of London's finest afternoon teas in a delightfully pretty and tranquil setting. Relax and watch the Mayfair world go by from the stunning conservatory. French chef Hélène Darroze, holder of three AA Rosettes for her food, is at the helm of the kitchens at the Connaught and keeps a watchful eye over each and every scone. A selection of twelve teas from Imperial Earl Grey to French Vanilla to Sencha Genmai Cha, and including the Espelette blend, awaits the dedicated connoisseur. Afternoon tea treats include: a mouth-watering selection of finger sandwiches, fresh scones from the Connaught Bakery, a selection of seasonal jams from Christine Ferber that include flavours such as raspberry and violet, melon-vanilla and Mirabelle, a delicious array of cakes and tarts, and pastries including poppy and strawberry choux, Baba in an orange and passion fruit jelly and much more.

To eat lunches, Chic & Shock afternoon tea, Champagne Afternoon Tea, themed teas

Open 3-5pm Mon-Fri; 1.30pm, 3.30pm, and 5.30pm sittings on Sat & Sun

Getting there 10-minute walk from Bond Street tube station or Green Park tube station

What to see Mayfair shops, changing the guard at Buckingham Palace, London museums

The Dorchester

The Tea Guild's Award of Excellence 2011

A time-honoured afternoon tradition in luxurious surroundings

Park Lane,
LONDON, W1K 1QA
Tel 020 7629 8888
e-mail restaurants@thedorchester.com
web www.thedorchester.com

Tea at The Promenade in the Dorchester is all that you would expect: tables set with fragile bone china laden with delightfully presented delicacies, sumptuous sofas and well-mannered staff. The beautiful setting of marble columns with Corinthian detailing, sweeping palms and gentle piano music playing in the background cannot fail to impress. Indulge in finger sandwiches, scones with clotted cream and jam, and fresh pastries made by the hotel's resident patissier, all served with speciality teas such as Chinese Bai Mai, Russian Country, or The Dorchester's own house blend. For that special occasion add a glass of Champagne. Winner of The Tea Guild's Top London Afternoon Tea Award 2002 and 2007.

To eat Afternoon tea, Champagne tea.

Open Daily. Tea served 2:30-6pm. Seating times are 1:15pm, 2:30pm, 3:15pm, 4:45pm and 5:15pm.

Getting there Nearest tube Hyde Park Corner, Green Park.

What to see Hyde Park, Mayfair, Bond Street.

Claridge's

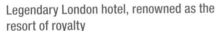
The Tea Guild's Top
London Tea Place 2011

**Legendary London hotel, renowned as the
resort of royalty**

Brook Street,
LONDON, W1K 4HR
Tel 020 7629 8860
e-mail info@claridges.co.uk
web www.claridges.co.uk

Claridge's sets the standards by which other hotels are judged and any visit here is a special occasion. Afternoon tea is served in the Art Deco Foyer, beneath the fabulous Dale Chihuly silver-white light sculpture, assembled from more than 800 hand-blown glass pieces, as well as in the Reading Room restaurant with its leather columns, suede walls and plush banquettes. Choose from over forty different teas from around the world, all carefully described on the tea menu and including Darjeeling First Flush, Dragon Pearl Jasmine, Pomegranate Oolong, and Royal White Silver Needles. The specialities of the house are the delightful finger sandwiches, using the best of British and organic produce on artisanal breads, French pastries and freshly baked raisin and apple scones. These are served with Marco Polo jelly and Cornish clotted cream.

To eat Afternoon tea, Champagne afternoon tea.

Open Daily. Tea served 3-5:30pm.

Getting there Nearest tube Bond Street.

What to see The Royal Academy, shopping in Mayfair, art galleries.

London Hilton on Park Lane

Chocoholics need search no longer for their
perfect afternoon tea

22 Park Lane,
LONDON W1K 1BE
Tel 020 7493 8000
e-mail info@podiumrestaurant.com
web www.hilton.co.uk or www.podiumrestaurant.com

Afternoon Tea at the London Hilton on Park Lane is a real treat. Served in the Podium Restaurant and Bar, a smart, modern space, decorated in bold, citrus tones, 'Confessions of a Chocoholic' is a chocolate-themed afternoon tea to die for. The new menu offers chocolate lovers a four course feast of elegantly exquisite treats. After the selection of traditional sandwiches (given a modern update with an 'open' presentation) you'll be presented with a contemporary tiered chrome stand piled with freshly baked chocolate chip scones (served with a home-made chocolate praline spread) chocolate cupcakes and miniature chocolate fancies, displayed on an edible chocolate plate. If you're not a chocoholic, a rather less chocolatey version is available, along with nut free, dairy free, gluten free, and vegetarian options.

To eat Afternoon Tea, Chocolate Afternoon Tea

Open Daily 2-6

Getting there Nearest tube stations Hyde Park Corner or Green Park

What to see Hyde Park, Knightsbridge, galleries and museums

Grosvenor House Park Room & Library

The Tea Guild's Award of Excellence 2011

Afternoon Tea in grand style in one of London's most famous hotels.

86-90 Park Lane,
LONDON, W1K 7TN
Tel 020 7499 6363
web www.londongrosvenorhouse.co.uk

The Park Room at Grosvenor House, A JW Marriott Hotel which overlooks Hyde Park, is certainly an elegant venue in which to enjoy an afternoon tea. Choose from the traditional Anna's Tea, named after the Duchess of Bedford who started the tradition of afternoon tea; Hendrick's Tea Time, which includes a Hendrick's Martini; or Grover's Tea Time which is created for children and includes a complimentary Grover toy to take home. If you don't want a set tea, you can choose your own favourites from home-made buttermilk scones with strawberry jam and organic Devon clotted cream, mini cakes and pastries. The wonderful selection of teas from around the world includes classics like Lady Grey and Assam, China teas such as Keemun and Long Jing Green, and floral teas - Flowering Red Amaranth, perhaps, or Flowering Osmanthus.

To eat Anna's Tea, Hendrick's Tea Time, Grover's Tea Times, Gluten Free Afternoon Tea.

Open Daily 2pm-6pm

Getting there Nearest tube Marble Arch or Hyde Park.

What to see Buckingham Palace, London Eye, Hyde Park.

Montagu at the Hyatt Regency, London - The Churchill

 The Tea Guild's Award of Excellence 2011

Tranquil and welcoming oasis in the heart of the West End

30 Portman Square,
LONDON, W1H 7BH
Tel 020 7299 2037
web www.london.churchill.hyatt.com

The calm and contemporary colours of The Montagu, where Afternoon Tea is served, offer a welcoming and relaxing contrast to the hubbub of Oxford Street, only a stone's throw away. Elegantly tiered stands bear a selection of traditional thinly sliced finger sandwiches, warm fruit and plain scones with strawberry jam and Cornish clotted cream, and a selection of pretty pastries, fruit tartlets and mini desserts. These are served with a fine selection of exquisite teas, including Sapphire Earl Grey, organic Bohea Lapsang, organic Silver Needles and hand-rolled Jasmine Pearls. For an extra special treat, guests can also add a glass of the sommelier's choice of Champagne. Booking is recommended.

To eat Afternoon Tea, Champagne Afternoon Tea

Open Daily 3pm-6pm

Getting there Nearest tube Marble Arch

What to see Buckingham Palace, Wallace Collection, Hyde Park

Walk

Mayfair – Laced With Luxury

A leisurely walk through wealthy Mayfair with plenty of opportunities to indulge yourself.

Start/finish: Bond Street tube station

Distance: 2.75 miles/4.4km

Level of difficulty: ● ● ●

Suggested map: AA Street by Street London

Walk directions

❶ Turn **L** outside tube station and sharp **L** into pedestrianised South Molton Street. At end turn **L** into Brook Street. Cross road and go along cobbled **R-H** alley, Lancashire Court, which opens into courtyard. Few paces past Hush restaurant is Elemis Day Spa.

❷ Turn **L** here and cross road to reach store, Fenwick. Turn **R** along Brook Street to Hanover Square. At statue of young William Pitt turn **R** into St George Street, past St George's Church and **L** at end into Conduit Street.

3 Take next **R** into road of fine suits, Savile Row. At end bear **L** and then **R** into Sackville Street. Turn **R** along Piccadilly and look for entrance to Albany's courtyard on **R**.

4 Just past auspicious-looking Burlington Arcade turn **R** into Old Bond Street and past several exclusive shops including those of Cartier, Mont Blanc and Tiffany. Turn **L** after Asprey into Grafton Street; which takes 90-degree **L** bend, later becoming Dover Street.

5 Turn **R** along Hay Hill and then **R** again towards Berkeley Square, going over 2 crossings with square on **R**, to reach handsome Charles Street. Beyond Chesterfield Hotel turn **L** along Queen Street and then **R** into Curzon Street.

6 Turn **R** into South Audley Street and Counter Spy Shop, past Grosvenor Chapel, then, at Purdey's (gunmakers), turn **L** into Mount Street. At end turn **R** along Park Lane, past Grosvenor House Hotel.

7 Turn **R** into Upper Grosvenor Street, past American Embassy on Grosvenor Square, then turn **L** into Davies Street. Next, take 1st **R** into Brooks Mews and go **L** along narrow Avery Row. This leads to Brook Street. From here retrace steps along South Molton Street, to Bond Street at start.

BURLINGTON ARCADE

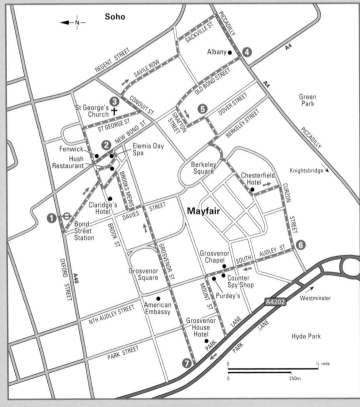

The Lanesborough

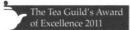

The Tea Guild's Award
of Excellence 2011

Award-winning teas in splendid surroundings

Hyde Park Corner,
LONDON, SW1X 7TA
Tel 020 7259 5599
e-mail info@lanesborough.co.uk
web www.lanesborough.com

The classically beautiful Apsley's in this luxury hotel is the setting for a superb afternoon tea. The Lanesborough Tea includes a generous selection of sandwiches, pastries and cakes as well as freshly-baked scones served with clotted cream and home-made strawberry jam. Don't miss the Lanesborough's famous home-made lemon curd. The tea sommelier will advise on your tea preferences and explain the exceptional variety of teas offered on the tea menu. These include Dragon Well Green Tea, Puerh, Rose Congou, Silver Needles, and rare Iron Buddah Tieguanyin Oolong. For a real occasion enjoy the "Belgravia Tea" which also includes strawberries with cream and a glass of Champagne. Winner of The Tea Guild's Top London Afternoon Tea Award 2008.

To eat Afternoon tea, Champagne tea, Belgian tea

Open Daily. Tea served Mon-Sat 3:30pm-6pm, Sun 4pm. Closed 25 Dec.

Getting there Nearest tube Hyde Park Corner.

What to see Buckingham Palace, Knightsbridge shops, Royal Academy.

The Langham Hotel – The Palm Court

The Tea Guild's Award of Excellence 2011

A decadent and indulgent experience in one of the most elegant rooms in London

1c Portland Place, LONDON W1B 1JA
Tel 020 7636 1000
e-mail reservations@palm-court.co.uk **web** www.palm-court.co.uk

A recent £80 million restoration has taken place at this elegant hotel, which first opened in 1865, and has served afternoon tea for over 140 years. Winner of The Tea Guild's Top London Afternoon Tea in 2010, the dazzling Palm Court is like an intricately decorated jewel box, with mirrored tables, sparkling chandeliers and velvet sofas. Light meals are available all day and there is an extremely extensive Afternoon Tea menu which features vegan, diabetic and gluten free teas as well as the Wonderland Tea and the G and Tea Time – which features a tea blend based on Beefeater gin. And of course there is the truly splendid Bijoux Afternoon Tea – described as 'super, luxurious, irresistible and indulgent' – which includes amazing sandwiches (foie gras and truffle parfait or duck egg mayonnaise with Secretts Farm mustard cress). The selection of scones includes one with raisins soaked in Louis Roederer champagne, and another with chocolate and marinated orange. The pastries, inspired by jewellery – Chanel pearl, Asprey diamonds, delices de Cartier, are almost too pretty to eat. There are 40 tea blends to choose from as well, with the help of the tea sommelier.

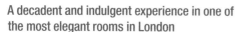

To eat Food available all day. Lunches, set teas – Bijoux Afternoon Tea, Wonderland Tea, G and Tea Time, high tea

Open 7am-11pm Mon-Fri, 8am-11pm Sat-Sun

Getting there Oxford Circus tube station

Things to see British Museum, Regents Park, Oxford Street

Le Méridien Piccadilly

A wonderful location and an atmosphere of elegance

21 Piccadilly,
LONDON, W1J 0BH
Tel 020 7851 3085
e-mail piccadilly.terrace@lemeridien.com
web www.lemeridien.com/piccadilly

Ideally located in the heart of the West End, Le Meridien Piccadilly has recently been transformed by a dramatic refurbishment programme. The new design is a dramatic marriage of classic and contemporary style, featuring classic Victorian details juxtaposed with bold modern décor and furnishings. Afternoon tea is served in the first floor Terrace Restaurant, a light-filled room with views of bustling Piccadilly below. The Terrace Afternoon Tea features a selection of classic finger sandwiches, warm homemade scones with strawberry jam and Cornish clotted cream, a selection of French pastries, and your choice from the tea menu. Add a glass of Champagne for the Champagne tea. The Light Tea is for smaller appetites and doesn't include sandwiches. The well kept and accurately described teas include Jing Tien Shan Hua, Russian Caravan, and Taiwanese High Mountain Oolong.

To eat Afternoon Tea, Champagne Afternoon Tea

Open Mon-Sat in Terrace Restaurant 12pm-6pm. Sun in Oak Room 12pm-6pm

Getting there Nearest tube Piccadilly Circus.

What to see Oxford Street, Theatreland, Buckingham Palace.

The Park Lane Hotel -
The Palm Court Lounge

The Tea Guild's Award
of Excellence 2011

Art deco elegance overlooking Green Park

Piccadilly,
LONDON, W1J 7BX
Tel 020 7290 7328
e-mail palmcourt.parklane@sheraton.com
web www.sheraton.com/parklane

The Palm Court Lounge is one of the most wonderful settings in which to take afternoon tea. The art deco style and the stunning ceiling, polished waiter service and resident harpist combine to create an atmosphere of timeless elegance. Three sets of teas are offered, each accompanied by one of a fine selection of exotic teas. The selection includes The Park Lane Afternoon Tea, which finishes with a glass of Champagne, and the venue also creates a themed afternoon tea to celebrate each season.

To eat Park Lane afternoon tea, Art Deco afternoon tea.

Open Daily. Tea served 3pm-6pm.

Getting there Nearest tube Green Park, Hyde Park Corner.

What to see Green Park, Hyde Park, Buckingham Palace, Knightsbridge.

The Ritz

The Tea Guild's Award of Excellence 2011

Quintessentially the Ritz experience, but advance planning is vital

150 Piccadilly,
LONDON, W1J 9BR
Tel 020 7493 8181
e-mail enquire@theritzlondon.com
web www.theritzlondon.com

It's what afternoons were made for, according to London's glitzy Ritz Hotel, and their invitation to tea is one that few will forget in a hurry. Smart clothes are necessary – jeans and trainers just won't do, and men should wear a jacket and tie – and booking is up to 10 weeks in advance for weekend reservations (slightly less for week days). The spectacular Palm Court makes an elegant setting and serves a tea to match: finely cut sandwiches without a crust in sight, freshly baked scones with jam and clotted cream, delicate pastries and an excellent selection of tea. To add to the experience, finish off with a glass of sparkling Champagne.

To eat Afternoon tea, Champagne tea. Chocolate tea

Open Daily. Tea served at 11am, 1:30pm, 3:30pm, 5:30pm, 7:30pm.

Getting there Nearest tube Green Park.

What to see Royal Academy of Art, Fortnum & Mason, Burlington Arcade.

Rubens at the Palace

A friendly hotel where afternoons can be spent rewardingly

39–41 Buckingham Palace Road,
LONDON, SW1W 0PS
Tel 020 7958 7725
e-mail bookrb@rchmail.com
web www.rubenshotel.com

Located directly opposite the mews of Buckingham Palace, as its name suggests, this well-regarded hotel offers stylish comfort in a busy tourist area. Enter its portals to be greeted by a smart commissionaire, and head for the Palace Lounge and Bar where light meals are served during the day. Everything doesn't quite stop for tea, but you feel it would if it had to. The full afternoon set meal incorporates finger sandwiches, freshly-baked scones, pastries, fruit cake and a pot of tea chosen from a range that includes Orange Pekoe, Lapsang Souchong and that ubiquitous favourite, Earl Grey. The warm, relaxing colours and background music ensure you will be in no hurry to leave. The Dom Perignon afternoon tea is served in the Leopard Champagne Bar. Booking recommended.

To eat Traditional afternoon tea, original crumpet tea, Royal afternoon tea, Dom Perignon afternoon tea.

Open Mon-Fri 2pm-4:30pm, Sat-Sun 1pm-4:30pm.

Getting there Nearest tube Victoria.

What to see Buckingham Palace, Houses of Parliament, Westminster Abbey.

Park Plaza Sherlock Holmes London

A boutique hotel in a central London location

108 Baker Street,
LONDON, W1U 6LJ
Tel 020 7958 5210
e-mail ppsh@pphe.com
web www.parkplazasherlockholmes.com

A totally contemporary look is achieved at this elegant hotel, with clean lines, natural colours and muted tones. It is convenient for the West End shops and theatres and many other places of interest. Sherlock's Grill is open for breakfast, lunch and dinner, and afternoon tea can be taken in the lounge or Sherlock's Bar – a popular venue just inside the main entrance. The house speciality is a luxury tea, including a glass of Champagne along with freshly cut sandwiches, scones with preserves, cream and berries, and petits fours. Booking required.

To eat Afternoon tea, Champagne tea. Breakfast, lunch and dinner.

Open Daily. Tea served 2:30pm-5pm.

Getting there Nearest tube Baker Street.

What to see Madame Tussaud's, London Zoo, West End theatres.

Royal Albert Hall

Sotheby's, Bond Street

The Wolseley

Fine food in an impressive triple-arched building on Piccadilly

160 Piccadilly,
LONDON, W1J 9EB
Tel 020 7499 6996
web www.thewolseley.com

Built in 1921, this stately Grade II-listed building was commissioned by Wolseley Cars as their London showroom – hence the name. Tea is served in a variety of elegant rooms: the main dining room, the salon, reception and the bar. Admire the striking décor while you indulge in a cream tea with fruit scones and a wide choice of teas, or a full afternoon tea with assorted finger sandwiches and a selection of pastries. Don't forget to glance through the dessert and patisserie menus too – there are inviting delights on offer. A refreshing alternative to Champagne is fresh lemonade, available by the glass or pitcher.

To eat Afternoon tea, cream tea, Champagne tea.

Open Daily. Tea served Mon-Fri 3pm-6:30pm, Sat 3:30pm-5:30pm, Sun 3:30pm-6:30pm. Closed 25 Dec, August Bank Holiday.

Getting there Nearest tube Green Park.

What to see Royal Academy, Bond Street, Green Park.

The Milestone

The Tea Guild's Award
of Excellence 2011

A popular small hotel in the heart of Royal London

1–2 Kensington Court,
LONDON, W8 5DL
Tel 020 7917 1000
e-mail conciergems@rchmail.com
web www.milestonehotel.com

Expect to be treated like royalty at this luxurious hotel overlooking Kensington Palace and Gardens – their motto is "no request too large, no detail too small". With its roaring fire on cooler days and stately home atmosphere at all times, it is the perfect place in which to enjoy afternoon tea. Come with friends for a chat, or curl up on your own with a book and relax as you enjoy the expert service. Tea comes in a variety of flavours, from Darjeeling to camomile, accompanied by an assortment of traditional foods; with the cream tea come freshly baked scones with Devonshire clotted cream and strawberry preserve, while afternoon tea includes a selection of finger sandwiches (smoked salmon on honey and sultana bread perhaps), scones and French pastries. For that added touch of luxury you can enjoy a glass of Champagne while your tea brews. Other light meals and drinks are also served, and booking is recommended.

To eat Cream tea, traditional afternoon tea, Champagne afternoon tea. Also, Afternoon Seduction (for two people), Little Prince and Princess Tea (for children under 12).

Open Daily. 3pm-6pm.

Getting there Nearest tube High Street Kensington.

What to see Kensington Palace, Diana Princess of Wales Memorial Fountain, Natural History Museum.

Royal Garden Hotel

Landmark modern hotel next to the Royal Gardens
of Kensington Palace and Hyde Park

2–24 Kensington High Street,
LONDON, W8 4PT
Tel 020 7937 8000
e-mail sales@royalgardenhotel.co.uk
web www.royalgardenhotel.co.uk

The Royal Garden is a sophisticated, modern hotel with a spacious, elegant foyer and stylish dining rooms. Afternoon tea takes place in The Park Terrace Restaurant, Lounge and Bar, which has a wonderfully open feel, with broad windows looking out over Kensington Palace gardens. The set-price tea comprises a selection of freshly made finger sandwiches, fluffy scones with clotted cream and a choice of home-made preserves, as well as a range of delicious cakes and pastries. Champagne is an optional extra.

To eat Afternoon tea, Champagne tea.

Open Daily. Tea served 2:30pm-5:30pm. Snacks and Oriental dishes also available.

Getting there Nearest tube High Street Kensington.

What to see Kensington Palace, Royal Albert Hall, High Street Kensington.

The Montague on the Gardens

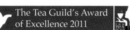

The Tea Guild's Award of Excellence 2011

A Georgian-fronted hotel serving classy teas

15 Montague Street, Bloomsbury,
LONDON, WC1B 5BJ
Tel 020 7637 1001
e-mail bookmt@rchmail.com
web www.montaguehotel.com

An intimate atmosphere pervades this town house, which feels more like a country hotel than one in central London. The beautiful gardens help to foster this impression, while indoors the stylish public rooms are staffed by a dedicated and discreet team. Tea in the conservatory should not be missed, or you can go one better in the summer and sit on the terrace under a large sunshade overlooking the gardens. The Montague special tea, which includes a selection of finger sandwiches, scones and pastries served on a silver cake stand with elegant china plates and tea cups, is a reminder of past grandeur. The traditional afternoon tea features scones and lashings of Devonshire clotted cream.

To eat Traditional afternoon tea, cream tea, Champagne high tea.

Open Daily. Tea served 3pm-6pm.

Getting there Nearest tube Russell Square.

What to see British Museum, Covent Garden, Dickens House Museum.

The Savoy

The Tea Guild's Award
of Excellence 2011

Splendidly luxurious hotel on the banks of the Thames

The Strand,
LONDON WC2R 0EU
Tel 020 7836 4343
e-mail savoy@fairmont.com
web www.fairmont.com/savoy

The Savoy has recently undergone an incredible £100 million restoration, and the hotel seamlessly blends elements of the original and the new while the stunning Edwardian and Art Deco interiors sparkle with timeless elegance and glamour. The Thames Foyer is the heart of the hotel - the perfect venue for light, informal dining. Its reinstated glass cupola, based on a guest's drawing, once again allows natural daylight to flood in on even the darkest day. The centrepiece of the room is the magnificent new winter garden gazebo. Afternoon Tea is served in this comfortable and intimate spot, accompanied by the hotel's resident pianist. Afternoon Tea at The Savoy is an enduring custom, and guests can choose from a wide range of almost 30 teas served with finger sandwiches, homemade scones with clotted cream and jam, and a mouth-watering selection of cakes and pastries. Savoy Tea, the new store in the Upper Thames Foyer, is the place to buy beautifully packaged tea to take home with you.

To eat Afternoon Tea, High Tea

Open Afternoon Tea 2:30pm-6:30pm

Getting there Nearest tube station is Charing Cross or Embankment

What to see Trafalgar Square, London Eye, Royal Festival Hall, the West End, Covent Garden

Swissôtel The Howard, London

Luxury hotel in a prime location

Temple Place,
LONDON, WC2R 2PR
Tel 020 7836 3555
e-mail ask-us.london@swissotel.com
web www.london.swissotel.com

A smart hotel between Westminster and the City of London, the Swissôtel has panoramic views from the Houses of Parliament to St Paul's Cathedral, across London's historic skyline. Covent Garden and the West End with their bars, restaurants and shopping are all within easy reach. Afternoon Tea is served in Mauve, the cosmopolitan cocktail lounge, with its contemporary setting. On Saturdays, a modern high tea, Afternoon Beats, is offered while a local DJ spins a variety of funky tunes. During the summer months, enjoy afternoon tea in the Garden Courtyard with its waterfalls and exotic plants.

To eat Afternoon Tea, Champagne Tea, Afternoon Beats.

Open Daily. Tea served 2:30pm-5:30pm. Afternoon Beats Sat 4pm-7pm.

Getting there Nearest tube Temple.

What to see Houses of Parliament, London Eye, Tower Bridge.

Windmill Tea Room

A tea room and bakery next to a fully working windmill makes for an interesting day out

Bircham Windmill,
GREAT BIRCHAM (near King's Lynn), PE31 6SJ
Tel 01485 578393
e-mail info@birchamwindmill.co.uk
web www.birchamwindmill.co.uk

The Windmill at Bircham is fully restored and bread is baked for sale in the bakery. It is ideal for families as there is plenty to do and see including exhibitions, ponies, sheep, chickens, guinea pigs and a well-kept garden. Visitors can also climb up to the sail stage and, on a windy day, can see the milling machinery turning. The tea rooms were built on the site of the granary and along with 17 blends of tea, also serve light lunches, snacks, sandwiches, scones and cakes. The Windmill bread is a speciality.

To eat Cream tea. Light lunches and snacks.

Open Daily 10am-5pm Etr-Sep

Getting there Great Bircham is on the B1153. Nearest main road A148. Own car park.

What to see Royal Sandringham, Kings Lynn Arts Centre and Town House Museum, Houghton Hall, Norfolk Lavender, Peddars Way and Norfolk Coast Path.

Norfolk Coast Path

Congham Hall Country House Hotel and Spa

A Georgian manor house near the Sandringham Estate

Lynn Road,
GRIMSTON, PE32 1AH
Tel 01485 600250
e-mail info@conghamhallhotel.co.uk
web www.conghamhallhotel.co.uk

Congham Hall is a fine country house set in 30 acres of parkland, orchards, gardens and a famous herb garden with 700 different herbs, including over 50 varieties of mint. Log fires provide a warm welcome in the public rooms, and full afternoon tea is served in the lounges, or out on the terrace in warmer weather. Full afternoon tea comprises sandwiches, cake, biscuits, scones with home-made preserves, and seasonal fruit tartlets. A range of home-made produce and Norfolk delicacies is offered for sale, including preserves, pot pourri, lavender, books and herb plants (May–September). Dogs are allowed on the terrace. Parking provided. Booking required for full afternoon tea

To eat Set tea.

Open Daily. Tea served 3pm-6pm.

Getting there Northeast of King's Lynn on A148, turn right towards Grimston and hotel is on the left.

What to see Royal Sandringham, African Violet Centre, Kings Lynn Arts Centre and Town House Museum, Peddars Way and Norfolk Coast Path.

The Owl Tearoom & Bake Shop

Friendly tea room within easy reach of the beautiful north Norfolk coast

Church Street,
HOLT, NR25 6BB
Tel 01263 713232

The Owl Tearoom proudly states that they "make all our products in-house, from raw ingredients right down to the jam you put on our scones." The menu includes three course lunches as well as light bites and teas. Booking is not essential and children are welcome, as are those with special dietary requirements.

To eat Cream tea. Light lunches and snacks.

Open Mon-Sat 9am-5pm.

Getting there Holt is on the A148. Parking in the town.

What to see North Norfolk Railway, Baconsthorpe Castle, Felbrigg Hall (National Trust), Muckleburgh Collection Museum, Blakeney Point.

Wroxham Barns - The Old Barn Restaurant Café

Tea room housed in a converted barn on the Norfolk Broads

Wroxham Barns, Tunstead Road, HOVETON, NR12 8QU
Tel 01603 777106 **e-mail** info@wroxham-barns.co.uk
web www.wroxhambarns.co.uk

Wroxham and its neighbour Hoveton, on opposite sides of the River Bure, have almost merged into one town, and together they form the main centre for cruising the Norfolk Broads; boats can be hired from several firms. The comfortable Old Barn Restaurant and Café is close to Wroxham and set in extensive parkland. Wroxham Barns is essentially a collection of 18th-century barns that have been reborn as small shops and working craft galleries and is the sort of place you will want to wander, shop, sit and drink in the scenery, or maybe a classic cup of tea. Breakfast, lunch, snacks, sandwiches, scones and cakes are available and so is a children's menu.

To eat Cream tea. Light lunches and snacks. Breakfast

Open Daily 10am-5pm. Closed 25,26 Dec & 1 Jan.

Getting there The Barns are signposted off the A1151, north of Wroxham. Own car park.

What to see: Wroxham Broad, Horning, Bure Valley Railway, Norwich.

Blakeney

Northamptonshire

The Apothocoffee Shop

Quaint, intriguing tea rooms in an historic setting

Jeyes on The Square,
26-28 The Square,
EARLS BARTON, NN6 0NA
Tel 01604 810289
web www.dollylodge.com

You will be surprised to find, on The Square in Earls Barton, under the gaze of the famous Saxon Tower of All Saints' Church, and behind the chemist's door at Jeyes, this traditional Apothocoffee Shop. The Blossom Tea Lounge in the conservatory, with its walled garden, provides refreshment for all the family throughout the day. A speciality gluten-free menu is also available and groups are welcome.

To eat Set tea. Full lunchtime menu.

Open Mon-Fri 8:30am-5:30pm. Sat 8:30am-5pm. Closed Sun.

Getting there Earls Barton is half-way between Northampton and Wellingborough, just off A45. Nearest motorway M1, Jnct 15. Parking in the village.

What to see Museum of Village Life, Keepsake Gift Shop, The Dolly Lodge, Potty About Flowers, Fotheringhay, Sywell Reservoir, Eleanor Cross, Hunsbury Hill, Skewbridge.

Tasty Bite Victorian Tea Shop

Spare some time to browse in this old-fashioned tea shop

34–36 High Street,
THRAPSTON, NN14 4JH
Tel 01832 7330070

Victorian-style black and white outfits, home-made cakes and a focus on presentation, including original Victorian glass cake stands, all add up to create a nostalgic and delightful environment. There are 15 different types of tea and a wealth of items available for purchase, including history books by local author John N. Smith, souvenirs featuring scenes from the Victorian period right up to World War II, and maritime and military art by local artist Keith Hill.

To eat Set tea. Cakes and light snacks.

Open Mon-Fri 9am-5pm. Sat 9am-4:30pm.

Getting there Off the A14. Parking at the Co-op nearby.

What to see Elton Hall, Stahl Theatre, Oundle Museum, Barnwell Country Park, Lowick Pocket Park.

St Mary and All Saints, Fotheringhay

Towcester Tea Rooms

**An expert tea room offering a great
variety of teas**

169 Watling Street,
TOWCESTER, NN12 6BX
Tel 01327 358200
e-mail mail@towcestertearooms.co.uk
web www.towcestertearooms.co.uk

The exquisite Towcester Tea Rooms fulfil all of the expectations
of a truly English establishment, as its founders, Sharon and
Tony, have fashioned the business on the traditional English
tearoom. There is an extraordinary range of tea to try with
cream tea menus or a divine slice of home-made cake.
Refreshing cold drinks include organic ginger beer and
elderflower sparkling pressé. Both gluten-free and vegetarian
choices are available. Freshly made buffets can also be made for
delivery as part of their outside catering operation.

To eat Tea selection. Lunches.

Open Mon-Sat 9am-3pm. Closed Bank Holiday Mondays.

Getting there Off the A5. Parking available within the town.

What to see Althorp House, Castle Ashby, Stoke Bruene
Village (with Canal Museum), Towcester Racecourse,
Silverstone Circuit.

Althorp House

Tea and Health

A number of recent scientific studies have suggested that tea is good for your health

It's always nice to discover that something you like might not be doing you any harm – and may even be doing you good! Although the results of these studies are preliminary findings with more research still to come, there are indications that tea has a number of health and nutritional benefits.

Many people don't drink enough fluid every day. Regular consumption of at least three cups of tea (which is 99.5% water) each day will help. It used to be believed that any quantity of tea was a diuretic – but this is not the case – you'd need to be drinking a much larger amount for it to have any diuretic effect.

It is often suggested that green tea is healthier than black tea, but in fact there is no real difference between the health benefits offered. If you take milk with your tea you may be augmenting the levels of vitamins and minerals present in tea (potassium, manganese, riboflavin and niacin) and will additionally increase your calcium levels. (You should add the milk first so as not to scald the fats in it, and use semi-skimmed if you want to limit the additional calories to just 13.)

A natural source of fluoride, tea is good for your teeth, helping to prevent decay (unless you add sugar!). The tannins and flavenoids it contains help to limit the build up of plaque, and there have been suggestions that tea may contribute to the prevention of oral cancer.

It may also help prevent heart disease and strokes – although the evidence is not conclusive, it is believed that the flavenols in tea may work together with other dietary advice to reduce the risks of developing cardio-vascular disease.

Antioxidants such as those found in tea can promote general health and well-being, enhancing the benefits of eating five portions of fruit and vegetables a day. Tea is a major source of antioxidants such as flavenols, and supplement those from other sources which might be a factor in reducing the onset of Parkinson's and Alzheimer's diseases, as well as helping the prevention of cancers and cardiovascular disease.

If you want to find out more, visit www.tea.co.uk/tea-4-health

Northumberland

Matfen Hall

Magnificent country house hotel set amid landscaped parkland

MATFEN, NE20 0RH
Tel 01661 886500
e-mail info@matfenhall.com
web www.matfenhall.com

Built in the 1830s, Matfen Hall has been transformed into a fine hotel with some of the best leisure facilities in the county, including its own 18-hole golf course. Tea is served both in the drawing room and in the conservatory. The menu offers a cream tea and a full afternoon tea, the latter comprising scones with clotted cream and preserves, toasted teacakes, rich fruit cake, an assortment of sandwiches and a pot of tea or freshly brewed coffee. As well as traditional "black" tea and Earl Grey, there's peppermint and liquorice, sweet camomile and berry. Booking recommended.

To eat Set tea, cream tea, full afternoon tea.

Open Daily. Tea served 2:30pm-5:30pm
(Sun 4:30pm-5:30pm).

Getting there From the A1, take the A69 Hexham, Carlisle road. At Heddon on the Wall take the B6318 west. Eventually there'll be a sign for Matfen. The hotel is just before the village.

What to see Hadrian's Wall, Belsay Hall, Castle and Gardens, Prudhoe Castle.

The Chantry Tea Rooms

Genuine hospitality and a pleasing atmosphere in the tea rooms of the unique Morpeth Bagpipe Museum

9 Chantry Place,
MORPETH, NE61 1PJ
Tel 01670 514414
e-mail info@bagpipemuseum.org.uk
web www.bagpipemuseum.org.uk

It is always a pleasure to find a place like The Chantry, where you are assured of a warm welcome and attentive service. There are 11 blends of tea available, including the Chantry's own "Northumbrian" blend, to accompany the range of sandwiches, scones, cakes and light meals on the menu. Once you've settled in and tickled your taste buds, look around at the original paintings and photos on the walls, many of which are for sale.

To eat Afternoon tea. Light lunches and snacks.

Open Mon-Sat 9:15am-4:30pm.

Getting there Morpeth is on the A1(M). There is parking in the town.

What to see Morpeth Chantry Bagpipe Museum, Wallington Hall, Belsay, Cragside, the Northumbrian coast, Hadrian's Wall, Northumberland National Park.

Cragside

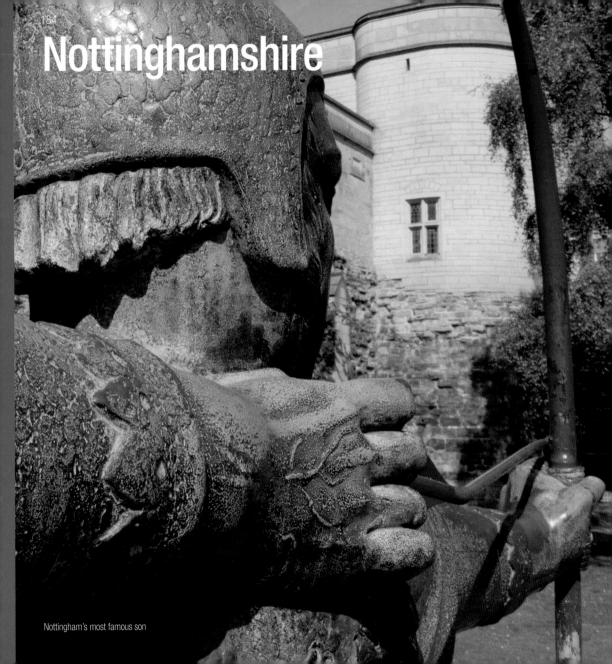

Nottinghamshire

Nottingham's most famous son

Old School Tearoom

Old school artefacts and wonderful home baking

CARBURTON (near Worksop), S80 3BP
Tel 01909 483517

This peaceful country tea room is housed in a converted 1930s school, where many original features have been used to delightful effect. The menu is written on an old blackboard and easel, and the original hand basins have been kept in the washrooms. Where once reference books and stacks of homework sat on the school shelves, displays of local woodwork, prints and greetings cards are now on sale. Home-baked fruit pies, cakes, scones and fine teas feature on the interesting menu, and the savoury tea (cheese scones with cheese, celery and chutney) makes a tasty alternative to the set cream tea.

To eat Set teas. Cakes and savoury snacks.

Open Mid-Jan to Oct, Tue-Sun and Bank Holiday Mondays 10am-4:30pm (Oct-Dec closes 4pm). NB: Afternoon tea not served 12-2pm. Closed two weeks Christmas and New Year.

Getting there On B6034 Worksop to Ollerton, opposite entrance to Clumber Park.

What to see Clumber Park, Sherwood Forest, Dukeries Garden Centre.

Walk

Sherwood Forest – a merrie tale

Walk among the oaks of this legendary forest

Start/finish: Grid ref SK 626676

Parking: Sherwood Forest Visitor Centre (pay-and-display)

Distance: 5.5 miles/8.8km

Level of difficulty: ● ● ●

Suggested map: OS Explorer 270 Sherwood Forest

Walk directions

1 Facing main entrance to Visitor Centre from car park, turn **L** and follow well-signposted route to Major Oak.

2 Go along curving path as it completes semi-circle around impressive old tree and continue as far as junction with public bridleway (signposted). Turn **L** here, then walk this straight and uncomplicated route for 0.25 mile (400m), ignoring paths off.

3 At green notice board, warning of nearby military training area, main path bears **L**. Instead go straight ahead, past metal bar gate, for path that continues over crossroads to become wide, fenced track through pleasant open country of heather and bracken known as Budby South Forest.

4 At far side go through gate and turn **L** on to unmade lane, walk this route for 0.75 mile (1.2km).

5 At major junction just before plantation begins, turn **L**, indicated 'Centre Tree'. With rows of conifers on **R**, and good views across Budby South Forest on **L**, keep to this straight and obvious track. Where track divides into 2 parallel trails, gravelly track on **R** is technically cycle route, while more leafy and grassy ride to **L** is bridleway, but either can be used.

6 When you reach Centre Tree – huge spreading oak – 2 routes converge to continue past bench down wide avenue among trees. Don't go down this, but instead turn **L** and, ignoring paths off **R** and **L**, carry straight on along main track back into heart of forest.

7 After almost 0.75 mile (1.2km) you pass metal bar gate on **R** and then meet bridleway coming in from **L**. Ignoring inviting path straight ahead (which returns to the Major

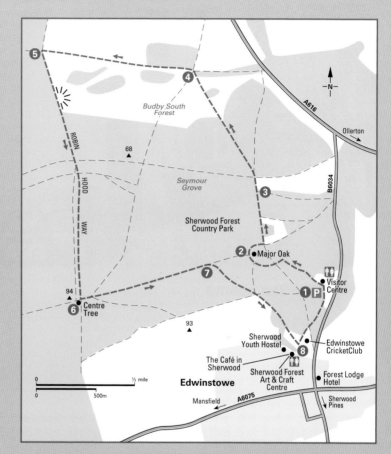

Oak) bear **R** on main track, past bare holes and dips hollowed out by children's bikes. At large junction of criss-crossing routes go straight on (signposted 'Fairground') so that open field and distant housing becomes visible **R**. This wide sandy track descends to field by Edwinstowe cricket ground. The Art

and Craft Centre and Sherwood Youth Hostel are on far side, and village centre beyond.

8 To return to visitor centre and car park, follow well-walked, signposted track back up past cricket ground.

Lock House Tea Rooms

Indulge in a little culinary nostalgia with a range of old favourites

Trent Lock, Lock Lane,
LONG EATON, NG10 2FY
Tel 0115 972 2288
e-mail mt@lockhousetearoom.demon.co.uk

Idyllically set where the rivers Trent and Soar meet, in attractive Nottinghamshire countryside, these tea rooms specialise in good old-fashioned cooking. The house dates from 1794, and although it has been modernised over the years by successive lock keepers, there is still evidence of the blacksmith's forge and stabling for barge horses which were an early feature. The Ashby family offer a warm welcome and a menu to delight visitors. There is a choice of over 60 teas and a selection of speciality coffees. Choose from Cornish clotted cream teas, hot toasties, tripe and onions, jacket potatoes, and specials including rabbit stew, fresh poached salmon, and various salads, as well as the famous prawn tea. Relish the knickerbocker glory – reputedly the largest for miles around. In summer, the Victorian style ice cream cart offers a variety of unusual ice cream flavours - many of them homemade.

To eat Set teas. Hot and cold meals.

Open Wed-Fri 10am-4pm, Sat-Sun 10am-6pm (summer). Closes one hour earlier in winter. Tea served all day. Last orders 30 minutes before closing.

Getting there Off M1 junct 24. Just outside Long Eaton at junction of River Trent and Erewash Canal.

What to see Donington Grand Prix Collection, Royal Crown Derby Visitor Centre, Shardlow Heritage Centre.

Ollerton Watermill Tea Shop

The Tea Guild's Award
of Excellence 2011

**The only working watermill in Nottinghamshire,
with a delightful tea shop serving delicious wholesome food**

Market Place,
OLLERTON, Newark, NG22 9AA
Tel 01623 822469

The old millwright's workshop and watermill, built in 1713 and now fully operational, is the wonderfully atmospheric setting for this friendly tea shop. The old mill has been put to work again after the Mettam family – owners and millers since 1921 – decided to restore it and open it to the public. The tea shop was an inspirational stroke of genius when it was set up to offer refreshments to mill visitors, and its popularity quickly spread. The owners are particular about the teas and produce they offer and the result is home-baked cakes, quiches, salads and mouth-watering puddings; the cream tea with plain or fruit scones, jam, cream and strawberries is a perennial winner. The views from the window looking upstream to the waterwheel and mill race are delightful.

To eat Set teas. Lunchtime snacks.

Open Wed-Sun 10:30am-4pm. Tea served all day; Closed Mon, except Bank Holidays, mid-Dec to Feb.

Getting there 20 miles north of Nottingham on A164, 12 miles west of Newark on A616. Tea shop in village centre.

What to see Rufford Country Park, Sherwood Forest, Newark (historic market town).

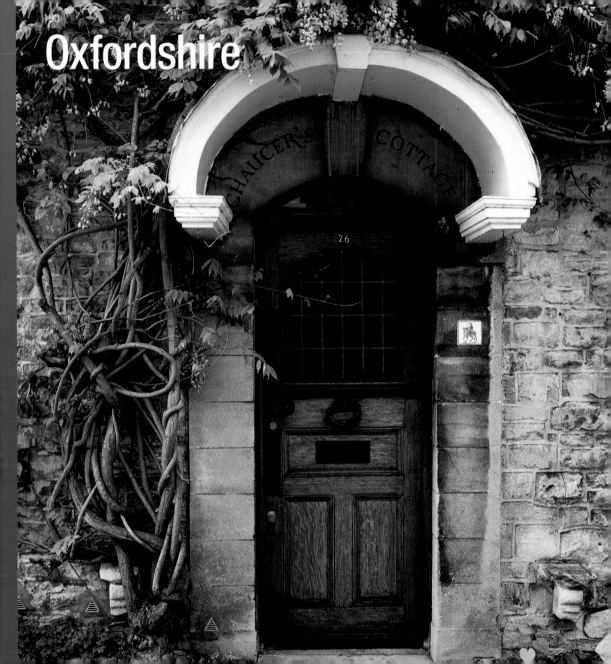

Oxfordshire

The Pear Tree Teashop

Hand-made cakes, patisserie and light lunches served in the Waterperry Gardens teashop

Waterperry Gardens,
near WHEATLEY, OX33 1JZ
Tel 01844 338087
e-mail teashop@waterperrygardens.co.uk
web www.waterperrygardens.co.uk

Enjoy hand-made cakes and patisserie in the magical gardens of the Waterperry Estate, whether you choose to wander there or not. The teashop's loose-leaf teas are much recommended and include Assam, Earl Grey made from real Bergamot orange, and Darjeeling. Enjoy your choice of tea with a slice of farmhouse cake or one of Waterperry's famous fruit scones. The teashop serves light lunches daily between 12 and 2pm as well as soup and sandwiches. All food is freshly prepared on the premises and a variety of soft drinks is also available, including Waterperry apple juices, grown and pressed on the estate.

To eat Cream tea.

Open Mar-Oct, daily 10am-5pm, Nov-Feb 10am-4pm (last orders 15 minutes before closing)

Getting there The Gardens can be accessed from junctions 8 and 8A of the M40. Parking available.

What to see Waterperry Gardens, museum, gallery and garden shop, Courthouse (National Trust), Shotover Hill, Rycote Chapel, Thame, Aylesbury.

Old Parsonage Hotel

For guests at this welcoming hotel, afternoon tea is a definite priority

1 Banbury Road, OXFORD, OX2 6NN
Tel 01865 310210
e-mail info@oldparsonage-hotel.co.uk
web www.oldparsonage-hotel.co.uk

This beautiful town house hotel dates in part from the 16th century, and offers comfortable seating areas for day visitors. Afternoon tea is served in the cosy club-like restaurant, or on warm summer days, on the terrace of one of the two small garden areas. A special menu offers a choice of Light Tea (scones with cream and preserves, various teas including Old Parsonage Blend, and coffees), or Very High Tea (sandwiches, home-baked cakes, and scones with cream and preserves, and tea or coffee); a Champagne Tea is also available. Other tea time offerings include toasted crumpets, home-made ice creams and sorbets, and hot chocolate or toddy to keep out the winter chill. Booking recommended at weekends.

To eat Light tea, Champagne tea, Very High tea.

Open Daily. Tea served Mon-Fri 3pm-5pm. Sat-Sun 3:30pm-5pm.

Getting there 5 minutes' walk from city centre on Banbury Road, next to St Giles Church.

What to see Oxford University Colleges, Ashmolean Museum, Pitt Rivers Museum.

Harriet's Cake Shop and Tea Rooms

A Cotswold experience in an appealing setting close to Oxford

20 High Street,
WOODSTOCK, OX20 1TF
Tel 01993 811231
e-mail harriets@btopenworld.com

An abundance of charm oozes from this quaint tea room, with its interior of wood panelling and exposed stone, complete with original fireplaces, a vintage bread oven and tea served by waitresses dressed in traditional black and white. Wherever possible, the ingredients have a Cotswold origin with special cream teas using Cotswold clotted cream and honey sourced from a local farmer. The shop itself sells a fascinating range of teapots, home-made preserves, cakes and confectionery.

To eat Afternoon tea.

Open Mon-Fri 8:30am-5pm, Sat 8:30am-5:30pm, Sun 10am-5:30pm.

Getting there Woodstock is on the A44, north of Oxford. Parking in high street.

What to see Blenheim Palace, Sir Winston Churchill's grave in Bladon, Church of St Mary Magdalene, Chaucer's house.

Blenheim Palace, Woodstock

Ethical Sourcing of Tea

Consumers are increasingly concerned about the ethical implications of the products they buy. Tea is mostly grown in developing countries where social and economic conditions can leave a lot to be desired.

The tea industry employs between 18 and 20 million people worldwide. In some countries, much of the tea is grown by independent smallholders, whose living conditions may be desperately poor. In recent years a number of organisations have been working to improve living and working conditions.

Many of the tea companies in Britain belong to the Ethical Tea Partnership (ETP), a non-profit making organisation which works with producers in 12 countries to drive positive change and ensure that members' tea comes from sustainable sources. The ETP has been monitoring the estates in the supply chains of its members since 1997. Their regional managers work with the producers to address any issues raised by the monitors, and support sustainability improvements. Among the areas they monitor are minimum age and wage levels, education, maternity, and health and safety. They also aim to implement best practice in the environmental management of water, waste, energy, soil and agrochemicals.

As well as monitoring estates itself, the ETP works with technical specialists, development agencies, and government and UN organisations to improve the lives of tea workers. As members of the ETP are also increasingly interested in selling tea that is labelled under a particular certification scheme, such as Fairtrade, Rainforest Alliance and UTZ CERTIFIED, the ETP has developed relationships with these programmes, in order to share resources and raise standards in even more tea estates. If an ETP member is interested in part of their supply chain becoming certified and the tea estate is interested in certification, the ETP will work with the producer and certification body in question to achieve this as efficiently as possible.

Shropshire

Rocke Cottage Tearoom

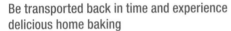

The Tea Guild's
Top Tea Place 2011

Be transported back in time and experience delicious home baking

Craven Arms, Abcott, CLUNGUNFORD SY7 0PX
Tel 01588 660631
e-mail kr.clarke@brinternet.com   **web** www.rockecottagetearoom.co.uk

This charming 400-year-old tea room exists in a timewarp where it is forever 'between the wars', full of 1920s and 1930s details and memorabilia. Rocke Cottage offers a wide range of fresh leaf teas and genuine home baking as well as a proper cup of coffee. Most of the food is locally sourced and, as well as the cakes and scones, they offer a range of light lunches - locally smoked trout, smoked salmon platters, home-made quiches, patés and pies. There is always a choice of at least twenty teas, including Nuwara Eliya, Shropshire Blend and Lucky Green Dragon plus changing guest teas that might include Golden Monkey or Pai Mu Tan. They also offer a range of local chutney, pickles and honey to take home. You could start the day here with a special breakfast – scrambled eggs with smoked salmon, fresh baby scones, toast, croissants, preserves, fresh orange juice and your choice from the selection of teas. Take time to experience the full afternoon tea of sandwiches, cakes and crumpets to accompany the classic cream tea (with Herefordshire clotted cream) all served with the tea or coffee of your choice. Breakfast or afternoon tea must be booked in advance.

To eat light lunches, set teas

Open 10am-5pm Wed-Sun & Bank Holidays

Getting there From A49 at Craven Arms take B4368 towards Clun. Left after 1.5m onto B4367 towards Clungunford. After 3m go through the village and over the bridge, Rocke Cottage is on the right.

What to see Ludlow, Stokesay Castle, Ironbridge, Powis Castle

Walk

Clee Hill – the real bedlam

In Shropshire's high and charismatic hills

Start/finish: Grid ref SO 595753

Parking: Car park/picnic site/viewpoint opposite turning for Kremlin Inn on A4117 on eastern edge of Cleehill village

Distance: 8.25 miles/13.3km

Level of difficulty: ● ● ●

Suggested map: OS Explorer 203 Ludlow

Walk directions

1 Walk up track opposite picnic area, towards Kremlin Inn. After 100yds (91m), pass through rusty bridle gate on **L** along track. After 220yds (201m), right of way runs to **L** of it, but can be difficult and most walkers use track.

2 Meet radar station access road by Hedgehog House and turn **R**. Walk to end of Rouse Boughton Terrace and go through gate on **L**. Cross cattle grid then bear **R** along pasture edge. Continue along next field edge and through gate in corner to Shropshire Way, which goes to **R**. Ignore it and go ahead, skirting stream and gorse; cross stile in fence before returning to **L-H** hedge-line.

3 Green track develops, swinging **R** and down to cross Benson's Brook at bridge. Follow track up again, passing abutments of former tramway bridge (Titterstone Incline on OS maps), before arriving at Bedlam.

4 Turn **L** into hamlet, then immediately fork **R**. Pass Hullabaloo House as you climb track to cattle grid. Follow track up to farm then bear **L** up green track.

5 Reaching Bitterley Incline again, climb on to embankment, joining Shropshire Way. Follow it uphill. At ruined quarry buildings, go **R** on level path. Pass last building, fork **L** and climb slightly. Go straight on, crossing access road twice at bend, then swing **L** before another quarry, with radar station beyond.

6 Some 100yds (91m) north of trig pillar are remains of cairn, Giant's Chair. From this bear **R**, above scree slopes, then swing **L** on clearer path; continue across brackeny moorland to red-roofed farm (Callowgate).

7 Before you reach Callowgate, leave Shropshire Way and turn sharp **R** by moorland edge. Joining lane at Cleetongate, turn **R** and walk to Cleeton St Mary. Turn **R**, looping round church and along almshouses, then **L** on to Random bridleway, which runs along moorland edge. Follow vague paths parallel to fence, except where you need to cut corner – obvious when you come to it.

8 When fence makes sharp **L** turn, keep ahead to meet radar station access road. Turn **L** to Rouse Boughton Terrace; retrace steps to start.

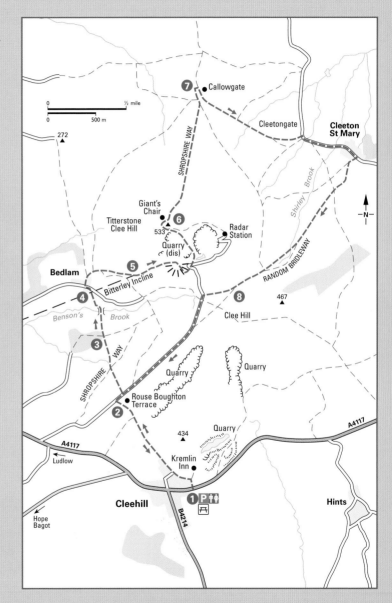

Acorn Wholefood Restaurant and Coffee House

All natural, home-made food in a unique location

26 Standford Avenue,
CHURCH STRETTON, SY6 6BW
Tel 01694 722495

The ivy covered entrance of this charming retreat leads to the Little Oaks and Acorn Coffee Lounges and to the peaceful tea garden. An enthusiastic wholefood menu is provided using local ingredients. The pastries, cakes, scones and puddings are made with organic wholemeal flour and dishes can be geared to specialist diets and tastes. There are 25 blends of tea on offer, plus a light lunchtime menu of sandwiches, scones and cakes.

To eat Afternoon tea. Light lunches, snacks, sandwiches, scones and cakes available.

Open Thur-Tue and Bank Holidays 9:30am-5pm. Closed Weds, 25 Dec, 26 Dec

Getting there Church Stretton is signposted off the A49. Parking in the town.

What to see Stokesay Castle, The Acton Scott Farm Museum, Attingham Hall and Park, Boscobel, Wroxeter Roman City.

Stokesay Castle

Church Stretton

De Grey's

An old-fashioned bakery and tea shop serving a wide choice of pastries, cakes and speciality teas

5-6 Broad Street,
LUDLOW, SY8 1NG
Tel 01584 872764
web www.degreys.co.uk

Located just below the Buttercross clock tower, De Grey's is housed behind a picturesquely beamed bakery. Inside the tea shop you can sample a pot of one of the carefully chosen speciality teas, or try an iced green or mandarin tea. The splendid afternoon tea consists of a sandwich, fancy cake, and fruit scone with jam and cream, or you can pick your own selection from toasted teacakes, pastries, scone and buns. Light and full meals are served throughout the day. The menu includes Welsh rarebit or club sandwiches, as well as home-made lasagne, salads and baked potatoes.

To eat Set teas. Light and full meals.

Open Mon-Thu 9am-5pm, Fri-Sat 9am-5:30pm, Sun 11am-5pm. Tea served all day.

Getting there In town centre, on Broad Street, near Buttercross Clock Tower.

What to see Ludlow Castle, Stokesay Castle, St Lawrence's Church.

Somerset

The Somerset Levels

Regency Tea Rooms

The Tea Guild's Award of Excellence 2011

A cream tea here will transport you back to the world of Jane Austen

40 Gay Street,
BATH, BA1 2NT
Tel 01225 442187
web www.janeausten.co.uk/tearooms

A visit to the Jane Austen Centre can now be enhanced by a visit to the elegant Regency Tea Rooms, where you can take "Tea with Mr Darcy" or taste the "Jane Austen" blend of tea. The whole experience takes place within the beautiful surroundings of a Georgian townhouse, into which Bath's busy streets fail to intrude. Sip real leaf tea, indulge in a slice of home-made cake and then visit the gift shop for a souvenir. Gluten free scones and crumpets are also available.

To eat Cream Teas, Tea with Mr Darcy, Savoury Teas.

Open Daily 10am-5:30pm (closes 4:30pm in winter).

Getting there In heart of Bath by Queen Square. Parking nearby. In centre of city, off Brock Street. From M4 junction 18 take A46 into the city, or use park-and-ride system.

What to see Roman Baths and Pump Room, Bath Abbey, Building of Bath Museum, Jane Austen Centre, No 1 Royal Crescent.

Searcy's at The Pump Room

The Tea Guild's Award
of Excellence 2011

Classical music, elegant surroundings and
fine teas

Stall Street,
BATH, BA1 1LZ
Tel 01225 444477
web www.searcys.co.uk/the-pump-room/

For over two centuries the great and the good have come to drink the waters in this striking neoclassical room. The hot spa water they came to find is still on sale here, and many swear by its healing properties. Of more interest to Bath's modern visitors is the mouth-watering food served with impeccable style by Searcy's. High on the list of favourites comes afternoon tea; a traditional platter of finger sandwiches, freshly baked scones with local preserves and clotted cream; also delicious home-made cakes and pastries, and even a champagne tea served with smoked salmon and cucumber blini with shallot crème fraiche, all accompanied by a pot of tea. All this and live classical music from the Pump Room Trio or pianist. You can make reservations during the week but not at weekends.

To eat Traditional Pump Room tea, Searcy's Champagne tea.

Open Daily 9.30am-close (to 9pm Jul-Aug). Tea served 2:30pm-close. Closed 25-26 Dec.

Getting there From M4 junction 18 take the A46 into the city. Parking within 5 minute walk. Alternatively, use park-and-ride system.

What to see Roman Baths, Assembly Rooms & Fashion Museum, Bath Postal Museum.

The Royal Crescent Hotel

Smart surroundings for an equally refined afternoon tea

16 Royal Crescent,
BATH, BA1 2LS
Tel 01225 823333
e-mail info@royalcrescent.co.uk
web www.royalcrescent.co.uk

World-famous for its fine Georgian architecture, the Royal Crescent is a striking landmark at the top of the city, and part of it is occupied by this elegant hotel. The grandeur of the surroundings is matched by the glamour of afternoon tea served in the drawing room or the Dower House. The simple cream tea is easily outdone by the traditional afternoon tea, featuring sandwiches, scones with jam and cream, cakes and pastries, Bath buns and a choice of classy teas. For special occasions, add a glass of Champagne. Booking required.

To eat Set tea, cream tea, traditional afternoon tea.

Open Daily. Tea served 3-5pm.

Getting there In centre of the city, off Brock Street. From M4 junction 18 take the A46 into the city. or use park-and-ride system.

What to see Roman Baths and Pump Room, Bath Abbey, Sally Lunn's Kitchen Museum (free to patrons), Building of Bath Museum, Jane Austen Centre, No 1 Royal Crescent.

Old Bakehouse

With its bakery heritage, this place certainly won't disappoint at teatime

CASTLE CARY, BA7 7AW
Tel 01963 350067

The old walls, bay windows, wooden tables and chairs all make for a cosy atmosphere at the Old Bakehouse. The menu is strictly dedicated to home cooking, from wholesome English to traditional Thai cuisine, which can be enjoyed best of all under the grapevines in the courtyard garden. The Old Bakehouse has a convivial and welcoming ambience, both day and night. During the day, sixteen blends of the finest tea, can be accompanied by the home-made sandwiches, scones, cakes and light meals that are available here.

To eat Afternoon tea. Light lunches and snacks.

Open Daily 10am-4pm.

Getting there Castle Cary is off the A359 and A371 roads. Nearest motorway M5. Street parking and town car parks.

What to see Hadspen Garden and Nursery, Haynes International Motor Museum at Sparkford, Fleet Air Arm Museum at Yeovilton, Lytes Cary Manor at Kingsdon.

Derrick's Tea Rooms

The Tea Guild's Award of Excellence 2011

Lovely surroundings and excellent teas

The Cliffs, CHEDDAR BS27 3QE
Tel 01934 742288
e-mail enquiries@derrickstearoom.co.uk
web www.derrickstearoom.co.uk

Derrick's Tea Room nestles below Lion Rock in the beautiful surroundings of Cheddar Gorge. Dating back to the 1500s, the building was originally three stone masons' cottages and the original cheese shop. Owned and run by Simon and Bonnie, it has a secluded terraced garden, seating 30 people in a covered area, full of plants and flowers in summer. There are around 15 types of tea plus fruit and herbal infusions. The original Derrick's cream tea is a choice of plain or fruit scones served with clotted cream and strawberry and champagne jam, together with a pot of tea. Alternatively try the Gentleman's cream tea – a cheese scone with cream cheese and chutney plus tea, or Chocolate Heaven – a chocolate chip scone with clotted cream and chocolate spread. Gluten and wheat-free scones are also available. Afternoon tea adds sandwiches to a cream tea, and the high tea, served on a three tier stand, offers a selection of savoury finger sandwiches, slices of home-made cake and scones with jam and clotted cream. Wash this down with tea, a glass of wine or, a bottle of champagne. There is also a shop, selling pickles, jams and cooking sauces, as well as food to take away, including a 'cream tea in a bag'.

To eat breakfast, lunch, set teas

Open all week
Jan 10am-4pm, Feb & Mar 10am-5pm, Apr-Jul 10am-5.30pm, Aug 10am-6pm, Sep-Oct 10am-5pm Nov 10am-4pm. (Nov-Jan 10am-5pm wknds only). Closed Xmas

Getting there From Wells follow the A371, then turn right onto the B3135, Cliff Street, follow the road towards the Gorge until you see Derrick's on the left.

Things to do Explore the caves and Gorge

Wishing Well Tea Rooms

Enjoy light lunches and teas at this busy tea room.

The Cliffs,
CHEDDAR, BS27 3QA
Tel 01934 742142

After the highlight of driving down the spectacular Cheddar Gorge, you can enjoy the simple but appetizing fare at this family-run tea room. There are at least 10 blends of tea on offer and the good-value afternoon tea includes home-made cakes and scones. Light lunches, jacket potatoes and snacks are also on the menu, and hot chocolate is a speciality. Service is attentive and the atmosphere friendly – but in the high season it does get very busy.

To eat Afternoon Tea, Fruit Tea, Deluxe Cream Tea. Light lunches and snacks.

Open Apr to mid-Oct, daily 10am-5pm; mid-Oct to Nov and Feb-Mar weekends only. Closed Dec-Jan.

Getting there Cheddar is on the A371. Nearest motorway M5. Parking in the village.

What to see Cheddar Caves, Cheddar Gorge, Wookey Hole, walking in the Mendip Hills, Wells Cathedral and Bishop's Palace.

Settle

A cheery traditional tea shop where everything is home-made

16 Cheap Street,
FROME, BA11 1BN
Tel 01373 465975

Standing in the heart of an old paved street with a little stream running down the middle, this tea shop has a busy, bustling and cheerful atmosphere. Everything on the menu is home-made and the range of cakes and pastries is incredibly diverse, not to mention the toasted and untoasted sandwiches, snacks and light lunches. Then, of course, there's the traditional cream tea. Particular highlights are the local specialities, including cream from Jersey cows and local apple juice.

To eat Cream tea. Light lunches and snacks.

Open Mon-Sat 9am-5pm; also 7:30pm-8:45pm Thu-Sat. Closed Bank Holidays.

Getting there Frome is on the A359 and A362 roads. Nearest motorway M4. Limited street parking.

What to see Nunney Castle, Longleat, Brokerswood Country Park at Wesbury, Farleigh Hungerford Castle.

Cheddar Gorge, Somerset

Ston Easton Park

An architectural gem is the setting for elegant afternoon teas

STON EASTON, (near Bath), BA3 4DF
Tel 01761 241631

The hotel, a Palladian mansion of noted architectural distinction, is set in landscaped grounds not far from Bath. It is easy to see how time can lose all importance as one is seated in the elegant drawing room sipping tea from china cups. A variety of teas is on offer and the culinary treats are all home-made. As well as afternoon teas with jam and cream, you can get snacks and light meals. Reservations are advisable.

To eat Traditional full afternoon tea, Gourmet full afternoon tea. Light lunches and snacks.

Open Daily. Afternoon tea served 3:30pm-5:30pm.

Getting there Bath can be reached on the A4, A36 and A46 roads. Nearest motorway M4. Parking.

What to see Bath, Corsham Court, Lacock, Longleat, Dereham Manor, The American Museum at Claverton Manor.

The Castle at Taunton

Elegant teas are served in this historic hotel, which really was a castle

Castle Green,
TAUNTON, TA1 1NF
Tel 01823 272671

The stonework of this former castle is today so festooned by a magnificent wisteria that you might not immediately realise its historic pedigree. The welcome and service given to residents and non-residents alike is fit for a king, though. Somerset Cream Tea consisting of scones, jam and cream, and a pot of tea, can be taken in the warmth of the lovely Rose Room, decorated with paintings, tapestries and fresh floral displays. Ten blends of tea are available to accompany the sandwiches, scones and snacks on offer.

To eat Somerset Cream Tea. Light lunches and snacks.

Open Daily 3:30pm-5:30pm.

Getting there Taunton is on the A38 and A358 roads, just off the M5 motorway. Large car park in front of the hotel.

What to see Hestercombe Gardens, Blackdown Hills, Willow and Wetlands Visitor Centre at Stoke St Gregory.

Bridge Cottage

A delightful haven in an unspoilt Somerset village

WINSFORD, TA24 7JE
Tel 01643 851362
web www.bridgecottageexmoor.co.uk

A relaxing tea room in the heart of picturesque Winsford serving delicious, traditional food at affordable prices. As well as afternoon teas, they also serve brunch and lunch, and everything is home-made from fresh local ingredients. The attractive tea garden is the perfect place to relax on a sunny day, and dogs (on a lead) are welcome there. The tea room is big enough to accommodate large parties, and special diets present no problem. Children also are welcome.

To eat Cream tea. Lunch and snacks.

Open Etr-Sep 10:30am-5:30pm (winter Fri-Sun 10:30am-3:30pm).

Getting there Off the A396 Tiverton–Minehead road, south of Wheddon Cross. Parking available next door.

What to see Exmoor National Park, The Wambarrows, The Caractacus Stone and local guided walks.

Porlock Vale, Exmoor National P0ark

Tarr Steps, Exmoor National Park

Suffolk

Bailey's 2

Small intimate place in the centre of
Bury St Edmunds

5 Whiting Street,
BURY ST EDMUNDS, IP33 1NX
Tel 01284 706198

This restaurant and tea room is on one of Bury St Edmunds'
quaint narrow streets close to the town centre. Simple cane
chairs and plain china make for an easy-going charm. You will
receive friendly service from the smiling staff, and it is an
altogether enjoyable experience. Real food is the emphasis
here, and light lunches and snacks such as quiches are served,
as well as sandwiches and home-baked scones and cakes –
all made using local produce.

To eat Light lunches, snacks.

Open Mon-Sat 9am-4pm. Closed BH

Getting there Bury St Edmunds is situated on the A45.
Parking is limited, and controlled in the busy town centre.

What to see Moyse's Hall Museum (and Art Gallery), Abbey
Gardens, St Edmundsbury Cathedral, Guildhall, Corn Exchange.

Hintlesham Hall Hotel

Country house elegance in the heart of Suffolk

George Street,
HINTLESHAM, IP8 3NS
Tel 01473 652334
e-mail reservations@hintleshamhall.com
web www.hintleshamhall.com

Set in a large area of wonderful countryside, this Grade I listed
Elizabethan manor house has Georgian additions, which
include the splendid façade. Afternoon tea is served in one of
the elegant lounges or al fresco, overlooking the beautiful
gardens. A selection of finger sandwiches (chicken and
watercress, cured ham and grain mustard, cream cheese and
chive, smoked salmon and capers) is followed by home-made
scones with chantilly cream and preserves, and chocolate chip
and marmalade brownies. A good choice of teas is available,
supplemented by fruit and mint tisanes. Staff are friendly and
professional. Booking is possible, but not essential.

To eat Full afternoon tea, Chantilly cream tea.

Open Daily. Tea served 3pm-6pm, but available at other times
on request.

Getting there West of Ipswich on A1071 to Hadleigh and
Sudbury.

What to see Lavenham, Snape Maltings, Long Melford.

Guildhall, Lavenham

The Granary

View local prints and paintings as you enjoy tea and cake in a converted granary building

Snape Maltings,
SNAPE, IP17 1SR
Tel 01728 687171
e-mail info@snapemaltings.co.uk
web www.snapemaltings.co.uk

Snape Maltings is a collection of Grade II listed Victorian buildings nestled beside the River Alde. It houses a wonderful collection of shops, galleries and the famous Concert Hall. The Granary teashop offers made to order sandwiches, light snacks, home-made cakes and pots of loose leaf tea. Most of the ingredients are sourced from local producers. Farmers Markets are held on the first Saturday of each month.

To eat Sandwiches, snacks.

Open Daily 10am-5pm.

Getting there Snape is on the B1094 off the A12. The site has a large car park.

What to see Concert Hall, River Alde boat trips during the summer, Aldeburgh, Easton Farm Park, Minsmere Reserve.

Aldeburgh

Resident beachcombers

Flying Fifteens

The Tea Guild's Award of Excellence 2011

Popular seafront tea rooms with a lovely garden overlooking the beach

19a The Esplanade,
LOWESTOFT, NR33 0QG
Tel 01502 581188

These popular tea rooms offer full waitress service. All the food is home-cooked using the best ingredients, and chips are banned from the menu. Specialities include locally smoked salmon, local oak smoked ham and, on Saturdays, fresh Cromer crab. There are no set meals, just a good choice of sandwiches, soup, omelettes, baguettes and cakes, with favourites such as strawberry scones, very large meringues and boozy fruitcake, plus over 40 wonderful loose leaf teas from around the world. The name "Flying Fifteens" comes from a sailing boat designed by Uffa Fox in the 1940s, "fifteen" relating to its length. Teas, gifts and greeting cards are sold. Dogs are permitted in the garden.

To eat Afternoon tea. Light meals, available all day

Open Spring Bank Holiday to mid-Sep Wed-Sun. Easter-Spring Bank Holiday weekends only. Tea served 10:30am-4:30pm. Closed winter.

Getting there On South Beach seafront promenade, between South Pier and Claremont Pier, near Hotel Hatfield. Parking nearby.

What to see Lowestoft town centre, East Anglian Transport Museum, Pleasurewood Hills Amusement Park, Africa Alive, Somerleyton Hall and Gardens, Oulton Broad.

Surrey

Pennyhill Park Hotel & The Spa

The Tea Guild's Award of Excellence 2011

An indulgent afternoon tea in luxurious surroundings

London Road, BAGSHOT GU19 5EU

Tel 01276 471774

web www.pennyhillpark.co.uk

Pennyhill Park is a luxury country house hotel with an award-winning Spa, set in 123 acres of rolling Surrey parkland. In a great location, between Ascot, Sunningdale and Wentworth, it's just 45 minutes from the centre of London, and offers everything from tennis and amazing spa breaks and treatments, to its own golf course. The excellent staff really go out of their way to make sure you get what you want from a stay or a visit. The Ascot Bar, with its relaxed and sociable atmosphere, is a haven of tranquillity and elegance, and is the ideal place to indulge in a decadent, homemade afternoon tea, served on a tiered cake stand with a glamorous sense of tradition and occasion. If it's too nice a day to sit inside, why not enjoy the sunshine on the pretty terraces. Traditional Ascot Afternoon Tea includes a pot of tea of your choice, with freshly cut sandwiches, assorted pastries, freshly baked scones with clotted cream and strawberry preserve, plus a choice of cakes from the trolley. Trade up to the Royal Ascot which includes a glass of Champagne or a Champagne cocktail. For a special occasion, the Celebration Afternoon Tea features an individual birthday cake baked by the hotel's pastry chef to put the finishing touches on a memorable afternoon (please give 24 hours notice).

To eat Light lunches, snacks, set teas

Open Ascot bar from 9am, Afternoon tea 1pm-5pm

Getting there Exit M3 at Junct 3 (signed Woking, Bracknell, Lightwater), take 1st exit at rdbt onto A322 (signed Bracknell, Bagshot). At traffic signals, left onto B3029 (signed Bagshot, Windlesham) entering Bagshot. At rdbt, 2nd exit onto Guildford Road - B3029. At T-junction turn left onto London Road - A30. After 0.5m Pennyhill Park is signed on right.

What to do Golf; racing at Ascot; Windsor Castle

The Original Maids of Honour Ltd

A cake's royal past and an original recipe make this a tea shop to remember

288 Kew Road, KEW GARDENS, TW9 3DU
Tel 020 8940 2752

The Original Maids of Honour Tea Shop is steeped in nearly three-hundred years of Richmond history. The famous Maid of Honour cake itself dates back to Henry VIII, who first used its name when at the Royal Household of Richmond Palace and reportedly helped to keep its recipe a secret. The tea shop has been on these premises since 1860, and is the perfect place to come for a traditional English afternoon tea. The staff pride themselves on baking daily from their own original recipes and there is a large selection of both sweet and savoury treats with which any visitor can be spoilt.

To eat Traditional afternoon tea. Light lunches. Snacks.

Open Mon-Sat 9am-6pm, Sun 8:30am-6pm. Afternoon tea served 2:30pm-5:30pm.

Getting there Kew Gardens is well signposted from all major roads. The A205 and the A307 (Kew Road) both border the gardens. Ample on street parking is available.

What to see The Royal Botanic Gardens Kew, The London Butterfly House, The London Wetland Centre, The Aquatic Experience.

Fanny's High Tea House and Farm Shop

A unique high tea experience in a delightful setting

Markedge Lane,
MERSTHAM, (near Redhill), RH1 3AW
Tel 01737 554444
e-mail fannysfarm@yahoo.co.uk
web www.fannysfarm.com

A tree house at Fanny's Farm treats up to nine adults with a special "Winnie the Pooh" style afternoon tea adventure and provides a delightfully secluded setting for an afternoon tea party of sandwiches, scones, clotted cream, jam and, of course, a pot of tea. This magical tea house is located next to Fanny's Farm Shop, which sells a vast range of home-made fare, including speciality honey, preserves, eggs, cheeses and cakes. Gift baskets can also be made to order. Booking is essential for the High Tree House.

To eat Morning coffee and high tea for adults and children.

Open By appointment only. Farm Shop daily 8am-6pm.

Getting there Markedge Lane is off Gatton Bottom Road, accessible from the A23 & A217. Parking available.

What to see Gatton Park, Mercers Country Park, North Downs Way, Reigate Priory Museum, East Surrey Museum.

The Royal Botanic Gardens Kew

Bingham

The Tea Guild's Award of Excellence 2011

Chic refinement overlooking the River Thames

61–63 Petersham Road,
RICHMOND UPON THAMES,
TW10 6UT
Tel 020 8940 0902
e-mail info@thebingham.co.uk
web www.thebingham.co.uk

The River Thames provides the atmospheric backdrop to this chic, contemporary Georgian townhouse, now a boutique hotel. The grandeur of the handsome lounge bar is accentuated by expansive mirrors, sofas covered with rich furnishings, a hand blown glass chandelier and a contemporary silver-leafed ceiling. The traditional afternoon tea consists of sandwiches, scones and home made preserves, and a selection of cakes and pastries. A wide selection of loose leaf teas is available, ranging from Assam Breakfast to Flowering Red Amaranth.

To eat Pink Afternoon Tea, Laduree Afternoon Tea

Open Mon-Sat 3:30-5:30pm, Sun 4-6pm.

Getting there 10 minutes' walk south from Richmond Station along George Street into Petersham Road or 5 minutes on the No 65 Kingston bus.

What to see Kew Gardens, Hampton Court Palace, Richmond Park.

Oatlands Park Hotel

In a country setting, but with easy access to the motorway network and airports

146 Oatlands Drive,
WEYBRIDGE, KT13 9HB
Tel 01932 847242
e-mail info@oatlandsparkhotel.com
web www.oatlandsparkhotel.com

Indulge in a little bit of English tradition, in this quintessentially English setting, and enjoy the mouth-watering delights of an afternoon tea served in a tranquil country house hotel, originally built by King Henry VIII for Anne of Cleves. Finely cut sandwiches, freshly-baked scones with jam and clotted cream, and a range of delicate pastries.

To eat Set tea.

Open Daily. Tea served 3-5pm.

Getting there Through Weybridge High Street to the top of Monument Hill. Hotel on left.

What to see Wisley RHS Gardens, Brooklands Museum, Hampton Court Palace, Painshill Park, Mercedes Benz World, Thames Path.

Thames path, Hampton Court

Hampton Court Palace

The Role of The Tea Taster

The role of tea taster is a fascinating one. Like so many aspects of tea production, most of us know little or nothing about the people whose skill and knowledge ensures our favourite blend is always consistent. All kinds of things affect the flavour and colour of tea – the type of tea plant, the topography of the estate, climate, and the methods used in the processing. It takes at least five years to train as a tea taster, learning how to identify all these different elements and judge the quality of the tea. Some tasters work for the tea factory, testing the tea after processing, and attributing quality gradings which will affect the price, while others work for the tea companies, deciding whether the quality is suitable and whether their company should buy it, and if so, whether it can be sold as an individual tea variety, or is more suitable as part of a blend. Testing a tea thoroughly involves far more than just having a mouthful and identifying the type. Tea has texture, character and 'mouthfeel' as well as complex flavours and aromas. Tea tasters are advised to avoid smoking, drinking alcohol and eating spicy foods, as all these things can affect the sense of taste.

If you want to experience tea tasting for yourself, there are various courses available. Jane Pettigrew runs Masterclasses (usually held at the Chesterfield Hotel in London) where you can learn how to identify the differences between varieties of teas as well as discovering more about the history of tea and how it is made. To find out more visit www.tea.co.uk

If a course doesn't appeal, and you want to do some tasting at home, here are some things to look out for: check the dry leaf to make sure it isn't musty, dull or lifeless; once made, the liquid should be clear and sparkling, with a bright rim; and the brightness, colour, taste and aroma of the tea should help you tell whether it's a good example of the blend/variety.

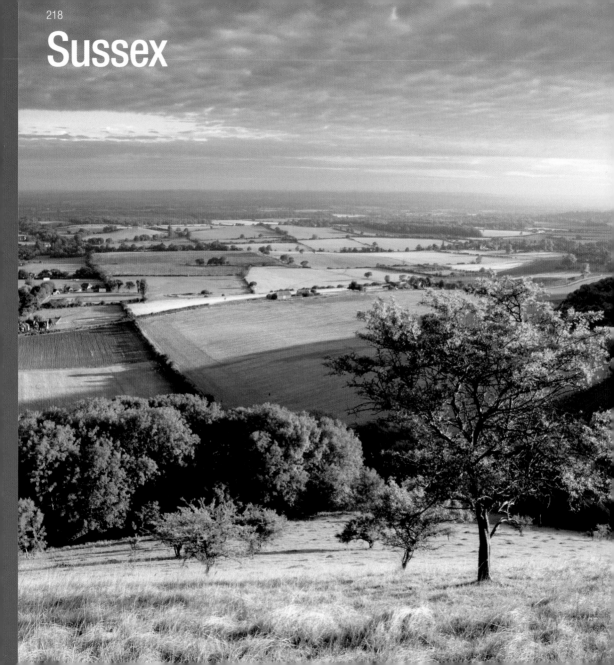

Sussex

The Tudor House

Tea, light lunch and evening meals in the picturesque setting of the South Downs

High Street,
ALFRISTON (near Polegate), BN26 5SY
Tel 01323 870891
e-mail booking@tudorhouse-restaurant.co.uk
web www.tudorhouse-restaurant.co.uk

A mellow 14th-century building with many original features, The Tudor House stands in the main street of the picturesque village of Alfriston. The two rooms for taking tea are peaceful and traditional in character whilst, in the summer, the pleasant garden with views over the Downs is an inviting setting in which to enjoy some refreshment. Choose from the 10 blends of tea to accompany a traditional afternoon tea or indulge in a Sussex cream tea.

To eat Afternoon tea, Sussex cream tea. Light lunches and snacks.

Open Daily 10:30am-5pm.

Getting there Alfriston is well signposted off the A27. There is a car park in the village.

What to see Alfriston village green, Alfriston church, Sussex Downs, Firle Place, Drusillas, Clergy House (National Trust), The Long Man of Wilmington.

The Mock Turtle

Welcoming tea shop in an historic seaside location

4 Pool Valley,
BRIGHTON, BN1 1NJ
Tel 01273 327380

After touring the Lanes area of historic Brighton, wander down the narrow streets to find The Mock Turtle nestled just off East Street, very close to the Grand Parade and seafront. The atmosphere is most convivial and there are so many varieties of tea, speciality meringues, tasty cakes and breads that you'll soon lose count. It is deservedly popular with locals and often the first port of call for regular visitors to the city. In the summertime, seating spills out onto the pavement to create an enjoyable experience for everyone.

To eat Afternoon tea, cream tea, Mock Turtle tea.

Open Tue-Sun 9am-6:30 pm.

Getting there Brighton is off the A23 and A237 roads. Nearest motorway M23. Meter parking and public car parks. The Mock Turtle is very close to Pool Valley bus station.

What to see Royal Pavilion, Brighton Pier, Sea Life Centre, The Lanes, The North Laine shopping area, Brighton Toy and Model Museum.

Brighton Pier

Walk

Birling Gap – to Beachy Head

A magnificent clifftop walk exploring a scenic stretch of the Sussex coast.

Start/finish: Grid ref TQ 554959

Parking: Free car park at Birling Gap

Distance: 7 miles/11.2km

Level of difficulty: ● ● ●

Suggested map: OS Explorer 123 Eastbourne & Beachy Head

Walk directions

1 Walk from car park, keeping road on **L**. Ignore South Downs Way sign by road and continue on grassy path. Keep **R** of next car park and follow path between trees.

2 Keep parallel to road and when you see junction with concrete track, take next **L** path to meet it. Follow bridleway signposted 'East Dean Down'. Glance back for view of old Belle Tout lighthouse. Pass fingerpost and continue ahead.

3 Follow concrete track as it bends **R** towards Cornish Farm, avoiding bridleway going straight on. Look for gate on **R** and head east,

keeping fence on **R-H** side. Make for next gate and continue ahead. Pass alongside bushes before reaching next gate. Traffic on A259 zips by on skyline. Pass access track to Bullockdown Farm and along here you can see flint walls enclosing fields and pastures.

4 Pass beside barrier to road and turn **R**, following grassy verge. On reaching 2 adjoining gates on **R**, cross road and take path to waymarked junction. Follow path towards Eastbourne, signposted 'seafront'; soon meet South Downs Way (SDW).

5 Bear sharp **R** here and follow long-distance trail as it climbs steadily between bushes and vegetation. Keep **R** when another path comes in from **L** and make for viewpoint, with Beachy Head lighthouse below. Cross grass, up slope to trig point. Before you now are Beachy Head pub and Beachy Head Countryside Centre.

6 Return to SDW and follow it west. Path ahead runs over undulating cliff top. Keep Belle Tout lighthouse in your sights and follow path up towards it. Keep to **R** of old lighthouse and soon car park at Birling Gap edges into view, as do Seven Sisters cliffs. Bear **R** at SDW post and follow path down and round **L**. Swing **L** just before road and return to car park.

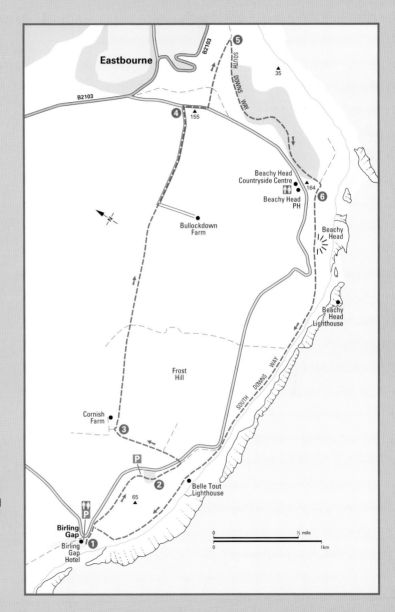

Gravetye Manor Hotel

Stone-built Elizabethan mansion with beautiful gardens

EAST GRINSTEAD, RH19 4LJ
Tel 01342 810567
e-mail info@gravetyemanor.co.uk
web www.gravetyemanor.co.uk

One of the first ever country house hotels, Gravetye Manor remains a shining example of its type. Delightful public rooms with oak panelling, fresh flowers and open fires provide the perfect setting for afternoon tea. Alternatively, in fine weather, guests can sit outside in the garden. An à la carte selection of sandwiches, cakes, biscuits and scones with cream and preserves is offered along with a choice of teas and coffees. The set afternoon tea includes all of the above plus Gravetye Spring Water. Please note that tea is served to non-residents by prior arrangement only and booking is required. Gravetye preserves are available to purchase at reception.

To eat Set tea.

Open Daily. Tea served 3pm-5pm daily.Closed 25-26 Dec, 1 Jan.

Getting there M23 junct 10. A264 towards East Grinstead. At 2nd rdbt take 3rd exit (Turners Hill, B2028). After Turners Hill, left at fork in road, left again and Hotel is on the right.

What to see Wakehurst Place, Chartwell, Hever Castle.

Exceat Farmhouse

A farmhouse tea shop with its own courtyard garden close to the picturesque countryside of the South Downs

Exceat, Seven Sisters Country Park,
SEAFORD, BN25 4AD
Tel 01323 870218

This lovely 17th-century farmhouse nestles in the heart of the sheltered Cuckmere Valley and is a lovely place to stop for tea or a light lunch. There is a selection of teas to choose from and everything on offer at this agreeable tea house is made on the premises from the best ingredients. The atmosphere is peaceful and the service friendly.

To eat Afternoon tea, cream tea.

Open Daily 10am-5pm. Earlier closing in winter.

Getting there The farmhouse and park are signposted off the A259, Seaford-Eastbourne road. Nearest motorway M23. Car park.

What to see Michelham Priory, Battle Abbey, Pevensey Castle, Alfriston, Ashdown Forest, The Long Man of Wilmington, South Downs Way.

Ashdown Park Hotel and Country Club

The Tea Guild's Award of Excellence 2011

A magnificent house and grounds set in the heart of Ashdown Forest

Wych Cross,
FOREST ROW, RH18 5JR
Tel 01342 824988
e-mail reservations@ashdownpark.com
web www.ashdownpark.com

The tradition of afternoon tea is proudly maintained at Ashdown Park Hotel, which offers an à la carte tea menu in the relaxing and elegant surroundings of the hotel's drawing rooms or outside on the terrace. Options range from simple tea and crumpets to a Champagne Tea – finger sandwiches, scones served warm with clotted cream and a choice of preserves, and a selection of cakes, tea breads and pastries accompanied by a glass of chilled Champagne and fresh strawberries with cream, all to be enjoyed with a pot of tea from the superb choice on offer. If you wish to treat someone else to afternoon tea at Ashdown Park, gift certificates are available at reception and booking is possible.

To eat Afternoon tea and Champagne tea.

Open Daily. Tea served 3pm-5:30pm.

Getting there A264 to East Grinstead, A22 to Eastbourne. South of Forest Row at Wych Cross lights, turn left to Hartfield. Hotel on right

What to see Wakehurst Place, Sheffield Park, Bluebell Railway.

The Grand Hotel

An impressive Victorian hotel overlooking Eastbourne's beach and seafront

King Edward's Parade,
EASTBOURNE, BN21 4EQ
Tel 01323 412345
e-mail reservations@grandeastbourne.com
web www.grandeastbourne.com

Traditional afternoon tea can be enjoyed in the grand style in the Great Hall with its lofty ceiling and fluted pillars and column. Light piano music provides a restful background. On the last Sunday of the month (except June, July and December) the Palm Court Strings play in the Great Hall at teatime. Enjoy a selection of teas, sandwiches (with interesting breads), fresh scones with preserves and clotted cream, Eton Mess or Quich Tartlets according to season, and a selection of freshly made cakes and pastries. As an extra treat, glasses of chilled Champagne add to the sense of occasion. Booking is highly recommended.

To eat Set teas.

Open Daily. Tea served 2:45pm-6pm. Closed to non-residents 23-26 Dec.

Getting there On seafront, west of Eastbourne, close to railway station.

What to see South Downs Way, Beachy Head Countryside Centre, The Long Man

April Cottage Tearoom

An intimate 16th-century cottage in a village with wonderful views of the Weald and South Downs

West Street,
MAYFIELD, TN20 6BA
Tel 01453 872160

East Sussex has its share of traditional tea rooms, but few are as old as April Cottage, tucked away on a side turning in the village of Mayfield. Inside, the tea room is cool and rustic, with white-washed walls, beams, a fireplace that stretches the width of the room and classic dark wood tables and chairs. At teatime, the freshly prepared set teas are all delicious. A walk around the village with its lovely views is a must.

To eat Set teas.

Open Fri-Tue 3pm-5:30pm. Closed Wed.

Getting there The village is south of Tunbridge Wells on the A267. Car parking in the village.

What to see Mayfield Church, Uckfield, Crowborough, Pashley Manor, Scotney Castle (National Trust).

South Downs

St Martin's Tearooms

Georgian city centre Historic tearooms serving a range of loose teas and organic home-made fare

3 St Martin's Street,
CHICHESTER, PO19 1NP
Tel 01243 786715
web www.organictearooms.co.uk

The county town of West Sussex, Chichester, is also a cathedral town and this very charming, unique tearooms is in the city centre. The tearooms building is medieval in origin with an 18th-century façade typical of many of the area's historic vernacular buildings. It also has a pretty brick stone paved garden for eating alfresco. Welsh rarebits are a speciality and the scones and cakes are delicious.

To eat Afternoon tea.

Open Mon-Sat 10am-6pm.

Getting there Chichester is on the main A27 and A286 roads. Car parking restricted to the town's car parks.

What to see Chichester Cathedral (and the Lady Chapel), Chichester District Museum, Goodwood Motor Racing Circuit, South Downs.

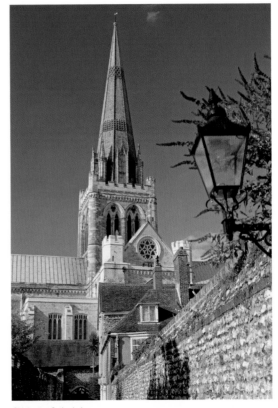

Chichester Cathedral

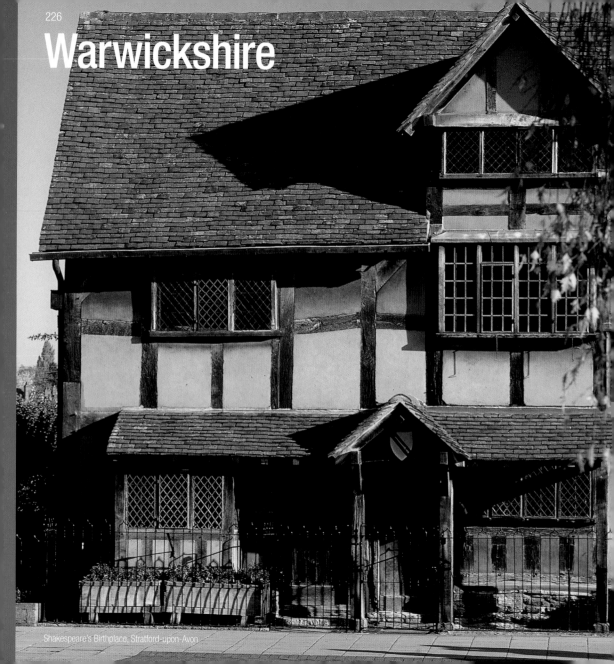

Warwickshire

Shakespeare's Birthplace, Stratford-upon-Avon

Henley Tea Rooms

Attractive tea rooms famous for their Henley ice cream

152 High Street,
HENLEY-IN-ARDEN, B95 5BT
Tel 01564 795172

This traditional 16th-century establishment is home to the famous Henley Ice Cream, which comes in over 40 flavours, and can be enjoyed in a friendly and welcoming environment. Henley cream teas, hand-made cakes and both hot and cold snacks are available whether you wish to sit in or out. In warm weather, one of their popular Henley Ice-cream milk shakes can be very refreshing.

To eat Set tea. Lunchtime snacks.

Open Apr-Sep Mon-Fri 9am-6pm, Sat 9:30am-6:30pm, Sun 10am-7pm; Oct-Mar Mon-Fri 9:30 am-5pm, Sat 9:30am-5:30pm, Sun 10am-5:30pm. Times may vary in school holidays or during Winter. Phone for details.

Getting there Between the A4189 and the A3400. Parking available off the High Street.

What to see Warwick Castle, Mary Arden's House, Coughton Court, Hatton Country World, Stratford-upon-Avon.

Mary Arden's farm

Thomas Oken Tea Rooms

Three set teas to choose from with a large variety of tea

20 Castle Street,
WARWICK, CV34 4BP
Tel 01926 499307

Formerly an old dolls museum, this tea shop is brimming with historic ambience and a sense of traditional Englishness. Choose from Oken's afternoon tea, Oken's cream tea or a Warwick cream tea, all served with a giant sultana scone and a dollop of strawberry preserve and clotted cream. They boast 22 different types of tea so you will have no problem finding one to suit your fancy and the Bei and Nannini coffee is also a pleasant alternative. There is a delicious selection of sandwiches, such as Warwickshire Truckle cheese, and light snacks as well.

To eat Set teas. Light lunches and snacks.

Open Mon-Fri 10am-5:30pm, Sat-Sun 10am-6pm.

Getting there Off the A429. Parking nearby.

What to see Warwick Castle, Stratford-upon-Avon, National Agricultural Centre, Lunt Roman Fort, Stoneleigh.

Warwick Castle

Boston Tea Party

This famous event on 16 December 1773 has been credited with leading eventually to the War of American Independence

The background is complex, but lies in the resentment felt by Americans against the taxes on imported tea they were forced to pay to an unpopular Britain. They disliked taxation without representation, and wished instead to be able to raise taxes themselves. Boycotts against taxed goods, such as tea, encouraged the growth of smuggling, and the colonists finally decided to refuse to import any tea where tax would have to be paid.

This particular dispute was sparked by the arrival in Boston harbour of three ships from the East India Company, all carrying tea on which tax would have to be paid. The local Governor of Massachusetts insisted the tea be unloaded and the tax paid. He even blockaded the port to make sure this happened. A huge protest meeting in Boston was incensed by this action and the people decided to take matters into their own hands.

A group of American patriots boarded the ships and efficiently, yet without violence, emptied all 342 casks of tea into the waters of the harbour. The value of the tea at

today's prices was almost £1 million. They even tidily swept the decks of the ships afterwards. Later they rowed round the harbour beating the tea under the water to ensure it was unusable.

The Tea Party caused a crisis in relations between Britain and America. The British government felt that the people of Boston should be punished and charged the ringleaders of the protest with High Treason. The response in America

Above: The modern-day dunking of tea over the side of the Boston Tea Party Ship, a faithful replica of the brig *Beaver II*, one of the ships boarded in the protest against the British East India Company of the 1770s.

was to unite more people in their support for independence from Britain, and two years later the War of American Independence started. Eight years afterwards Britain was defeated and a new nation was born.

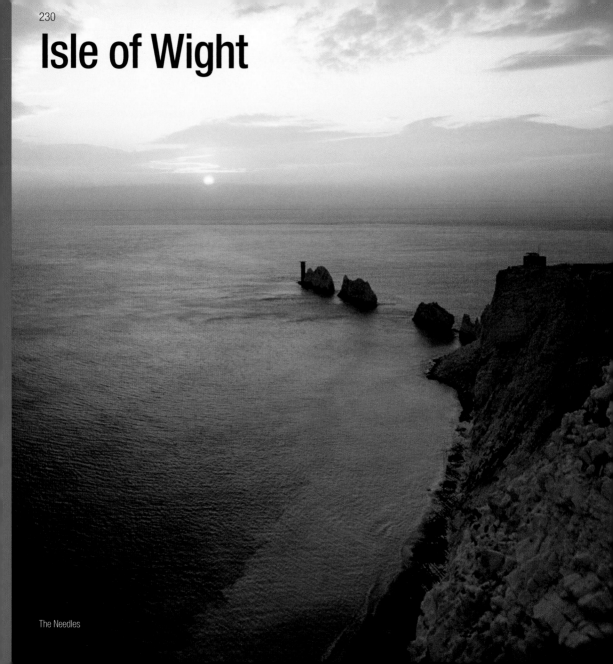

Isle of Wight

The Needles

The Bat's Wing Tea Room

It would be a shame to miss this little gem
of a tea shop

High Street,
GODSHILL (near Ventnor), PO38 3HH
Tel 01983 840634

This modest, almost plain, cottage tea shop is in danger of
being eclipsed by the burgeoning collection of assorted tea
experiences. Visitors who do find it, however, are always
grateful. In the traditionally furnished, low beamed rooms, you
will find families and groups of friends reading, munching or
quietly chatting. Choose from a selection of teas, snacks,
sandwiches, cakes and scones.

To eat Cream tea. Light lunches and snacks.

Open Mar-Oct, daily 10am-5pm.

Getting there Godshill is on the A3020 west of Shanklin.
Parking in the village.

What to see Botanic Garden at Ventnor, Blackgang Chine,
Dinosaur Isle, Bembridge Windmill, Appuldurcombe House.

The Old Thatch Tea Shop

A delightful place to stop for a pot of tea and
a bite to eat

4 Church Road,
Old Village,
SHANKLIN, PO37 6NU
Tel 01983 863184

Sunshine drifts into this cottage, lighting up the intriguing little
corners. After a day at the beach or in the town the Old Thatch
glows in the warmth of the afternoon. Inside, fine food and
good company await. This is tea as we dream of it – gentle
and welcoming to all. There's also a delightful garden,
accessed through the main entrance.

To eat Afternoon tea. Light lunches.

Open Mar-Nov, daily 10am-5pm.

Getting there Shanklin is on the A3020 and A3055.
Parking is limited in the area.

What to see Shanklin Chine, Appuldurcombe House,
Dinosaur Isle, Bembridge Windmill, Butterfly World.

Bembridge Windmill

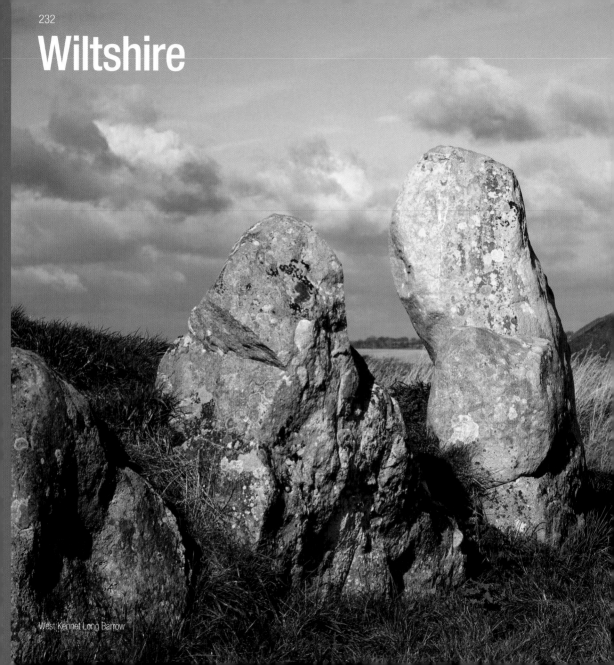

Wiltshire

West Kennet Long Barrow

The Bridge Tea Rooms

The Tea Guild's Award of Excellence 2011

An award-winning tea shop where top-quality teas are served in elegant fine bone china cups

24a Bridge Street,
BRADFORD-ON-AVON, BA15 1BY
Tel 01225 865537

The afternoon ritual of serving tea has been developed to a fine art here. The afternoon ritual of serving tea has been developed to a fine art here, and is so accomplished that the Bridge Tea Rooms was the 2009 winner of The Tea Guild's Top Tea Place award. Think of delicate fine bone china, the finest leaf teas, and friendly staff in Victorian costumes serving home-made cakes, pastries and sandwiches. Housed in a former 17th-century blacksmith's cottage, the Bridge Tea Rooms positively oozes atmosphere. Interesting light meals are also served throughout the day, but the famous Bridge cream tea is the main attraction here: expect large scones topped with Dorset clotted cream and strawberry preserve, and a pot of one of 26 fine loose-leaf teas presented to perfection in a beautiful teapot. They also serve Champagne Afternoon Tea, Master and Misses (for children) Savoury Afternoon Tea and Victorian Afternoon Tea. Postcards and a range of loose leaf teas are on sale.

To eat Bridge cream tea, Bridge full afternoon tea, Victorian afternoon tea, Champagne afternoon tea.

Open Mon-Sat 9:30am-5:30pm, Sun 10am-5.30pm. Tea served all day. Closed 25-26 Dec.

Getting there Next to the old town bridge and lock-up.

What to see Saxon church, tithe barn, Westwood Manor, City of Bath.

Walk

Calne – exploring Bowood Park

A visit to one of Wiltshire's grandest houses

Start/finish: Grid ref ST 998710

Parking: Choice of car parks in Calne

Distance: 7 miles/11.3km

Level of difficulty: ● ● ●

Suggested map: OS Explorer 156 Chippenham & Bradford-on-Avon

Walk directions

❶ Find library on The Strand (A4); head south along New Road to roundabout. Turn **R** along Station Road and take footpath **L** opposite fire station. Turn **C** on Wenhill Lane and follow it out of built-up area.

❷ Nearing cottage, follow waymark **L** and along field edge. Beyond cottage, climb bank and keep **L** along field edge to plank bridge and stile. Keep to **L-H** field edge; soon bear **L** to stile. Follow

path R, through rough grass around Pinhills Farm to stile opposite bungalow and turn **L** along drive.

3 At junction, turn sharp **R** along drive and continue for 1 mile (1.6km). Near bridge, take footpath **R**, through kissing gate; go through parkland beside pond. Cross bridge, go through gate and turn **R** alongside Bowood Lake.

4 Bowood House ahead, bear **L** to gate and cross causeway to gate. Keep straight on up track, following it **L** and then **R** to cross driveway to Bowood House.

5 Beyond gate, keep ahead along field edge, soon follow path **L** across Bowood Park. Keep **L** of trees and field boundary to gate. Turn **R** along drive beside Bowood Golf Course. Where drive turns sharp **R** to cottage, keep on into woodland.

6 Swing immediately **R**, then follow path **L**, downhill through clearing (can be boggy) along telegraph poles. Turn **L** at bottom of hill and follow woodland path uphill beside golf course. Turn **R** through break in trees and go through main gates to Bowood House into Derry Hill.

7 Turn **R** along Old Road. At A4, turn **R** along pavement. Soon cross to opposite pavement and continue

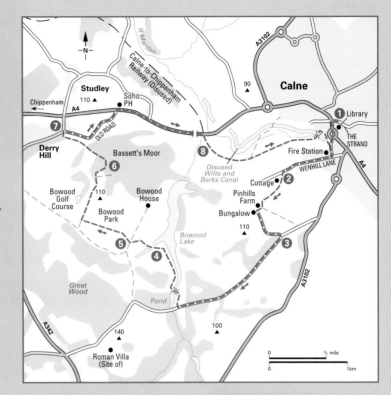

downhill. Pass under footbridge; take drive **R**.

8 Join former railway line at Black Dog Halt. Turn **L** and follow this towards Calne. Cross disused canal and turn **R** along towpath. Where path forks keep **R** to Station Road. Retrace your steps to start.

Manor House Hotel and Golf Club

The Tea Guild's Award of Excellence 2011

Stone-built, 14th-century manor house, surrounded by rolling Cotswold countryside

CASTLE COMBE, SN14 7HR
Tel 01249 782206
e-mail enquiries@manorhouse.co.uk
web www.exclusivehotels.co.uk

Enjoy afternoon tea in any one of the hotel's six lounges – cosy rooms with roaring fires in winter – or the leather furnished comfort of the Full Glass bar. In summer you can sit outside in the garden. An excellent selection of fine loose-leaf teas is available and there is a choice between the cream tea or the full set afternoon tea, comprising sandwiches, freshly baked scones with clotted cream and strawberry preserve, teacakes and Bath buns. In summer there might be an afternoon tea party on the lawn with gifts for the children.

To eat Full afternoon tea, cream tea.

Open Daily. Tea served 3pm-6pm.

Getting there Castle Combe is off the B4039, northwest of Chippenham.

What to see Castle Combe racetrack, Lacock Abbey, Corsham Court, Westonbirt Arboretum.

King John's Hunting Lodge

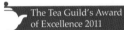

The Tea Guild's Award
of Excellence 2011

A centuries-old stone cottage in the centre of this beautiful village

21 Church Street,
LACOCK, SN15 2LB
Tel 01249 730313
web http://kingjohnslodge.2day.ws/

This is the oldest house in this unspoilt, medieval village. It dates back to the 13th century, and was added to during the Tudor period. The award-winning tea room, with a pleasant, secluded garden, has built a reputation for fine, traditional cooking. A number of specialist teas are served along with filter coffee, light lunches and high cream teas. Meals are created from Margaret's recipes, old and new, and a recipe book *Tea with the Bennets* is available for purchase. During the winter months a roaring log fire warms the tea rooms.

To eat King John's Royal Tea, Margaret's Cream Tea. The Bennets Cream Tea, Light lunches.

Open Feb-Dec, Wed-Sun 11am-5:30pm.

Getting there Lacock is just off the A350 Melksham to Chippenham road. Nearest motorway M4. Parking in the village.

What to see Church of St Cyriac, Lacock Abbey, Fox Talbot Museum, Bowood House and Gardens, Calne.

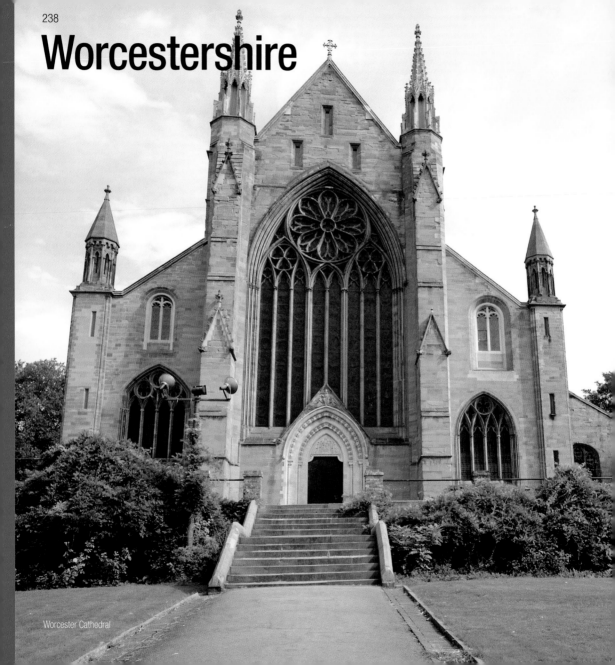

Worcestershire

Worcester Cathedral

Tisanes Tea Room

A traditional English tea shop in the old village of Broadway

Cotswold House,
21 The Green,
BROADWAY, WR12 7AA
Tel 01386 853296
web www.tisanes-tearooms.co.uk

An elegant shop that specialises in both useful and frivolous tea accessories for home and table, including a wide variety of teapots, china, and a range of fine teas too numerous to list. It occupies a 17th-century Cotswold stone building full of olde worlde charm and atmosphere. A light lunch menu that includes snacks, sandwiches, cakes and scones with jam and cream is offered, along with full waitress service. Gluten-free versions of many of the cakes are available, as is gluten-free bread for sandwiches. Specialities include brie and herb rolls and soup.

To eat Set teas. Light lunches.

Open Daily 10am-5pm. Closed Christmas Day.

Getting there Broadway is on the A44, southeast of Evesham. Parking in the village.

What to see Walks on the Cotswold Way, Broadway Tower Country Park.

The Lygon Arms

Beautiful building full of historic character

High Street,
BROADWAY, WR12 7DU
Tel 01386 852255
e-mail stay@barcelo-hotels.co.uk
web www.barcelo-hotels.co.uk/lygonarms

Built as an inn in 1532, the Lygon Arms is the archetypal country house hotel, with inglenook fireplaces, oak panelling and a wealth of antique furniture. It is located in the village of Broadway, surrounded by all the delights of the Cotswolds and by its own lovely garden. Tea is available in the lounges and courtyard every day. There is a set traditional afternoon tea and a Champagne tea, both with home-made cakes, scones and sandwiches, served on a three-tier cake stand.

To eat Set teas, including Champagne tea. Light lunches.

Open Daily 9am-5:30pm. Afternoon Tea served 3-5.30pm.

Getting there On High Street; Broadway is near Evesham off A44.

What to see Walks on the Cotswold Way, Broadway Tower Country Park.

Sugar and Spice

Full of all things nice, with friendly service

20 High Street,
PERSHORE, WR10 1AB
Tel 01386 553654

The entrance to this welcoming, informal tea room is through a glassware and china shop. The tables always look inviting with lace cloths and Wedgwood china and the light lunch menu of cakes, sandwiches and scones with jam and cream provide plenty of choice. Service is kind and thoughtful and there are several varieties of tea to choose from.

To eat No set tea. Lunches, cakes and scones.

Open Mon-Sat 9am-5pm.

Getting there Pershore is on the B4084 and A4104. Nearest motorway M5. Town car parks.

What to see Pershore Abbey, Pershore Bridge, Tyddesley Wood, The River Avon, Coughton Court, Snowshill Manor.

Cotswold Way

The Elms

A stunning location for afternoon tea, with idyllic views

Abberley,
WORCESTER, WR6 6AT
Tel 01299 896666

The Elms is a country house hotel near Abberley in Worcestershire, that actually feels like a home from home. That is, if your home is a lovely Queen Anne house set in ten acres of well kept gardens and lawns with ornate moulded ceilings, carved fireplaces and stained glass windows. There are more than ten different varieties of tea served alongside a light lunch menu with snacks, sandwiches, cakes and an afternoon tea with scones, jam and cream.

To eat Set afternoon tea. Light lunches and snacks.

Open Daily 3pm-6pm.

Getting there Abberley is on the A443 and A451 roads. Nearest motorway M5. Ample car parking.

What to see Witley Court, Abberley's churches, The Riverside Meadows, The Staffordshire and Worcestershire Canal, The Basins area.

Broadway Tower

Abberley Hill

Yorkshire

Bettys Café Tea Rooms

The Tea Guild's Award
of Excellence 2011

The first of the six Bettys, opened in 1919

1 Parliament Square,
HARROGATE, HG1 2QU
Tel 01423 502746
web www.bettysandtaylors.co.uk

When young confectioner Frederick Belmont travelled from Switzerland to find his fortune he came to Harrogate accidentally – by catching the wrong train. He liked the place well enough to stay, married a local lass and opened the first Bettys. Today's unique Swiss/Yorkshire menu continues to reflect the heritage of the family business. Sister company Taylor's of Harrogate, imports and blends all the excellent teas served, and each of the tea rooms has a shop selling teas, coffees, speciality breads, cakes, pastries and chocolates, all hand made at Bettys Craft Bakery. Cookery courses are also available at Bettys Cookery School, also in Harrogate. No dogs except guide dogs.

To eat Set tea, cream tea.

Open Daily 9am-9pm. Tea served all day. Closed 25-26 Dec, 1 Jan.

Getting there Harrogate is on the A61 and A59 roads. Parking in town centre.

What to see RHS Garden Harlow Carr, Royal Pump Room Museum, Knaresborough Castle and Museum, Harewood House, Fountains Abbey.

Bettys at RHS Garden Harlow Carr

The Tea Guild's Award of Excellence 2011

A fabulous setting for the latest addition to this famous family business

Crag Lane,
HARROGATE, HG3 1QB
Tel 01423 505604
web www.bettysandtaylors.co.uk

Bettys is a Yorkshire institution, a third-generation family business that is justly famous. This is Bettys' sixth tea room, and the first new one to open for more than 30 years. The Royal Horticultural Society's 58-acre Harlow Carr Garden is the location, and the existing building was transformed with Lloyd Loom chairs, marble topped tables, palm trees, and a terrace overlooking the garden. There is also a tea house in the middle of the gardens, plus a Bettys shop and deli. The sister company, Taylor's of Harrogate, buys and blends its own teas from all over the world, and provides the perfect brew for the set traditional or cream tea. A pianist plays on Sundays from 10am to 1pm.

To eat Set tea, cream tea.

Open Daily 9am-5:30pm. Tea served all day. Closed 25-26 Dec, 1 Jan.

Getting there Off B6162 Otley Road.

What to see RHS Garden Harlow Carr, Royal Pump Room Museum, Knaresborough Castle and Museum, Harewood House, Fountains Abbey.

Ripley Castle Tea Rooms

Home of the Ingilby family since 1320, with a characterful tea room

Ripley Castle,
RIPLEY, HG3 3AY
Tel 01423 770152

After looking around the castle and gardens, a visit to the tea rooms is a must. Fashioned from the old kiln and potter's shop in the stable yard, the tea rooms cater for thousands of visitors every year, and yet everything is freshly made on the premises. You can sip one of seven blends of tea with your traditional cream tea or a light lunch. There's also a menu of sandwiches, if you prefer a savoury snack. Booking is necessary for groups.

To eat Cream tea. Light lunches and snacks

Open Mon-Sat 10am-5pm.

Getting there Ripley is North of Harrogate on the A61 and A651 roads. Parking in the castle grounds.

What to see Ripley Castle, Brimham Rocks, Newby Hall, the Yorkshire Dales National Park, Harrogate.

The Garden Restaurant at Scampston

Innovative operation within the walled garden at Scampston Hall

Walled Garden, Scampston Hall,
MALTON YO17 8NG
Tel 01944 759000
e-mail restaurant@scampston.co.uk
web www.scampston.co.uk

A range of teas, coffee and light lunches are served in this light and airy modern establishment, using produce from the gardens and ingredients from other local sources. You can buy home-made pickles, jams, cookery books, crockery and paintings, and cookery courses and demonstrations are a feature in a specially designed kitchen. Book for groups and private functions.

To eat Afternoon tea. Light lunches and snacks.

Open Tue-Sun and Bank Holiday Mon 10am-5pm. Tea served all day.

Getting there On A64 between Scarborough and Malton, near Rillington.

What to see Scampston Hall and Walled Garden, Castle Howard, Wolds Way Lavender.

Ripley Castle

The Black Swan Tearoom & Patisserie at The Black Swan Hotel

The Tea Guild's Award of Excellence 2011

A fine classic tearoom in an historic Yorkshire hotel

Market Place,
HELMSLEY, YO62 5BJ
Tel 01439 770466
e-mail enquiries@blackswan-helmsley.co.uk
web www.blackswan-helmsley.co.uk

You can't miss the Black Swan Hotel in Helmsley's Market Square. It has been here for centuries and has been a coaching inn since the 1750s. The Tearoom and Patisserie is the most recent development and is a smart room attended by friendly and knowledgeable staff. Enjoy your choice of tea from the excellent tea menu, accompanied by one of the artisan cakes created by the hotel's patisserie chef, or sample home-made fruit scones. Alternatively, splash out on the Full Black Swan Afternoon Tea, presented on silver-tiered cake stands. The Tea Guild's Winner of Top Tea Place 2010.

To eat Cream tea, Black Swan Full Afternoon Tea. Light lunches and snacks.

Open Daily (except 25 Dec) 10am-6pm

Getting there East of Thirsk on A170 towards Scarborough

What to see Helmsley Castle, Duncombe Park, Helmsley Walled Garden

Walk

Ilkley Moor – Twelve Apostles

Discover some ancient standing stones and plenty of history on Ilkley Moor

Start/finish: Grid ref SE 132467

Parking: Car park below Cow and Calf rocks

Distance: 4.5 miles/7.2km

Level of difficulty: ● ● ●

Suggested map: OS Explorer 297 Lower Wharfedale

Walk directions

1 Walk up road; 150yds (137m) beyond Cow and Calf Hotel, where road bears **L**, fork **R** up grassy path. Scramble on to ridge and follow it west past Pancake Stone, enjoying extensive views over Ilkley and Wharfedale. Dip across path rising along shallow gully and continue beyond Haystack Rock, joining another path from **L**. Keep **L** at successive forks, swinging parallel to broad fold containing Backstone Beck, over to **R**.

2 After gently rising for 0.75 mile (1.2km) across open moor, path eventually meets Bradford–Ilkley Dales Way link. Go **L** here, along section of duckboarding. Pass boundary stone at top of the rise, and continue to ring of stones known as Twelve Apostles, just beyond crest.

3 Retrace steps from Twelve Apostles, but now continue ahead along Dales Way link. Bear **R** at fork and cross head of Backstone Beck. Shortly, beyond crossing path, way curves **L** in steep, slanting descent off moor below ridge, levelling lower down as it bends to White Wells.

4 Turn **R** in front of bathhouse and follow path across slope of hill past small pond and falling below clump of rocks to meet metalled path. Go **R**, taking either branch around The Tarn to find path leaving up steps at end. After crossing Blackstone Beck, ignore rising grass track and continue up final pull to crags by Cow and Calf rocks.

5 It's worth taking a few minutes to investigate the rocks and watch climbers practising their belays and traverses. From here paved path leads back to car park.

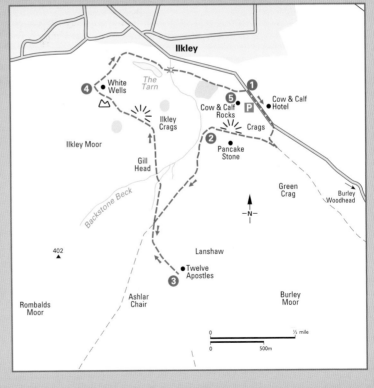

Bettys Café Tea Rooms

The Tea Guild's Award
of Excellence 2011

A strikingly attractive tea room on the tree-lined Grove

32–34 The Grove,
ILKLEY, LS29 9EE
Tel 01943 608029
web www.bettysandtaylors.co.uk

One of the six famous Bettys, the Ilkley incarnation has a wrought-iron canopy and an extensive tea and coffee counter stacked with antique tea caddies. Of particular interest are the specially commissioned stained-glass windows, depicting wild flowers from Ilkley Moor, and the large teapot collection. The tea room is a favourite with ramblers, tired, hungry and thirsty from a tramp across the moors. The guiding principle of Bettys' founder, Frederick Belmont, was that "if we want things just right we have to do it ourselves", and Bettys Bakery still makes all the cakes, pastries, chocolates, breads and scones served in the tea rooms, all best enjoyed with a pot of tea from the wide range on offer. No dogs except guide dogs.

To eat Set tea.

Open Daily 9am-5:30pm. Tea served all day. Closed 25-26 Dec, 1 Jan.

Getting there Ilkley is on the B6382 road, off the A65.

What to see Ilkley Moor, Haworth Parsonage, National Museum of Photography, Film and Television.

Bettys Café Tea Rooms

Elegant Cafe and Palm Room

188 High Street,
NORTHALLERTON, DL7 8LF
Tel 01609 775154
web www.bettysandtaylors.co.uk

The Tea Guild's Award of Excellence 2011

The Northallerton branch of Bettys is situated in a Grade II listed Georgian building with a domed glass roof, huge window mirrors and a Chusan Palm. During the warmer months you can enjoy afternoon tea 'alfresco' in the walled courtyard. Two set teas are offered: a Yorkshire Cream Tea with two sultana scones, butter, strawberry preserve and Yorkshire clotted cream, or the Bettys Traditional Afternoon Tea with a choice of sandwiches, a sultana scone with butter, preserve and cream, followed by a selection of miniature cakes. In both cases, the tea in the pot is Bettys Tea Room Blend of top class African and Assam teas; Bettys also offers an excellent choice of teas to revisit or experiment with. Children are not only welcome, but good facilities are provided to keep them fed, cleaned, changed and entertained. No dogs except guide dogs.

To eat Set teas.

Open Daily 9am-5:30pm (opens at 10am Sun). Tea served all day. Closed 25-26 Dec, 1 Jan.

Getting there From the A167, turn on to the B1333 and then onto Northallerton High Street.

What to see North York Moors National Park, Flamingo Land, Rievaulx Abbey.

Swinton Park

The Tea Guild's Award of Excellence 2011

Castle hotel in extensive parkland, gardens and lakes, on the fringe of the Yorkshire Dales National Park

MASHAM, HG4 4JH
Tel 01765 680900
e-mail enquiries@swintonpark.com
web www.swintonpark.com

The ancestral home of the Cunliffe-Lister family dates from the 17th century but was extended in later times. The estate is surrounded by beautiful moorland, dales and rivers. The bar and lounge menu includes sandwiches, light meals and desserts, plus a range of iced teas, leaf teas and freshly ground coffees. Four set teas are served in the lounge: a cream tea, Wensleydale tea (with locally made fruit cake and Wensleydale cheese), full afternoon tea comprising a selection of fine teas, sandwiches, cakes and scones with clotted cream and jam, and Royal Garden Party Afternoon Tea, which comes with a glass of Champagne. Bookings taken.

To eat Cream tea, traditional Wensleydale tea, full afternoon tea, Royal Garden Party Afternoon Tea.

Open Daily. Tea served 3pm-6pm.

Getting there From A1 north of Ripon, B6267 to Masham. Follow signs through town centre.

What to see Fountains Abbey, Newby Hall, Castle Howard.

Bettys Café Tea Rooms

The Tea Guild's Award of Excellence 2011

Bettys in York – a flagship café in the heart of the city

6–8 St Helen's Square,
YORK, YO1 8QP
Tel 01904 659142
web www.bettysandtaylors.co.uk

In 1936 Frederick Belmont, Bettys founder, travelled on the maiden voyage of the Queen Mary, during which time he was planning a new café in York. The luxury liner provided the required inspiration, and the ship's interior designers were commissioned to recreate the magnificent panelling, pillars and mirrors in the elegant new premises. Favourite dishes to accompany a fine selection of well-chosen teas include Swiss rösti, Alpine macaroni, Yorkshire sausages and Yorkshire Rarebit, plus a fine selection of cakes, patisserie and desserts. Children have always been welcome, and there's a "Little Rascals" menu, books, toys, organic baby food and baby-changing facilities for mums and dads. A café pianist enhances the atmosphere during the evenings. No dogs, except guide dogs.

To eat Set tea. Light lunches.

Open Daily 9am-9pm. Tea served all day. Closed 25-26 Dec, 1 Jan.

Getting there From the A19 turn onto the A1036, turn left onto Lendal and St Helen's Square is on the left.

What to see York Minster, York Castle Museum, National Railway Museum, The Shambles, Jorvik, The ARC.

Bullivant of York

The Tea Guild's Award of Excellence 2011

All-day home-cooked fare in a city centre location

15 Blake Street,
YORK, YO1 2QJ
Tel 01904 671311

A fine choice of carefully-brewed teas is served at this friendly tea room, which has fine weather seating in the courtyard outside. The menu lists an extensive selection of meals, sandwiches and snacks prepared to order, plus an enticing range of home-made desserts. Set teas include a traditional high tea, cream tea and the speciality, Chocolate Heaven – a chocolate chip scone with Yorkshire clotted cream and luxury praline chocolate spread served with hot chocolate. The high tea offers baked beans on toast or griddled eggs with toasted soldiers as an alternative to sandwiches. Reservations accepted. Home-made cheese, chocolate chip or fruit scones are available to buy.

To eat Cream tea, high tea, Chocolate Heaven. Light lunches and snacks.

Open Mon-Fri 9:30am-5pm, Sat 9am-5pm (Sun 11am-5pm). Closed 25-26 Dec. Please phone to check opening times Jan-Mar

Getting there From the A19, turn onto the A1036 and then turn left on Blake Street.

What to see York Minster, York Castle Museum, National Railway Museum, The Shambles, Jorvik, The ARC, Yorkshire Museum, York City Art Gallery, The York Dungeon.

Little Bettys

The Tea Guild's Award of Excellence 2011

A listed building in medieval Stonegate close to the Minster

46 Stonegate,
YORK, YO1 8AS
Tel 01904 622865
web www.bettysandtaylors.co.uk

There are six versions of Bettys, two of them in York, and this is the smallest of all – hence the name. The café is reached via a flight of winding stairs and has a delightful interior characterised by wooden beams and roaring fires. Hot dishes, speciality sandwiches and an extensive range of cakes and patisserie are served, with the Yorkshire Fat Rascal – a large fruity scone with citrus peel, almonds and cherries – a house speciality. The teas on the excellent tea menu are supplied by Bettys' sister company, family tea merchants Taylors of Harrogate, including some UK exclusives. Bettys is famously family-friendly, and children are made particularly welcome. No dogs, except guide dogs.

To eat Set tea. Lunches.

Open Daily 10am-5:30pm (from 9am Sat). Tea served all day. Closed 25-26 Dec, 1 Jan.

Getting there From the A19, turn onto the A1036. Go straight on to Blake Street, then left onto Stonegate.

What to see York Minster, York Castle Museum, National Railway Museum, The Shambles, Jorvik, The ARC, York City Art Gallery

Elizabeth Botham and Sons

 The Tea Guild's Award of Excellence 2011

Famous tea rooms specialising in Victorian recipes and fine teas

35–39 Skinner Street,
WHITBY, YO21 3AH
Tel 01947 602823
e-mail mj@botham.co.uk
web www.botham.co.uk

The invitation to take tea at Botham's is an irresistible one, involving wonderful cakes and pastries made from authentic Victorian recipes, and a huge range of rare and fine teas. Botham's was established in 1865 by Elizabeth Botham and is still run by her great-grandchildren. The first-floor tea rooms offer scones and teabreads, cream teas and toasts, special lunch of the day, jacket potatoes, salads and sandwiches. Afternoon tea comes with the house Resolution Tea, or you can find China Yunnan, Java Gunpowder and Darjeeling First Flush Badamtam and many others on the superb tea menu. Reservations are accepted.

To eat Cream tea, afternoon tea.

Open 9:30am-4:40pm (5pm May-Oct). Tea served all day. Closed Sun, Mon (Sep-Jun), Bank & Public Holidays.

Getting there From the A171 turn onto the A174. Turn right at the roundabout and left on to Skinner Street, which is on the west side of Whitby.

What to see Whitby Abbey, Captain Cook Museum, Pannett Museum, Robin Hood's Bay, North York Moors National Park.

Whitby Abbey

Wales

Pistyll Rhaeadr, Powys

Badgers

Llandudno's legendary tea room and patisserie is conveniently located among the town-centre shops

The Victoria Centre, Mostyn Street,
LLANDUDNO, Conwy, LL30 2RP
Tel 01492 871649
e-mail manager@badgerstearooms.co.uk
web www.badgerstearooms.co.uk

Badgers is the perfect place to rest, refuel and recuperate during a shopping expedition. Llandudno's Victorian traditions are upheld, with waitresses – called Badgers' Nippies – dressed in period costume. Regional specialities include Welsh rarebit, Welsh cakes, Welsh cheese salads, and bara brith, as well as home-roasted meats among the sandwich fillings. The Welsh Cream Tea comprises scones, jam and cream and bara brith, while the Victorian Tea adds a sandwich and an extra cake, all to be enjoyed with a pot of tea from the wide range on offer. All cakes and pastries, including swan meringues, dragon éclairs and ice mice, are made in the bakery upstairs and can be boxed to take away.

To eat Welsh cream tea, Victorian tea.

Open Mon-Sat 9:30am-5pm, Sun 11am-4pm. Tea served all day. Closed Easter Sun, 25-26 Dec, 1 Jan.

Getting there Turn off A470 onto A546, left on Clonmel Street and right into Mostyn Street. Parking nearby.

What to see Bodnant Gardens, Snowdonia National Park, Victorian Tramway to summit of Great Orme.

St Tudno Hotel and Restaurant

The Tea Guild's Award of Excellence 2011

Tea is served in the hotel lounge, with its wonderful sea views

The Promenade,
LLANDUDNO, LL30 2LP
Tel 01492 874411
e-mail sttudnohotel@btinternet.com
web www.st-tudno.co.uk

Situated on Llandudno's fine promenade, the St Tudno Hotel's afternoon tea is a delightful experience. The massive afternoon tea menu has pages of tempting choices, all of them truly delicious. The traditional Welsh tea and the "deluxe" selection come with a pot of loose-leaf speciality tea from around 14 classic choices – Assam and Darjeeling from India; Sri Lanka's Uva and Ceylon; and Formosa, Lapsang Souchong, Gunpowder and Keemun from China. Treats on offer include sandwiches, scones, bara brith, Welsh cakes and various other home-made cakes. Booking recommended for groups.

To eat Afternoon tea, De-luxe afternoon tea.

Open Daily. Tea served 2:30pm-5:30pm.

Getting there On the promenade, opposite the pier.

What to see Great Orme Copper Mines, Bodnant Gardens, Conwy Castle.

Walk

Conwy – castle stronghold

Conwy's castle and a remote Celtic fort

Start/finish: Grid ref SH 783775

Parking: Large car park on Llanrwst Road behind Conwy Castle

Distance: 6.75 miles/10.9km

Level of difficulty: ● ● ●

Suggested map: OS Explorer OL17 Snowdon

Walk directions

❶ From Conwy Quay head northwest along waterfront, past Smallest House and under town walls. Fork **R** along tarmac waterside footpath that rounds Bodlondeb Wood. Turn **L** along road, past school and on to A547. Cross road, then railway line by footbridge. Track beyond skirts wood to reach lane; turn **R**.

② At fork bear **R** past house to waymarked stile, from which footpath rakes up wooded hillsides up on to Conwy Mountain. Follow undulating crest of Conwy Mountain and continue past Castell Caer.

③ Several tracks converge in high fields of Pen-Pyra. Follow signposts for North Wales Path along track heading to southwest over **L** shoulder of Alltwen and down to metalled road traversing Sychnant Pass.

④ Follow footpath from other side of road, skirting woods on **L**. Over stile carry on past Gwern Engen to meet track. Go **R** and then bear **L**, dropping above lodge to reach lane. Turn **R** along lane, then turn **L** at next junction, into Groesffordd. Cross road, then take road ahead that swings to **R** past telephone box, then **L** (southeast) towards Plas Iolyn.

⑤ Turn **L** at end; leave opposite white house on path climbing to cottage. Cross track and continue upfield to B5106. Go **L** to Conwy Touring Park. Follow drive to hairpin, from which waymarked path climbs through trees, recrossing drive. Finally emerging through kissing gate, continue up field edge. Swing **L** along undulating ridge above successive pastures, finally meeting lane.

⑥ Turn **L**, shortly leaving **R** along

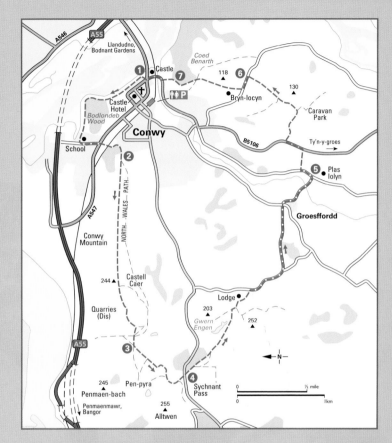

track past communications mast to Bryn-locyn. Continue at edge of fields beyond to stile by Coed Benarth, from which path drops beside wood.

⑦ Go over adder stile on **L-H** side and descend field to roadside gate at bottom. Turn **R** on to B5106 to return to quayside, or turn **L** to get back to main car park.

Tu Hwnt I'r Bont

A picturesque old cottage with a pretty garden

LLANRWST,
Conwy, LL26 0PL
Tel 01492 642322

Close to the bridge that spans the rushing River Conwy, this lovely 15th-century cottage is packed full of character, from its low beams and old fireplaces to the traditional Welsh dresser. The service is very welcoming, and the menu is refreshingly local – not surprisingly, Welsh rarebit is among the specialities, as is the ever popular fruit loaf known as 'bara brith'. To go with the cream teas or traditional afternoon tea, there are six blends of tea to choose from, including their own house blend.

To eat Afternoon tea, cream tea.

Open Mid-Mar to Nov, Tue-Sun and Bank Holiday Mon 10:30am-5:30pm. Nov-Dec weekends only.

Getting there Llanwrst is on the A470 and A548 roads. Car park is available.

What to see Gwydyr Uchaf Chapel, Conwy Valley Railway Museum, Betws-y-Coed, Trefriw Woollen Mills, Bodnant Garden, Conwy Castle, Snowdonia National Park.

Bodnant Garden

Swallow Falls, Betws-y-Coed

Cemlyn Tea Shop

The Tea Guild's Award
of Excellence 2011

Centrally located on Harlech's High Street

High Street, HARLECH,
Gwynedd, LL46 2YA
Tel 01766 780425
web www.cemlynrestaurant.co.uk

A tea shop with rooms, Cemlyn has superb views of Harlech's imposing 13th-century castle, Royal St David's Golf Course, the mountains and the sea. The owners have an uncompromising commitment to quality and are proud to offer a very fine choice of carefully selected loose leaf teas, alongside a selection of sweet and savoury bakery goods, all of which are made on the premises. There is a Terrace for outdoor seating on which dogs are welcome. Bed and breakfast accommodation is offered and tea, coffee, bara brith, guidebooks and other tea items are offered for sale, as is home made bread if ordered in advance.

To eat Morning coffee. Afternoon tea. Light lunches.

Open Mid March to end Oct, Wed-Sun 10:30am-5pm. Also Bank Holiday Mons. Tea served all day.

Getting there In town centre on B4573, between Post Office and chemist's shop.

What to see Harlech Castle, Llanfair Slate Caverns, Ffestiniog Railway, Portmeirion, the Lleyn Peninsula, Snowdonia National Park.

Plas Glyn-y-Weddw Gallery

Enjoy a splended afternoon tea surrounded by fine art

The Widows Glen,
LLANBEDROG,
Gwynedd, LL53 7TT
Tel 01758 740763

Plas Glyn-y-Weddw is one of those old-time, elegant houses that seem to age effortlessly. Now returned to its former glory as a gallery, you can browse the paintings, drawings and sculptures and, when the appetite for art has been satisfied, cross the hall to the tea room. Glowing with an antique charm, it is the setting for sumptuous teas involving all the usual treats – scones with jam and cream, cakes, sandwiches or the perhaps the speciality: fish cakes. The menu includes 13 blends of tea.

To eat Afternoon tea. Light lunches and sandwiches.

Open Feb-Dec, Wed-Mon 10am-5pm, also Tue in peak season.

Getting there Llanbedrog is on the A497/A499 roads. Own car park

What to see Lleyn Peninsula, Plas-yn-Rhiw, Criccieth Castle.

Criccieth Castle

Lleyn Peninsula

The Angel Hotel

The Tea Guild's Top City & Country Hotel 2011

Elegant former coaching inn on the edge of the Brecon Beacons

15 Cross Street,
ABERGAVENNY, NP7 5EN
Monmouthshire
Tel 01873 857121
e-mail mail@angelhotelabergavenny.com
web www.angelhotelabergavenny.com

The elegant Angel Hotel is in the centre of Abergavenny. Afternoon Tea is served in the restaurant at tables set with crisp linen and bone china, in the Sitting Room or, in fine weather, in the secluded courtyard. Specialist baker Sally Lane and her team bake scones, cakes, pastries and savouries every day, from custard slices and orange sponge to the more unusual beetroot cake. A wide range of teas and infusions is on offer, with the seasonal addition of other drinks including homemade lemonade and mulled wine. Champagne Afternoon Tea is perfect for a special occasion and the most recent addition is High Tea which includes savouries such as devils on horseback, sausage rolls and tomato, mozzarella and pesto tartlets.

To eat Afternoon Tea, High Tea, Champagne Afternoon Tea, Champagne High Tea

Open Daily 9am-11pm. Tea served Mon-Fri 3pm-5.30pm, Sat-Sun 3.30pm-5.30pm

Getting there Good road, rail and bus links.

What to see Blaenavon World Heritage Site, Raglan Castle, Llanthony Priory.

Walk

Blorenge – bird's-eye view of Abergavenny

A short sortie and some marvellous views.

Start/finish: Grid ref SO 270109

Parking: Small car park at Carn-y-gorfydd

Distance: 3 miles/4.8km

Level of difficulty: ● ● ●

Suggested map: OS Explorer OL13 Brecon Beacons National Park Eastern area

Walk directions

1 From Carn-y-gorfydd Roadside Rest, walk downhill for 500yds (457m) and bear **L**, through green barrier, on to grassy track.

2 This leads easily uphill, through tangle of bracken, eventually allowing great views over Usk Valley towards outlying peak of Ysgyryd Fawr.

3 As path levels you'll pass small hut. Continue along escarpment edge, on one of series of terraces

that contour above steep escarpment, and enjoy views over Abergavenny and Black Mountains. Rough ground was formed by the quarrying of stone.

4 Return to hut and bear **R**, on to faint, grassy track that crosses flat ground and small boggy patch before climbing slightly and becoming stony. Away to **R**, you should be able to make out pronounced hump of Bronze Age burial cairn. Path now leads easily to trig point and huge cairn that mark summit.

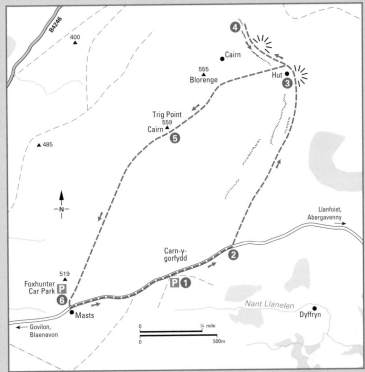

5 Continue in same direction, drop down past impressive limestone outcrop and towards huge masts on skyline. You should also be able to see extensive spoil heaps on flanks of Gilwern Hill, directly ahead.

6 At masts, you'll cross Foxhunter Car Park to meet road where you turn **L** and continue easily downhill, for 600yds (549m), back to start.

Carriages Tea Rooms – Old Station Tintern

The high quality of the teas here belies its past as a British Rail station

TINTERN,
Gwent, NP16 7NX
Tel 01291 689566

Railway food never tasted as good as it does at this unusual stop for tea, where you can choose to sit inside the old, carefully restored Victorian waiting room. Traditional cream teas are available, with strawberries in season, over a dozen blends of tea (including Fairtrade and herbal infusions) and the house speciality, the Tintern cheese platter. Booking is required for large groups. Outside is a picnic area with views of gently sloping hills, the signal box houses art exhibitions, and two old carriages have historical displays, a shop and tourist information.

To eat Cream tea. Light lunches.

Open Apr 1-Nov 1, daily 9:30am-5:30pm.

Getting there Tintern station is on the A466 Monmouth-Chepstow road. Car park is available.

What to see Tintern Abbey, Wye Valley, the Forest of Dean, Clearwell Caves and Ancient Iron Mines, Chepstow Castle, Nelson Museum and Local History Centre in Monmouth.

Old Printing House

From 'Just Off the Press' to 'Just Out of the Oven'

20 Main Street,
SOLVA,
Pembrokeshire, SA62 6UU
Tel 01437 721603
e-mail wendi_edwards@btinternet.com

The local paper was once produced in this 18th-century building, which has now been converted into a charming café. All the dishes are made by hand, and you are encouraged to ask where your food came from. A selection of Welsh food and drinks is served, such as bara brith (a tea bread) and Glengettie loose leaf tea. The Welsh cakes and scones are made every day and served with Sharon's home made jam and Drim Farm clotted cream. Look for the 'Just Out of the Oven' board to decide which of the freshly baked cakes to try. They also serve gluten-free cakes and a special savoury cream tea.

To eat Afternoon Tea, Savoury Cream Tea. Snacks.

Open Feb-Oct daily.

Getting there On main street in Lower Solva next to Window on Wales

What to see Solva Woollen Mill, St David's Bishop's Palace, Pembrokeshire Coast National Park.

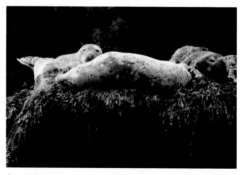

Grey seals

Llangoed Hall

Creeper-clad Jacobean/Edwardian great house

LLYSWEN,
Powys, LD3 0YP
Tel 01874 754525
e-mail enquiries@llangoedhall.com
web www.llangoedhall.com

The Welsh Parliament once stood on this spot, and the great country house that is now Llangoed Hall is suitably impressive. Tea is served in the gracious lounge, the bright garden room, the cheerful morning room, and the grand library. Reservations are accepted, but you can just turn up any afternoon for the cream tea and enjoy scones, clotted cream, jam and Welsh cakes. You will need to give 24-hours' notice for the speciality full afternoon tea, but it is well worth a bit of advance planning.

To eat Cream tea, full afternoon tea.

Open Daily. Tea served Mon-Fri 2pm-5pm, Sat-Sun 3pm-5pm.

Getting there On A470 between Brecon and Builth Wells.

What to see Brecon Beacons National Park, Brecknock Museum and Art Gallery in Brecon, Royal Regiment of Wales Museum in Brecon.

Gliffaes Hotel

A country house hotel, high in the Usk Valley

CRICKHOWELL,
Powys, NP8 1RH
Tel 01874 730371
web www.gliffaeshotel.com

A narrow winding road is the scenic route to this charming hotel, where the atmosphere is one of friendliness and informality. Great care is taken here to maintain the best standards of British cooking, and this extends to all the treats on offer for afternoon tea. All of the cakes are made on the premises, and there is a selection of teas to choose from.

To eat Afternoon tea. Light lunches and sandwiches.

Open Daily. Tea served 4pm-5:30pm.

Getting there The hotel is just off the A40 on the B4558. Own car park.

What to see Crickhowell Castle, Black Mountains, Brecon Beacons National Park, Tretower Court and Castle.

Old Stables Tearooms

 The Tea Guild's Award of Excellence 2011

Award winner in the world famous book town

Bear Street,
HAY-ON-WYE, HR3 5AN
Tel 01497 821557
e-mail info@chefontherunfoods.co.uk
web www.chefontherunfoods.co.uk

Chef on the run, Mike Carnell, with his wife Rachel and daughter Katie run this friendly award-winning tearoom serving fine food and, in particular, a splendid range of home made cakes and preserves, including an award-winning grapefruit and ginger marmalade. The atmosphere here is welcoming, and there is a pretty courtyard for warmer days. A range of set teas is available, which include bara brith (the traditional Welsh fruit cake), and a choice of 30 varieties of top quality teas, including their speciality, Rose Pouchong.

To eat Cream tea, Afternoon tea, High tea. Light lunches. Full meals Snacks

Open Bank Holidays and Tue-Sat 10:30am-4:30pm (summer) or 3pm (winter)

Getting there In town centre near Buttermarket and Bullring.

What to see Hay-on-Wye bookshops, Hay Castle, River Wye

The Drover's Rest Tea Rooms

A far tastier treat than the sulphur springs for which the town is known

The Square, LLANWRTYD WELLS,
Powys, LD5 4RA
Tel 01591 610264
e-mail foodfoodfood@lycos.com
web www.food-food-food.co.uk

The Drover's Rest has been welcoming travellers with courtesy, good food and a smile for many years, and long may it continue to do so. Along with its five blends of tea, you can enjoy a traditional afternoon tea, with Welsh cakes as the speciality – either instead of, or in addition to, the delicious scones with jam and cream. This place is deservedly popular, so it's advisable to make a reservation if you plan to visit in summer or on a Sunday.

To eat Cream tea, afternoon tea. Light lunches and sandwiches.

Open Tue, Thu-Sun 10.30am-4pm.

Getting there Llanwrtyd Wells is on the A483 road. Parking in the town.

What to see Elan Valley reservoirs, Brecon Beacons National Park, Brecknock Museum and Art Gallery in Brecon, Royal Regiment of Wales Museum in Brecon.

Bank Cottage Tea Rooms

The epitome of tea, tranquility and comfort

The Bank,
NEWTOWN,
Powys, SY16 2AB
Tel 01686 625771

In the rural heartland of Wales, this exceptional tea room offers a splendid range of cakes, pastries, sandwiches and light meals, with some 15 blends of tea to complete the experience. Welsh cream teas are a particular treat, especially for those who have worked up an appetite walking in the nearby countryside or exploring the town's historic heritage. The speciality of the house, though, is homity pie.

To eat Cream tea. Light lunches and snacks.

Open Mon-Fri 9am-5pm, Sat 10am-4pm.

Getting there Newtown is on the A483 and A489 roads. Parking in the town.

What to see Glansevern Hall Gardens at Berriew, Montgomery Castle, Powis Castle at Welshpool, Welshpool and Llanfair Light Railway.

Waterfall, Brecon Beacons National Park

Scotland

River Spey, Boat of Garten

The Coach House Coffee Shop

A village coffee shop on the western shore of Loch Lomond

Loch Lomond Trading Co Ltd,
LUSS,
Argyle and Bute, G83 8NN
Tel 01436 860341
e-mail enquiries@lochlomondtrading.com
web www.lochlomondtrading.com

Luss provides the delightful setting for Rowena Ferguson's café and gift shop, where you are likely to be welcomed by a log fire and Gaelic music. It is called a coffee shop, but has plenty to offer the tea connoisseur. Light meals and snacks with a Scottish flavour are served in generous portions accompanied by your choice of tea. Home-made soup, home-baked rolls and free range eggs from their own hens are featured. Speciality fruit cakes are laced with malt whisky or baked with ale and studded with crystallised ginger. Goods available for sale include teas, coffees, teapots, confectionary and cakes.

To eat Light meals and snacks.

Open Open daily. Tea served 10am–5pm.

Getting there Turn off A82 at signpost for Luss. Located next to the church. Parking available in the main village car park.

What to see Loch Lomond Cruises, Luss Glen, Ben Lomond and Ben Arthur, Lock Lomond and The Trossachs National Park.

The Grand Tea Lounge

The Tea Guild's Award of Excellence 2011

The welcome return of an Edwardian tradition

Turnberry Resort, Maidens Road, TURNBERRY KA26 9ZT
Tel 01655 331000
e-mail turnberry@luxurycollection.com
web www.luxurycollection.com/turnberry

When Turnberry first opened in 1906, the heart of this renowned hotel was the elegant Tea Lounge. It was here that the guests, freshly disembarked from the train at the hotel's own station, would savour afternoon tea while their servants prepared their rooms. The railway station may be long gone but the hotel is delighted to be reviving this fine tradition more than a hundred years later. Now, as then, the Grand Tea Lounge serves lunch and a truly memorable afternoon tea in an atmosphere of relaxed refinement. Let their tea sommeliers guide you through a choice of thirty or so teas, all brewed to order using a traditional samovar, and created in collaboration with Twinings. The selection might include Jasmine Pearls, White Silver Tips, Taiwanese High Mountain Oolong or Puerh, as well as their own Turnberry blend. The Grand Tea Lounge also has a choice of Champagne by the glass and a light menu of sandwiches and pastries. The Turnberry Tea includes finger sandwiches and Viennese bridge rolls, freshly baked scones and tea cakes with clotted cream and homemade strawberry preserve, as well as assorted pastries, all washed down by your choice of tea from the sommelier's trolley.

To eat Lunches, teas

Open 9am-5pm (Afternoon tea served 2pm-5pm)

Getting there Take A77 southbound towards Stranraer, 2m past Kirkoswald turn right for Turnberry

What to do Culzean Castle and Country Park; Golf; Robert Burns Museum in Alloway

Abbey Cottage Tea Rooms

The Tea Guild's Award
of Excellence 2011

Attractive cottage tea rooms next to Sweetheart Abbey

26 Main Street,
NEW ABBEY,
Dumfries, DG2 8BY
Tel 01387 850377
e-mail morag@abbeycottagetearoom.com
web www.abbeycottagetearoom.com

Quality is the watchword at this highly acclaimed tea rooms, where morning coffee, light lunches and afternoon teas are all freshly prepared on the premises, using the best of ingredients from mainly local suppliers. Home-made pâtés and organic bread, locally produced haggis and organic farmhouse cheeses are a speciality. They serve 11 different types of carefully brewed and selected teas, which in warm weather you can enjoy in the garden overlooking the Abbey. Abbey Cottage has its own well-stocked gift shop with fresh smoked local produce, an award-winning local butcher, and many other local organic sources. They also cater for vegetarians and other dietary needs.

To eat Set teas. Light lunches.

Open Apr-Oct, daily 10am-5pm. Nov, Dec, Feb & Mar Wed-Sun 11am-4pm

Getting there From Dumfries take A710 Solway Coast Road. Abbey Cottage is beside the car park of Sweetheart Abbey.

What to see Sweetheart Abbey, New Abbey Corn Mill, Shambellie House Museum of Costume.

Balmoral Hotel – Palm Court

The Tea Guild's Award of Excellence 2011

Edinburgh's most stylish afternoon tea

1 Princes Street,
EDINBURGH, EH2 2EQ
Tel 0131 556 2414
e-mail reservations.balmoral@roccofortecollection.com
web www.thebalmoralhotel.com,
web www.roccofortecollection.com

A harpist plays gentle music on the balcony of this very elegant setting with its Venetian chandelier and palm trees. The Balmoral Tea is served in the traditional style with an interesting choice of sandwiches, and delicious home made scones, such as fruit, heather honey and chocolate scones. The Balmoral Bakery prepares all these as well as many tempting pastries and cakes. A selection of twenty carefully selected loose leaf teas is on offer, and the tea can also be enjoyed with a glass of Champagne.

To eat Balmoral Afternoon Tea. Sandwiches

Open Daily 1:30pm-5:30pm

Getting there In Edinburgh city centre.

What to see Edinburgh Castle, Museum of Scotland, Palace of Holyrood House

Caledonian Hilton

Experience traditional afternoon tea with stunning views of Edinburgh Castle or Princes Street

Princes Street, EDINBURGH, EH1 2AB
Tel 0131 222 8888
e-mail guest.caledonian@hilton.com
web www.hilton.co.uk/caledonian

Originally built in 1903, as part of the Caledonian Railway Station, The Caledonian Hilton has long been a distinguished landmark on the Edinburgh skyline. Tea is served in the splendid and elegant Pompadour Restaurant. Friendly staff are eager to please and tea here is a treat for all the family – especially since the introduction of the specially designed Children's Afternoon Tea menu. For grown ups there's the Caley Afternoon Tea – freshly cut finger sandwiches, home-made fruit and plain scones with clotted cream and strawberry jam and followed by a delicious selection of cakes; strawberry tarts (a wonderful Scottish summertime tradition), fresh fruit and cream meringues, mini Battenberg, tea cakes and pistachio cream cakes to name a few. The well described and carefully chosen tea menu includes a great choice, from Caledonian Royal Scottish, Blue Lady and Nilgiri to China Teas including Keemun Congou and Lapsang Souchong. If you want to experiment a little the Display Tea Menu offers Chun Mee, Jade Pyramid, Snow Dragon and Jade Zeppelin. There really is a tea to suit everyone here. Booking is essential.

To eat Caley Afternoon Tea, Children's Afternoon Tea, Caley Celebration Afternoon Tea

Open daily, 2pm-5pm

Getting there Please see website for directions

What to see Shopping on Princes Street, Edinburgh Castle, the Royal Mile, Edinburgh Zoo

The Exchange at Sheraton Grand Hotel & Spa

Seasonal delights at this smart, central hotel

1 Festival Square,
EDINBURGH, EH3 9SR
Tel 0131 221 6422
e-mail grandedinburgh@sheraton.com
web www.sheratonedinburgh.com

The Exchange is the popular lounge bar of this central Edinburgh hotel. It is elegant and spacious – the ideal place to relax after sightseeing or shopping. Traditional Afternoon Tea comes with finger sandwiches, Viennoise bridge rolls, freshly baked scones and tea cakes with Devonshire clotted cream and preserves and a selection of the pastry chef's fine cakes. Fourteen different teas from around the world are available. An innovative idea is the Seasonal Afternoon Tea, using ingredients appropriate to the time of year.

To eat Traditional Afternoon Tea, Champagne Afternoon Tea, Seasonal Afternoon Teas.

Open Daily 2:30pm-5:30pm.

Getting there Off the west end of Princes Street on Western Approach Road just before the EICC.

What to see Edinburgh Castle, Royal Mile, Palace of Holyroodhouse.

Walk

Edinburgh New Town – luring the literati

A walk in the footsteps of literary giants

Start/finish: Grid ref NT 257739

Parking: Several large car parks in central Edinburgh

Distance: 3 miles/4.8km

Level of difficulty: ● ● ●

Suggested map: AA Street by Street Edinburgh

Walk directions

1 From tourist information centre, turn **L** and walk along Princes Street. Pass Scott Monument on **L**, cross road to reach Jenners department store. Continue along Princes Street; take **R** turn up Hanover Street.

2 Take second turning on **L** and walk along George Street to reach elegant Charlotte Square. Turn **R** and **R** again to go along Young Street. At end, turn **L** and walk down North Castle Street to reach Queen Street.

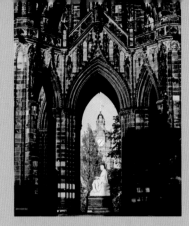

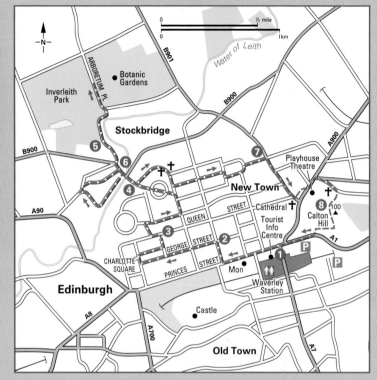

3 Cross road, turn **L**, then **R** down Wemyss Place and **R** into Heriot Row. When you reach Howe Street turn **L** and, before you reach church in middle of street, turn **L** and walk along South East Circus Place. Walk past sweep of Royal Circus and then down into Stockbridge.

4 Cross bridge, then turn **L** along Dean Terrace. At end, turn **R** into Ann Street. When you reach Dean Park Crescent turn **R** and follow road round into Leslie Place and into Stockbridge again. Cross main road, turn **L** and then **R** at traffic lights down St Bernard's Row. Follow this, then bear **L** into Arboretum Avenue.

5 Follow this road past Water of Leith down to Inverleith Terrace. Cross and walk up Arboretum Place to Botanic Gardens entrance on **R**. Turn **L** after visiting gardens and retrace your steps to Stockbridge.

6 Turn **L** at Hectors bar and walk uphill; turn **L** along St Stephen Street. At church follow road, cross over Cumberland Street then turn **L** along Great King Street. At end, turn **R**, then immediately **L** to walk along Drummond Place, past Dublin Street and continue ahead into London Street.

7 At roundabout turn **R** and walk up Broughton Street to reach Picardy Place. Turn **L**, walk past statue of Sherlock Holmes, then bear **L** towards Playhouse Theatre. Cross, continue **L**, then turn **R** into Leopold Place and **R** again into Blenheim Place. At church turn **R**, walk up steps and turn **L** at meeting of paths.

8 Go up steps on **R**, walk over Calton Hill, then turn **R** to pass canon. Go downhill, take steps on **L** and walk into Regent Road. Turn **R** and walk back into Princes Street and start.

Loopy Lorna's Tea House

The Tea Guild's Award of Excellence 2011

Eclectic décor, friendly atmosphere and excellent teas

372 Morningside Road, EDINBURGH, EH10 5HS
(also at The Church Hill Theatre, 33a Morningside Road, EH104DR)
Tel 0131 447 9217 / 0131 447 3042
e-mail hello@loopylornas.com **web** www.loopylornas.com

A friendly atmosphere and quirky surroundings, complimented by an amazing array of hand-knitted cosies keeping the excellent teas at just the right temperature! Loopy Lorna's Tea House (named after the owner's mother) has been widely acclaimed since opening in October 2008, winning awards and gaining a growing number of loyal customers. Loopy Lorna's pride themselves on serving delightful cakes, all baked on the premises, alongside an excellent selection of tea, working with a Master Tea Blender to obtain the best possible choices - 18 loose leaf teas are on offer. They are also proud of their excellent reputation for customer service. Due to increasing demand they opened a second premises in August 2010, combining the same warm ambience with enough space for buggies and a small play area, as well as catering for parties and private functions. Afternoon Tea includes a selection of dainty sandwiches, freshly baked scones served with Cornish clotted cream and homemade preserve, as well as a selection of home baked treats. Accompany this with a pot of tea from the main or speciality menus.

To eat Breakfast, lunches, snack and light bites plus Cream Teas and Traditional Afternoon Teas

Open 7 days 9am-5pm – breakfasts 9am-12noon, lunches / light meals 12noon-4.30pm

Getting there From the city centre, follow directions for Carlisle and Bigger and this will lead you to Morningside Road.

What to see Holyrood Park, Holyrood Palace, Princes Street, Edinburgh Castle

Kind Kyttock's Kitchen

Traditional Scottish tea rooms in an historic setting

Cross Wynd,
FALKLAND,
Fife, KY15 7BE
Tel 01337 857477
e-mail qdalrymple@yahoo.co.uk

The picturesque village of Falkland is dominated by Falkland Palace, the hunting palace of the Stuart monarchs, and close by is the very hospitable Kind Kyttock's tea rooms, where all the produce is made on the premises. A wide variety of snacks, soups, sandwiches, salads and sweets is served, and the set afternoon tea includes a pot of tea from a menu offering a choice of 15, including their own blend, together with a scone and pancake, plus a choice of home-made preserves and two home-made cakes. Specialities include Cloutie dumplings, apple tart and Irish soda bread. Children are welcome and high chairs are provided. A small selection of

items is offered for sale.

To eat Set tea. Light lunches.

Open Tue-Sun 10:30am-5:30pm. Tea served all day.

Getting there Falkland is on the A912. Nearest motorway M90. Street parking and car parks.

What to see Falkland Palace, Falkland Estate for country walks, Golf at St Andrews.

Walk

St Andrews – academic traditions
A town trail to an ancient monument

Start/finish: Grid ref NO 506170

Parking: Free parking along The Scores, otherwise several car parks

Distance: 4.5 miles/7.2km

Level of difficulty: ● ● ●

Suggested map: OS Explorer 371 St Andrews & East Fife

Walk directions

❶ With Martyrs Monument on The Scores in front of you, walk **L** past bandstand. At road turn **R**, walk to British Golf Museum, then turn **L**. Pass clubhouse of Royal and Ancient Golf Club on **L**, then bear **R** at burn to reach beach.

❷ Route now goes along West Sands. Walk as far as you choose, then either retrace your steps along beach or take any path through dunes to join tarmac road. Walk back to Golf Museum, then turn **R** and walk to main road.

3 Turn **L** along road and walk to St Salvator's College. Peek through archway at serene quadrangle – and look at initials PH in cobbles outside. They commemorate Patrick Hamilton, who was martyred here in 1528 – they say students who tread on the site will fail their exams. Cross over and walk to end of College Street.

4 Turn **R** and walk along Market Street. At corner turn **L** along Bell Street, then **L** again on South Street. Opposite Holy Trinity Church, turn R down Queens Gardens to reach Queens Terrace.

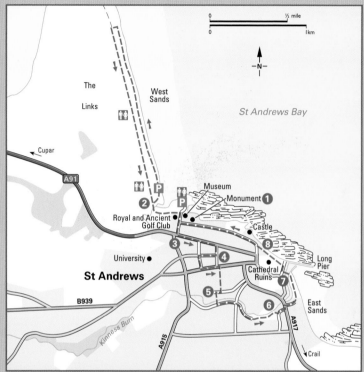

5 Turn **R** then immediately **L** down steeply sloping Dempster Terrace. At end cross burn, turn **L** and walk to main road. Cross and walk along Glebe Road. At park, take path that bears **L**, walk past play area and up to Woodburn Terrace.

6 Turn **L** to join St Mary Street and cross main road to follow Woodburn Place down towards beach. Just before slipway, turn **L** along tarmac path. Cross

footbridge and join road.

7 Bear **R** for few paces, then ascend steps on **L** to the remains of a church and famous ruined cathedral. Gate in wall on **L** gives access to site.

8 Route then follows beachfront past ancient castle on **R**, a former palace/fortress. Pass Castle Visitor Centre, then continue along The Scores to return to start.

The Old Course Hotel

Traditional afternoon tea with a surprising variation

ST ANDREWS,
Fife, KY16 9SP
Tel 01334 474371
e-mail reservations@oldcoursehotel.co.uk
web www.oldcoursehotel.co.uk

Afternoon tea at the Old Course Hotel is a world-class affair, with the world's most famous golf course serving as a truly unique backdrop. The award-wining experience offers a delicious selection of delicate pastries and cakes, created by the hotel's pastry chef, including plain and fruit scones, and lemon pancakes with clotted cream and strawberry and pink champagne preserve. Choose from a collection of rare teas, including the Flowering Sliver Tip Tea which blossoms as it infuses to reveal three Marigold flowers.

To eat Afternoon tea, Champagne afternoon tea.

Open Daily. Tea served 2pm-4pm.

Getting there Close to A91 on outskirts of the town when travelling from Cupar.

What to see St Andrews Museum, British Golf Museum, St Andrews Deer Centre.

Willow Tea Rooms

Stunning and beautiful tea room with food to match

97 Buchanan Street,
GLASGOW, G1 3HF
Tel 0141 204 5242
e-mail buchananstreet@willowtearooms.co.uk
web www.willowtearooms.co.uk

The Willow theme of placing strikingly beautiful furniture against a calm and tasteful background works as well here as at the sister tea shop in Sauchiehall Street (see page 287). The same architect, Charles Rennie Mackintosh, was responsible for the designs at the turn of the last century, when he created a series of tea shops for Kate Cranston. Upstairs is the blue Chinese Room with small furniture, while downstairs the amazing high-backed chairs are impossible to ignore. Tea is something of a distraction, though, with its classic afternoon selection served with a wide range of fine teas. There are plenty of savoury and sweet choices throughout the day too.

To eat Set teas. Light lunches.

Open Mon-Sat Tea served 9am-4:30pm. Sun 11am-4:15pm. Tea served all day.

Getting there In city centre off the A77, A80 and A82. Nearest motorway M8, M73 and M74. Meter parking and town car parks.

What to see House for an Art Lover, The Lighthouse, Clydebuilt, Glasgow Cathedral, Pollock House, Glasgow Science Centre.

The Willow Café & Gift Shop at Scotland Street School Museum

Modern tea room in Art Nouveau school

225 Scotland Street
GLASGOW, G5 8QB
Tel 0141 287 0502

Scotland Street School is one of Charles Rennie Mackintosh's iconic buildings. It was designed between 1903 and 1905, and is now a museum vividly demonstrating what education must have been like in those days. The proprietrix of the famous Willow Tea Rooms has opened a brand new tea room to enjoy while visiting this fascinating building. The décor is smart and modern, perfectly in keeping with the rest of the school. It is a welcoming place for families and is based on the principle that good food is not processed or manufactured miles away, but is made on the premises. Home made soups and bakeries are especially enticing – a far cry from old fashioned school dinners. The decorative stands of Afternoon Tea are particularly compelling as well as being reasonably priced. A wide selection of 26 loose leaf teas, herbal teas and infusions has been carefully selected for their flavours – a special MACS blend combines the best Ceylon and Assam teas.

To eat Afternoon Tea, snacks, lunches.

Open daily 10am-5pm (Fri, Sun open at 11am).

Getting there South side of River Clyde opposite Shields Road underground station and car park.

What to see Scotland Street School, Glasgow Science Centre, Burrell Collection.

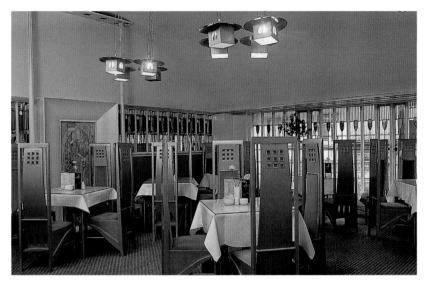

The Willow Tearoom

Stylish historic tea rooms in the heart of the city

217 Sauchiehall Street,
GLASGOW, G2 3EX
Tel 0141 332 0521
e-mail sauchiehallstreet@willowtearooms.co.uk
web www.willowtearooms.co.uk

Stunning designs, including tall silver chairs in futuristic styles and mirrored friezes, are a talking point when guests first enter this smart tea room. Located above a jewellery shop in this famous street, The Willow goes back to 1903, when Charles Rennie Mackintosh created a series of tea shops for owner Kate Cranston. The food served here is more than a match for the striking setting, and afternoon tea is a popular ritual with the city's many tourists. Enjoy a selection of sandwiches, scones with preserves and cream, a choice of cakes and a delicious pot of loose leaf tea chosen from the wide range available.

To eat Set teas. Light lunches.

Open Mon-Sat 9am-4:30pm, Sun 11am-4:15pm. Tea served all day.

Getting there In city centre off the A77, A80 and A82. Nearest motorways M8, M73 and M74. Meter parking and town car parks.

What to see Pollock House, Glasgow Science Centre, Glasgow School of Art, Glasgow Cathedral, Mugdock Country Park, People's Palace and Winter Gardens.

Cup Glasgow

Timeless tearoom, serving luxury blends in Glasgow's West End

311 Byres Road, Glasgow G12 8UQ
Tel 0141 357 2525
e-mail enquiries@cupglasgow.co.uk
web www.cupglasgow.co.uk

Located in the leafy and cosmopolitan West End of Glasgow, this tea room is decorated in a classically contemporary style and offers timeless tradition in ambience and service alike. Cup offers tea, coffee and food from early morning through to early evening. There is a great selection of over 30 teas (black, oolong, white, green and fruit infusions) sourced from luxury London tea retailer Tea Palace. Cup is the only tea room in Scotland serving these exquisite teas. The Afternoon Tea is available every day and includes freshly prepared sandwiches and home-baked scones, topped off with sweet delights including a Cup signature cupcake.

To eat: Afternoon Tea

Open: 10am–6pm

Getting there Located on Byres Road in the West End of Glasgow

What to see: Glasgow Botanic Gardens, Glasgow University, Kevlingrove Art Galleries, Loch Lomond

The Tea Guild Awards 2009

TOP TEA PLACE – AWARD WINNER:

BRIDGE TEA ROOMS (BRADFORD-ON-AVON, WILTSHIRE)

TOP LONDON TEA PLACE – AWARD WINNER:

THE ENGLISH TEAROOM AT BROWN'S HOTEL

The following establishments received an Award of Excellence in 2009

Abbey Cottage Tea Rooms
(New Abbey, Dumfries & Galloway)

The Angel Hotel
(Abergavenny, Monmouthshire)

Ashdown Park Hotel
(Wych Cross, East Sussex)

The Athenaeum
(London W1)

Badgers Café and Patisserie
(Llandudno, Conwy)

Bettys Café Tea Rooms
(Harrogate, North Yorkshire)

Bettys Café Tea Rooms
(Ilkley, West Yorkshire)

Bettys Café Tea Rooms
(Northallerton, North Yorkshire)

Bettys Café Tea Rooms
(York, North Yorkshire)

Bettys at RHS Gardens Harlow Carr
(Harrogate, North Yorkshire)

**The Black Swan Tea Tearoom
    at The Black Swan Hotel**
(Helmsley, Yorkshire)

Bullivant of York
(York, North Yorkshire)

Cemlyn Tea Room
(Harlech, Gwynedd)

Charlotte's Tea House
(Truro, Cornwall)

The Chesterfield, Mayfair
(London W1)

Claris's
(Biddenden, Kent)

The Corn Dolly
(South Molton, Devon)

De Grey's
(Ludlow, Shropshire)

de Wynn's
(Falmouth, Cornwall)

The Dorchester
(London W1)

Elizabeth Botham & Sons
(Whitby, North Yorkshire)

Flying Fifteens
(Lowestoft, Suffolk)

Gilbert White's Tea Parlour
(Selbourne, Hampshire)

Ginger & Pickles
(Nantwich, Cheshire)

The Goring
(London SW1)

Hazelmere Café & Bakery
(Grange-over-Sands, Cumbria)

Juri's – The Olde Bakery Tea Shoppe
(Winchcombe, Gloucestershire)

Kind Kyttock's Kitchen
(Falkland, Fife)

Lainston House Hotel
(Sparshot, Winchester, Hampshire)

The Lanesborough
(London SW1)

Little Bettys
(York, North Yorkshire)

Lock House Tea Rooms
(Long Eaton, Nottinghamshire)

Manor House Hotel
(Castle Combe, Wiltshire)

Marshmallow Tearooms & Restaurant
(Moreton-in-Marsh, Gloucestershire)

The Milestone
(London W8)

Moggerhanger Park Tearooms
(Moggerhanger Park, Bedfordshire)

Muffins Tea Shop
(Lostwithiel, Cornwall)

Old School Tearoom
(Carburton, Nottinghamshire)

Old Stables Tea Rooms
(Hay-on-Wye, Powys)

Ollerton Watermill Tea Shop
(Ollerton, Nottinghamshire)

Orange Pekoe
(Barnes, SW13)

The Palm Court at The Balmoral Hotel
(Princes Street, Edinburgh)

The Park Lane Hotel
(London W1)

Peacocks Tearoom
(Ely, Cambridgeshire)

Rectory Farm Tearooms
(Morwenstow, nr Bude, Cornwall)

The Ritz
(London W1)

The River Bar at The Lowry
(The Lowry Hotel, Salford, Manchester)

Roses Tea Rooms
(Heswall, Wirral, Cheshire)

Searcy at the Pump Room
(Bath, Somerset)

Swinton Park
(Swinton Park, Masham, North Yorkshire)

Tea on the Green
(Danbury, Essex)

The Tea Shop
(Wadebridge, Cornwall)

Tisanes Tea Rooms
(Broadway, Worcestershire)

The Wolseley
(London W1)

The Tea Guild Awards 2010

TOP TEA PLACE – AWARD WINNER:

THE BLACK SWAN TEAROOM & PATISSERIE (HELMSLEY, NORTH YORKSHIRE)

TOP LONDON TEA PLACE – AWARD WINNER:

THE LANGHAM (The Palm Court)

TOP CITY & COUNTRY HOTEL – AWARD WINNER:

THE MANOR HOUSE HOTEL (CASTLE COMBE, WILTSHIRE)

The following establishments received an Award of Excellence in 2010

Abbey Cottage Tea Rooms
(New Abbey, Dumfries)
Abbey Tea Rooms & Restaurant
(Tewkesbury, Gloucestershire)
The Angel Hotel
(Abergavenny, Monmouthshire)
The Ashdown Park Hotel
(Wych Cross, East Sussex)
The Athenaeum
(London W1)
**The Balmoral Hotel –
   The Palm Court**
(Princes Street, Edinburgh)
**Bettys at RHS
   Gardens Harlow Carr**
(Harrogate, North Yorkshire)
Bettys Café Tea Rooms
(Harrogate, North Yorkshire)
Bettys Café Tea Rooms
(Ilkley, West Yorkshire)
Bettys Café Tea Rooms
(Northallerton, North Yorkshire)
Bettys Café Tea Rooms
(York, North Yorkshire)
Bingham
(Richmond, Surrey)
The Bridge Tea Rooms
(Bradford-on-Avon, Wiltshire)

Brown's Hotel
(London W1)
Bullivant of York
(York, North Yorkshire)
Cemlyn Tea Room
(Harlech, Gwynedd)
Charlotte's Tea House
(Truro, Cornwall)
Cheristow Lavender Tea Rooms
(Hartland, Devon)
Claridge's
(London W1)
Claris's
(Biddenden, Kent)
The Corn Dolly
(South Molton, Devon)
Cream Tea Room
(Stow on the Wold, Gloucestershire)
Dartmoor Tearooms & Café
(Moretonhampstead, Devon)
De Grey's
(Ludlow, Shropshire)
de Wynn's
(Falmouth, Cornwall)
The Dorchester
(London W1)
Elizabeth Botham & Sons
(Whitby, North Yorkshire)

Flying Fifteens
(Lowestoft, Suffolk)
Gilbert White's Tea Parlour
(Selbourne, Hampshire)
The Goring
(London SW1)
Grosvenor House Park Room & Library
(London W1)
Hazelmere Café & Bakery
(Grange-over-Sands, Cumbria)
**Juri's – The Olde
   Bakery Tea Shoppe**
(Winchcombe, Gloucestershire)
The Landmark London
(London NW1)
The Lanesborough
(London SW1)
Little Bettys
(York, North Yorkshire)
Lock House Tea Rooms
(Long Eaton, Nottinghamshire)
**The Lowry - The River
   Bar & Restaurant**
(Salford, Manchester)
Mandarin Oriental Hyde Park
(London SW1)
**Marshmallow Tearooms
   & Restaurant**
(Moreton-in-Marsh, Gloucestershire)
The Milestone
(London W8)
Moggerhanger Park Tearooms
(Moggerhanger Park, Bedfordshire)
**The Montagu at Hyatt Regency
London – The Churchill**
(London W1)
Muffins Tea Shop
(Lostwithiel, Cornwall)
Old School Tearoom
(Carburton, Nottinghamshire)
Ollerton Watermill Tea Shop
(Ollerton, Nottinghamshire)

Orange Pekoe
(Barnes, SW13)
The Park Lane Hotel
(London W1)
Peacocks Tearoom
(Ely, Cambridgeshire)
Pennyhill Park Hotel & Spa
(Bagshot, Surrey)
The Quarterdeck at
The Nare Hotel
(Veryan, Cornwall)
Rectory Farm Tearooms
(Morwenstow, Nr Bude, Cornwall)
Regency Tea Rooms
(Jane Austen Centre, Bath, Somerset)
The Ritz
(London W1)
Rocke Cottage Tearooms
(Clungunford, Craven Arms,
Shropshire)
Roses Tea Rooms,
(Heswall, Wirral, Cheshire)
Searcy at The Pump Room
(Bath, Somerset)
Sofitel London St James
(London SW1)
Swinton Park
(Swinton Park, Masham,
North Yorkshire)
Tea on the Green
(Danbury, Essex)
The Tea Shop
(Wadebridge, Cornwall)
Tiffin Tearooms
(Alresford, Hampshire)
Tisanes Tea Rooms
(Broadway, Worcestershire)
Turnberry Resort –
The Grand Tea Lounge
(Turnberry, Ayrshire)
The Wolseley
(London W1)

The Black Swan Tearoom & Patisserie

Establishment Index

*Member of the Tea Guild

Establishment Index *continued*

Location Index

*Member of the Tea Guild

Location Index *continued*

Location Index *continued*

Acknowledgements

The Automobile Association would like to thank the following photographers, companies and picture libraries for their assistance in the preparation of this book.

Abbreviations for the picture credits are as follows – (t) top; (b) bottom; (c) centre; (l) left; (r) right; (AA) AA World Travel Library.

001r AA/John Freeman; 006tr Courtesy Rocke Cottage Tea Rooms; 007tl Courtesy The Tea Guild; 007tr Courtesy The Angel Hotel; 009 ImageDJ/Alamy; 010/011 Lou Linwei/Alamy; 012/013 Tim Whitby/Alamy; 014/015 Aflo Co. Ltd./Alamy; 016/017 AA/Michael Moody; 018 AA/M Birkitt; 019tl Courtesy Moggerhanger Park; 019tr Courtesy Moggerhanger Park; 020 AA/James Tims; 021br AA/Michael Moody; 022 IMAGEPAST/Alamy; 023tl Courtesy Bristol Marriott Royal Hotel; 024 AA/Michael Moody; 025tl AA/Derek Forss; 025tr Courtesy Compleat Angler Hotel; 026bl AA/James Tims; 027bl wda bravo/Alamy; 027r AA/M Birkitt; 028 AA/Tom Mackie; 029 Courtesy Peacocks Tearoom; 030tl Courtesy River Tea Rooms; 030tr Courtesy River Tea Rooms; 031r AA/Chris Coe; 032 AA/Jonathan Welsh; 033tl Courtesy The Chester Grosvenor & Spa; 033br AA/Jeff Beazley; 034tl Courtesy Roses Tea Rooms; 034tr Courtesy Roses Tea Rooms; 035tl Courtesy Ginger and Pickles; 035tr Courtesy Ginger and Pickles; 036 AA/Caroline Jones; 037tl Courtesy de Wynn's; 038tl Courtesy Muffins Tea Room; 038tr Courtesy Muffins Tea Room; 039bl AA/Caroline Jones; 040bl AA/Tom Teegan; 041cr Chris Fredriksson/Alamy; 042tl Courtesy Charlottes Tea House; 042tr Courtesy Charlottes Tea House; 043tl Courtesy The Edgcrumbe; 043r Courtesy Morwellham Quay; 044tl Courtesy Rectory Farm Tearooms; 044tr Courtesy Rectory Farm Tearooms; 045tl Courtesy The Tea Shop; 046tl Courtesy The Nare Hotel; 046tr Courtesy The Nare Hotel; 047 AA/Roger Coulam; 048tl Courtesy The Market Place Tea Shop; 049 AA/Roger Coulam; 050 AA/Peter Sharpe; 051tl Courtesy Rothay Manor; 051br AA/Anna Mockford & Nick Bonetti; 052b AA/S&O Matthews; 053br AA/Tom Mackie; 054bl AA/Roger Coulam; 055tl Courtesy Hazelmere Cafe and Bakery/Jonathan Bean Photography; 055tr Courtesy Hazelmere Cafe and Bakery/Jonathan Bean Photography; 056cl AA/Tom Mackie; 056bl AA/Anna Mockford and Nick Bonetti; 057r AA/

Cameron Lees; 058b AA/Anna Mockford & Nick Bonetti; 059br AA/Tom Mackie; 060tl Courtesy Gillam's Tearoom; 060tr Courtesy Gillam's Tearoom; 061 AA/Tom Mackie; 062tl Courtesy Northern Tea Merchants; 063br AA/Tom Mackie; 064tr AA/Andy Tryner; 064b AA/Tom Mackie; 066bl AA/Tom Mackie; 066br AA/Tom Mackie; 067bl AA/Tom Mackie; 067r AA/A J Hopkins; 068 AA/Nigel Hicks; 069br AA/Adam Burton; 070b AA/John Wood; 071br AA/John Wood; 072tl Courtesy Cheristow Lavender Tea Rooms; 072tr Courtesy Cheristow Lavender Tea Rooms; 073tl Courtesy Dartmoor Tearooms & Café; 073tr Courtesy Dartmoor Tearooms & Café; 074bl AA/Guy Edwardes; 075tl AA/Guy Edwardes; 076bl AA/Nigel Hicks; 077tr Courtesy Georgian Tea-Room; 077bl AA/Nigel Hicks; 078tl Courtesy The Corn Dolly Tea Shop; 079cr Robert Harding Picture Library Ltd/Alamy; 080 AA/Adam Burton; 081br AA/Adam Burton; 082tl Courtesy Mortons House Hotel; 082br AA/Andrew Newey; 083r AA/Andrew Newey; 084 AA/Caroline Jones; 085tl Courtesy Tea on the Green; 086tr Courtesy The Essex Rose Tea House; 087bl AA/Neil Setchfield; 087r AA/Neil Setchfield; 088 AA/Hugh Palmer; 089br AA/Steve Day; 090b AA/Richard Ireland; 091r AA/Richard Ireland; 092bl AA/Rebecca Duke; 093tl Courtesy The Dean Heritage Centre Teashop; 093br AA/Kenya Doran; 094tl Courtesy The Marshmallow; 095tl Courtesy The Cream Tea Rooms; 095tr Courtesy The Cream Tea Rooms; 096tl Courtesy Abbey Tea Rooms & Restaurant; 096tr Courtesy Abbey Tea Rooms & Restaurant; 097tl Courtesy Juri's - The Olde Bakery Tea Shoppe; 097tr Courtesy Juri's - The Olde Bakery Tea Shoppe; 098l AA/Steve Day; 100bl AA/Michael Moody; 101 AA/Steve Day; 102 AA/Colin Molyneux; 103tl Courtesy The Rocco Forte Collection/The Lowry Hotel Manchester; 103tr Courtesy The Rocco Forte Collection/The Lowry Hotel Manchester; 104 AA/Michael Moody; 105tl Courtesy Tiffin Tearooms Alresford; 105tr Courtesy Tiffin Tearooms Alresford; 106tl Courtesy The Montagu Arms Hotel; 106tr Courtesy The Montagu Arms Hotel; 107bl AA/Adam Burton; 107br AA/James Tims; 108tl Courtesy Four Seasons Hotels and Resorts/Four Seasons Hotel Hampshire; 108tr Courtesy Four Seasons Hotels and Resorts/Four Seasons Hotel Hampshire; 109tr Courtesy Tylney Hall Hotel; 109bl AA/Steve Day; 110tl Courtesy Gilbert

White's House & Garden and The Oates Collection/Tea Parlour; 110tr Courtesy Gilbert White's House & Garden and The Oates Collection/Tea Parlour; 111tl Courtesy Exclusive Hotels/Lainston House Hotel; 111tr Courtesy Exclusive Hotels/Lainston House Hotel; 112 AA/Michael Moody; 113tl Courtesy Down Hall Country House Hotel/Martyn Hicks Photography; 113br AA/M Birkitt; 114bl AA/Michael Moody; 115br AA/Clive Sawyer; 116 AA/Neil Setchfield; 117tl Courtesy Claris's Tea Room; 117tr Courtesy Claris's Tea Room; 118b/119bl Tony Watson/Alamy; 120tl Courtesy Secret Garden; 120tr Courtesy Secret Garden; 121 AA/Michael Moody; 122tl Courtesy Tiny Tim's Tearoom; 122tr Courtesy Tiny Tim's Tearoom; 123tr Courtesy The Oast House Tea Rooms; 123bl AA/M Busselle; 124tr Courtesy Fir Tree House Tea Rooms; 124bl AA/Michael Busselle; 125br AA/John Miller; 126tl Courtesy Food for Thought; 126tr Courtesy Food for Thought; 127bl AA/Peter Baker; 127br AA/Neil Setchfield; 128 AA/David Clapp; 129br AA/David Clapp; 130 AA/Andrew Newey; 131tl Courtesy Miss B's Tea Rooms; 131tr Courtesy Miss B's Tea Rooms; 132 AA/Tom Mackie; 133br AA/Tom Mackie; 134bl AA/James Tims; 135tl Tim Whitby/Alamy; 136 AA/Neil Setchfield; 137tl Courtesy The Landmark London Hotel; 137tr Courtesy The Landmark London Hotel; 138tl Courtesy Burgh House; 139tr AA/James Tims; 139bl AA/Sarah Montgomery; 140tl Courtesy The Goring/Christian Trampenau; 140tr Courtesy The Goring; 141tl Courtesy Mandarin Oriental Hyde Park, London; 141tr Courtesy Mandarin Oriental Hyde Park, London/Niall Clutton; 142bl AA/max Jourdan; 143tl AA/James Tims; 144tl Courtesy Sheraton Park Tower; 144tr Courtesy Sheraton Park Tower; 145tl Courtesy Sofitel St James London/The Rose Lounge; 146tl Courtesy The Capital Hotel/Niall Clutton; 146tr Courtesy The Capital Hotel/Tim Winter; 147l AA/Roy Victor; 147r AA/James Tims; 148tl Courtesy Blakes Hotel London; 148tr Courtesy Blakes Hotel London; 149br AA/James Tims; 150tl Courtesy Orange Pekoe/Panayiotis Sinnos; 150tr Courtesy Orange Pekoe/Panayiotis Sinnos; 151tl Courtesy The Athenaeum Hotel; 151tr Courtesy The Athenaeum Hotel; 152tl Courtesy Brown's Hotel/The English Tea Room/Adrian Houston; 152tr Courtesy Brown's Hotel/The English Tea Room; 153tl Courtesy The Chesterfield Mayfair; 154tl Courtesy Espelette at The Connaught; 155tl Courtesy The Dorchester London/The Promenade; 155tr Courtesy The Dorchester London/The Promenade; 156tl Courtesy Claridge's/Paul Raeside; 156tr

Courtesy Claridge's; 157 Courtesy Park Lane Hilton/Podium Restaurant; 157 Courtesy Park Lane Hilton/Podium Restaurant; 158tl Courtesy Grosvenor House Park Room & Library; 158tr Courtesy Grosvenor House Park Room & Library; 159tl Courtesy Hyatt Regency London - The Churchill/The Montagu/Neil Setchfield; 159tr Courtesy Hyatt Regency London - The Churchill/The Montagu; 160b AA/James Tims; 161tr AA/Sarah Montgomery; 162tl Courtesy The Lanesborough; 162tr Courtesy The Lanesborough; 163tl Courtesy The Langham Hotel/The Palm Court; 163tr Courtesy The Langham Hotel/The Palm Court; 164tl Courtesy Le Méridien Piccadilly; 164tr Courtesy Le Méridien Piccadilly; 164tl Courtesy The Park Lane Hotel/The Palm Court Lounge; 165tr Courtesy The Park Lane Hotel/The Palm Court Lounge; 166tl Courtesy The Ritz London/The Palm Court; 166tr Courtesy The Ritz London/The Palm Court; 167tl Courtesy The Rubens at the Palace/Palace Lounge; 167tr Courtesy The Rubens at the Palace/Palace Lounge; 168tr AA/James Tims; 168bl AA/Sarah Montgomery; 169tl Courtesy The Wolseley; 169tr Courtesy The Wolseley; 170tl Courtesy The Milestone Hotel; 171tl Courtesy Royal Garden Hotel/TimWinter; 172tl Courtesy The Montague on the Gardens; 173tl David Levenson/Alamy; 174tl Courtesy Swissôtel The Howard/Mauve Lounge; 175 AA/David Clapp; 176bl AA/Tom Mackie; 177tl Courtesy The Owl Tearoom & Bake Shop; 177br AA/Tom Mackie; 178 Elmtree Images/Alamy; 179tl Courtesy The Apothocoffee Shop; 179br AA/M Birkitt; 180tl Courtesy Towcester Tea Rooms; 180r AA/M Birkitt; 181br Piotr Skubisz/Alamy; 182 AA/Roger Coulam; 183tl Courtesy Matfen Hall Hotel; 183br AA/Roger Coulam; 184 eye35.com/Alamy; 185tl Courtesy Old School Tearoom; 186b Alan Pembleton/Alamy; 188tl Courtesy Lock House Tea Rooms; 189tl Courtesy Ollerton Watermill Tea Shop; 189tr Courtesy Ollerton Watermill Tea Shop; 190 AA/David Hall; 191tl Courtesy Old Parsonage Hotel; 192tl Courtesy Harriet's Cake Shop and Tea Rooms; 192r AA/Caroline Jones; 193br Kirsty McLaren/Alamy; 194 AA/Michael Short; 195tl Courtesy Rocke Cottage Tea Rooms; 195tr Courtesy Rocke Cottage Tea Rooms; 196bl AA/AA; 198bl AA/Rhea Thierstein; 198br AA/Caroline Jones; 199tl Courtesy De Greys Tea Rooms; 199tr Courtesy De Greys Tea Rooms; 200 AA/Richard Ireland; 201tl Courtesy The Jane Austen Centre/Regency Tea Rooms; 201tr Courtesy The Jane Austen Centre/Regency Tea Rooms; 202tl Courtesy The Pump Room, Bath;

203tl Courtesy The Royal Crescent Hotel; 203tr Courtesy Old Bake House; 204tl Courtesy Derrick's Tea Rooms; 204tr Courtesy Derrick's Tea Rooms; 205tl Courtesy The Wishing Well Tea Rooms; 205br AA/James Tims; 206tl Courtesy Ston Easton Park; 206tr Courtesy The Castle at Taunton; 207bl AA/Adam Burton; 207r AA/Nigel Hicks; 208 AA/Tom Mackie; 209br AA/Tom Mackie; 210bl AA/Tom Mackie; 210r AA/Tom Mackie; 211tl Courtesy Flying Fifteens; 212 AA/James Tims; 213tl Courtesy Pennyhill Park Luxury Hotel & Spa; 213tr Courtesy Pennyhill Park Luxury Hotel & Spa; 214bl AA/Neil Setchfield; 215tl Courtesy Bingham; 215tr Courtesy Bingham; 216r AA/James Hatts; 216bl AA/Derek Forss; 217b Robert Harding Picture Library Ltd/Alamy; 218 AA/John Miller; 219br AA/John Miller; 220b AA/John Miller; 222tl Courtesy Gravetye Manor/Jeremy Pelzer; 223tl Courtesy Ashdown Park Hotel & Country Club; 223tr Courtesy Ashdown Park Hotel & Country Club; 224tl Courtesy The Grand Hotel; 224br AA/Laurie Noble; 225tl Courtesy St Martin's Tearooms; 225br AA/Laurie Noble; 226 AA/Hugh Palmer; 227tr AA/AA; 227bl AA/Caroline Jones; 228tl Courtesy Thomas Oken Tea Rooms; 228r AA/Caroline Jones; 229cr Craig Ellenwood/Alamy; 230 AA/Simon McBride; 231br AA/Andrew Newey; 232 AA/Michael Moody; 233tl Courtesy The Bridge Tea Rooms; 234b AA/Caroline Jones; 235br AA/Michael Moody; 236tl Courtesy Manor House Hotel and Golf Club; 236tr Courtesy Manor House Hotel and Golf Club; 237tl AA/John Freeman; 238 AA/Michael Moody; 239tl Courtesy Tisanes Tea Room; 240tr Courtesy Sugar and Spice; 240bl AA/Steve Day; 241bl AA/Caroline Jones; 241r AA/David Hall; 242 AA/David Hall; 243tl Courtesy Bettys Harrogate; 243tr Courtesy Bettys Harrogate; 244tl Courtesy Bettys at RHS Garden Harlow Carr; 244tr Courtesy Bettys at RHS Garden Harlow Carr; 245 AA/David Clapp; 246bl AA/AA; 247tl Courtesy The Black Swan Tearoom & Patisserie; 247tr Courtesy The Black Swan Tearoom & Patisserie; 248b AA/Tom Mackie; 249tr AA/David Tarn; 250tl Courtesy Bettys Ilkley; 250tr Courtesy Bettys Ilkley/Victor de Jesus; 251tl Courtesy Bettys Northallerton; 251tr Courtesy Bettys Northallerton; 252tl Courtesy Swinton Park; 252tr Courtesy Swinton Park; 253tl Courtesy Bettys York; 253tr Courtesy Bettys York; 254tl Courtesy Bullivant of York; 255tl Courtesy Little Bettys, York; 255tr Courtesy Little Bettys, York; 256tl Courtesy Bothams of Whitby/Skinner Street Shop & Tea Room/Tony Bartholomew; 257 AA/Mike Kipling; 258/259 AA/Derek Croucher;

260tl Courtesy Badgers Tearooms; 260tr Courtesy Badgers Tearooms; 261tl Courtesy St Tudno Hotel/martin mccluskey; 261tr Courtesy St Tudno Hotel; 262b AA/Nick Jenkins; 263br AA/Mark Bauer; 264bl AA/Nick Jenkins; 264r AA/Mark Bauer; 265tl Courtesy Cemlyn Tea Shop; 265tr Courtesy Cemlyn Tea Shop; 266bl AA/Pat Aithie; 266r AA/AA; 267tl Courtesy The Angel Hotel; 267tr Courtesy The Angel Hotel; 268b/269bl forty40 photography/Alamy; 269br David Cheshire/Alamy; 270tl Courtesy Carriages Tea Room at Old Station Tintern; 270br AA/Michael Moody; 271tl Courtesy Llangoed Hall; 271tr Courtesy Gliffaes Hotel; 272tl Courtesy The Old Stables Tea Rooms; 272tr Courtesy The Old Stables Tea Rooms; 273tl Courtesy The Drovers Rest Riverside Tea Rooms; 273br AA/Ian Burgum; 274/275 AA/Jonathan Smith; 276tl AA/John Freeman; 277tl Courtesy Turnberry Resort/The Grand Tea Lounge/DKLT Worldwide Inc.; 277tr Courtesy Turnberry Resort/The Grand Tea Lounge/DKLT Worldwide Inc.; 278tl Courtesy Abbey Cottage Tea Rooms; 279tl Courtesy Balmoral Hotel, Edinburgh/Palm Court/KATIELEE ARROWSMITH; 279tr Courtesy Balmoral Hotel, Edinburgh/Palm Court; 280tl Courtesy Caledonian Hilton Edinburgh hotel/Pompadour Restaurant; 281tl Courtesy Sheraton Grand Hotel & Spa, Edinburgh/The Exchange/Julie Tinton; 281tr Courtesy Sheraton Grand Hotel & Spa, Edinburgh/The Exchange/Julie Tinton; 282b AA/Karl Blackwell; 283tl AA/Jonathan Smith; 284tl Courtesy Loopy Lorna's Tea House; 284tr Courtesy Loopy Lorna's Tea House/Brendan MacNeill; 285tl Courtesy Kind Kyttock's Kitchen; 285tr Courtesy Kind Kyttock's Kitchen; 286b/287bl AA/Derek Croucher; 288tl Courtesy The Old Course Hotel; 288tr Courtesy The Old Course Hotel/Hamish Campbell; 289tl Courtesy The Willow Tea Rooms in Buchanan Street; 289tr Courtesy The Willow Tea Rooms in Buchanan Street; 290tl Courtesy MACS at Scotland Street School Museum; 291tl Courtesy The Willow Tea Rooms in Sauchiehall Street; 291tr Courtesy The Willow Tea Rooms in Sauchiehall Street; 292tl Courtesy Cup Glasgow; 292tr Courtesy Cup Glasgow

Every effort has been made to trace the copyright holders, and we apologise in advance for any unintentional omissions or errors. We would be pleased to apply any corrections in a following edition of this publication.